If you have any queries please contact:

Helen Ramsey
John Wiley & Sons Limited
Baffins Lane
Chichester
West Sussex
PO19 1UD
England

Affix
Stamp
here

Customer Service Department
John Wiley and Sons Limited
Shripney Road
Bognor Regis
West Sussex
PO22 9SA
England

AVAILABLE

The programs described in this book are available on disk for your IBM PC (and most compatibles). They have been written in C and you will need to have a C compiler. (The author used Turbo C++ $^{(TM)}$.)

Order the Program Disk *today* priced £15.00 including VAT/$23.00 from your computer store, bookseller, or by using the order form below. (Prices correct at time of going to press.)

AMMERAAL: PROGRAMS AND DATA STRUCTURES IN C, 2ND EDITION — Program Disk

Please send me .... copies of the **Ammeraal: Programs and Data Structures in C, 2nd Edition** - Program Disk at £15.00 including VAT/$23.00 each.

0 471 93124 1

POSTAGE AND HANDLING FREE FOR CASH WITH ORDER OR PAYMENT BY CREDIT CARD

☐ Remittance enclosed .... Allow approx. 14 days for delivery

☐ Please charge this to my credit card (All orders subject to credit approval).
Delete as necessary:-
AMERICAN EXPRESS, DINERS CLUB, BARCLAYCARD/VISA, ACCESS/MASTERCARD

CARD NUMBER ☐☐☐☐☐☐☐☐☐☐☐☐☐☐☐☐ Expiry date ....

☐ Please send me an invoice for prepayment. A small postage and handling charge will be made.

Software purchased for professional purposes is generally recognized as tax deductible.

☐ Please keep me informed of new books in my subject area which is ....
....

NAME/ADDRESS ....
....
....

OFFICIAL ORDER No. .... SIGNATURE ....

PROGRAMS
AND DATA
STRUCTURES
IN C *Second Edition*

Based on ANSI C and C++

PROGRAMS AND DATA STRUCTURES IN C *Second Edition*

Based on ANSI C and C++

Leendert Ammeraal
Hogeschool Utrecht, The Netherlands

JOHN WILEY & SONS
Chichester • New York • Brisbane • Toronto • Singapore

Other Wiley Editorial Offices

John Wiley & Sons, Inc., 605 Third Avenue,
New York, NY 10158-0012, USA

Jacaranda Wiley Ltd, G.P.O. Box 859, Brisbane,
Queensland 4001, Australia

John Wiley & Sons (Canada) Ltd, 5353 Dundas Street West, Fourth
Floor, Etobicoke, Ontario M9B 6H8, Canada

John Wiley & Sons (SEA) Pte Ltd, 37 Jalan Pemimpin 05-04,
Block B, Union Industrial Building, Singapore 2057

**A catalogue record for this book is available
from the British Library**

ISBN 0 471 93123 3
ISBN 0 471 93124 1 (disk)

Printed in Great Britain by Courier International, East Kilbride, Lanarkshire

Contents

Preface

There are several good books that discuss algorithms and data structures using either Pascal or some fictitious language. Instead, I use the C language for this purpose, and although I feel no need to apologize, let me briefly explain this choice. Many years ago, authors who wanted to publish algorithms in a real programming language had to choose between a practical language, Fortran, which was not very suitable for that purpose, and a nice language (Algol 60), which was somewhat impractical. Wirth's publication of Pascal in 1968 was a major step forward. Not only did this language offer new facilities for dynamic data structures, but very soon efficient compilers and good textbooks for this language became available. However, Pascal has some serious shortcomings, such as, for example, the lack of facilities for random file-access, for bit operations and for separate compilation of procedures and functions. Every Pascal implementor has invented his own language extensions, at the cost of portability, and, consequently, Pascal cannot be regarded as a successor to Fortran. Though possibly a reasonable language for beginners, Pascal has some aspects that make it not an ideal language for teaching either. For example, my students are always inclined to test if a character is a newline-character *after* it has been read instead of using **eoln** beforehand, as Pascal requires, and it is a pity that we have to spend so much time teaching language peculiarities like the fact that a newline character should become available as a space-character. On the other hand, my teaching experiences with C are very positive. In comparison with some other high-level languages, C is rather closely related to machine architecture. Most programmers and students appreciate this relationship, although it does not make C attractive for those who loathe dealing with bits and bytes. Contrary to what people often think, C programs can be reasonably readable, provided that we pay some attention to this aspect; for example, by indenting in the same way as is customary in Pascal programming.

In short, C is an attractive language, not only in practice but also in teaching, because:

(1) It is suitable for expressing all kinds of algorithms and it does not require lengthy phrases to express something that can be said in a few words or symbols. It is also suitable for low-level programming, and in many cases it can be used instead of assembly language.

(2) It is widespread and supported by many efficient compilers, which all accept the same programs, provided these conform to the ANSI standard. Examples of such programs are those in this book, summarized in Appendix B.

When studying some intricate algorithm most students will appreciate having a ready-to-run version at their disposal, so that theoretical and experimental analysis may go hand in hand. This would not be possible with rudimentary sketches of algorithms and with 'programming details left as an exercise'. Incidentally, we should not use the term 'programming details' with any contempt. It would be no good if we could only *talk* about algorithms without being able to express them in correct and efficient programs. This book avoids any algorithmic vagueness by presenting complete programs. If desirable, the student can insert additional output statements to find out how the algorithm works. Besides, it is very instructive to investigate experimentally how a program's execution time depends on its input. As in physics, experiments are useful both to confirm theoretical results and to stimulate new theoretical investigations.

You will find many useful algorithms in this book. Many of them are related to what advanced professional programmers need in practice. Instead of mentioning some of these algorithms here, I would rather refer to the table of contents. Depending on the purpose for which the book is used, Chapter 9 might be studied very early, even before Chapter 2, since it does not use dynamic data structures and is not very difficult. I placed it at the end because otherwise the important subjects of linked lists and binary trees would have been delayed, and, once dealing with trees, the chosen order of the subjects in Chapters 6, 7, and 8 is the most logical one. It may also be noted that Chapter 8 does not depend on Chapters 5, 6, and 7, so this too might be given priority, if desired, especially since the programs in this chapter are perhaps easier than those in the three preceding chapters. It is curious that *dynamic programming*, discussed at the end of Chapter 3, is not included in most similar books. Not only is it a very useful subject; it is also instructive as an iterative solution to a recursive problem.

I have not attempted to be 'complete' in any sense, and you may miss some algorithms occurring in other textbooks. Incidentally, this is why I did not use the word *algorithm* in the title. However useful a cookbook of 'standard algorithms' may be, our capability to invent new algorithms will be at least as important, because there will always be new programming problems. This explains why I emphasize the *development* of algorithms, possibly giving you the impression that I invented them myself, which mostly was not the case. Most algorithms in this book (not the programs themselves) can be found in books by other authors, such as those mentioned in the Bibliography.

Although possibly a minority, there are universities and polytechnics where the C language is used in teaching. Students learn this language surprisingly quickly, as I know from experience, so there may be time left for the subject of programming itself. I hope that this book will be accepted as a reasonable textbook for this purpose; of course, any suggestions for improvements will be welcome.

Changes and New Features in the Second Edition

All programs have been rewritten in ANSI C, in such a way that they also conform to the C++ language rules. This is possible by using only those language elements that are available both in ANSI C and in C++. Some more information about this can be found in Appendix A.

An important new subject is *AVL trees* (including node deletion), dealt with in Section 5.4. Besides a recursive function to generate a complete list of permutations, there is now also an iterative function, **nextperm**, to generate only the next permutation. The same applies to combinations, for which there is a function **nextcomb**. There are numerous improvements, such as in program BTREE.C, which now displays a representation of the complete B-tree each time it is updated.

In comparison with the first edition, more use is made of standard library functions. For example, there is a discussion of the standard library function **qsort** and how this relates to our own quicksort functions.

L. Ammeraal

1

Programming Style, Iteration and Recursion

1.1 Introduction

Learning a programming language is normally done by studying examples and by solving little programming problems as exercises, so as soon as we are familiar with a programming language we know more or less what programming is about. However, it will then be desirable to improve our programming skill. Mastering a programming language is a prerequisite for advanced programming, so its importance should not be underestimated, but that alone is not sufficient. In the process of learning a language the examples and exercises are subordinate to the language elements under discussion. In this book it is the other way round. The reader is now assumed to be familiar with the C language, as explained in *C for Programmers* (Second Edition), listed in the Bibliography, and in many other books. When solving a programming problem, we will not only be interested in an *algorithm*, that is, a solution expressed in more or less abstract terms, but we will also want a ready-to-run C program or a C function that can be used as a tool in any application program. For most algorithms that we will be discussing it would not be practicable to express them in everyday English, so we need a formal language anyway. In mathematics, it is extremely convenient that we can use the single symbol ≤ for the phrase 'less than or equal to'. In the same way, many compact notations of the C language, possibly considered confusing or 'cryptic' by the uninitiated, provide us with a convenient means to express algorithms. In the early days of computing, many people used Algol 60 to publish algorithms, and had to convert them to (some old version of) Fortran to run the resulting programs efficiently. We are now in a much better position, since as soon as we have expressed algorithms in C we can run them efficiently on a great variety of computers.

1

There are many misconceptions about programming style. Sometimes people say that because of the speed of present-day computers we should not emphasize the aspect of program efficiency any longer, but rather focus on program readability. However well-intended, such general statements are confusing and misleading. We may as well argue that the increased speed of computers and their increased memory sizes give rise to the solving of larger programming problems, so that program efficiency is now more important than it used to be.

Besides simply measuring a program's running time, using either a watch or an 'internal clock', we can approach the subject of efficiency from an analytic angle. For many programs, the running time $T(n)$ is a function of the input size n. For example, a certain program to sort a sequence of n numbers, that is, a program to place these numbers in ascending order, may have a running time

$$T(n) = cn^2$$

where c is a constant. Although the value of c is not irrelevant, the fact that this running time is a quadratic function of the input size n is usually considered far more important. We therefore use the so-called 'big-oh' notation, and say that, in our example, the running time $T(n)$ is $O(n^2)$. In general, we say that $T(n)$ is $O(f(n))$ if there are nonnegative constants c and n_0 such that $T(n) \leq cf(n)$ whenever $n \geq n_0$. According to this definition, the fact that '$T(n)$ is $O(n^2)$' implies that '$T(n)$ is $O(n^3)$', but the latter is a weaker statement than the former, and in cases like this it customary to ignore such weaker statements. We also use the terms *growth rate* and *time complexity* for the function $f(n)$ used in the notation $O(f(n))$. In Chapter 2 we will see that there are sorting algorithms with time complexity $n \log n$ instead of n^2. It will be clear that this is an enormous improvement, provided that the length n of the sequence to be sorted is large. With present-day computers we can more easily accommodate such large sequences than we could, say, 20 years ago, so considerations of efficiency (or *complexity*, as computer scientists would rather say) are at least as important with fast modern computers as they used to be with slower computers of the past.

This discussion about efficiency is not meant to imply that the other aspect mentioned, namely program *readability*, should be of minor importance. Unreadable and incomprehensible programs will more often be incorrect than programs that we can read and understand, and it will be more costly to write and maintain them, so everyone is clearly in favor of program readability. However, there are two aspects of readability that many people seem to overlook. First, whether or not a C program is as readable as it should be can be judged only by those who are thoroughly familiar with the C language (and preferably with some other languages as well), and though there are a good many C programmers around today, there are also many computer people who have never used C themselves and whose opinions about the readability of C programs are therefore of little significance. Second, some algorithms, even when expressed in the best 'algorithmic language' possible, are too intricate to be fully understood quickly by every student and programmer. Incidentally, it may then be helpful to resort to the computer and first experiment a little with the algorithm under consideration. Such experiments may remove any suspicions about its correctness, and, especially if it runs faster than we had expected, encourage us to analyze it. The possibility of experimenting arises from discussing complete programs in a real programming language.

It is a good idea to discuss such concepts as efficiency and readability in the framework of concrete examples (not confined to sorting problems), and to be cautious with very general statements. Preferably, such examples should be more or less related to what we need in practice. However, not everyone needs the same things and, besides, unpractical examples may be very suitable to illustrate important concepts. Consequently, some programs and functions in the following sections are presented only to illustrate useful programming principles. Others, however, may well be suitable for real applications in their literal form.

1.2 Using a Sentinel in Linear Search

Some well-known solutions of certain programming problems are sometimes called *techniques* or *tricks*. The term 'technique' is too pompous for many little inventions, worthless from a scientific point of view, but nonetheless of some practical value. So for reasons of modesty, we will use the term *trick*, in spite of its bad connotations: our tricks are not meant to confuse or amuse (although they sometimes do, and hopefully the latter more often than the former).

Here is a well-known trick. Suppose that we are given the array **a** and the integer variable **x**, declared in

```
int a[N], x, i;
```

We now want to search array **a** for the value of **x**, or, more precisely, we want the smallest of all subscript values **i** (< N), if any, for which the value of **a[i]** is equal to **x**. If, on the other hand, all N array elements differ from **x**, the variable **i** is to take the value N. Here is the first solution:

```
i = 0;
while (i < N  &&  a[i] != x) i++;
```

It is clear that the variable **i** will be equal to the desired value if some array element **a[i]** is equal to **x**, for the first such element will cause the loop to stop just when the variable **i** has the desired value. If all array elements differ from **x**, the loop stops when **i** is equal to N, and then **i** again has the correct final value. Note that **&&** is a 'conditional' and-operator. The second operand **a[i] != x** is evaluated only if the first evaluates to 1 (which means *true*). When **i** becomes equal to N, if that should happen, there will be no evaluation of a comparison **a[i] != x**. Thanks to the 'conditional' behavior of **&&**, only existing array elements **a[0]**, **a[1]**, ..., **a[N−1]** (not **a[N]**) will be used in this comparison. By the way, this is not an extremely important point, for if it had been a problem we could simply have appended an extra element to array **a**. We will in fact do so in the following discussion, although for a completely different reason.

Correct as the above solution is, it is not the most efficient if N is large. The while-loop contains two tests for loop termination, but, with a little trick, one will do. We append one element to the array, and write

```
int a[N+1], x, i;
...
a[N] = x; i = 0;
while (x != a[i]) i++;
```

The three dots ... stand for some portion of program text, where the variables x and the first N elements of array **a** obtain their values. If **x** is equal to one of these N array elements, it is clear that the loop stops with the correct value of **i**. Should x be different from each of them, then the loop stops with the correct value i = N, since then the element **a[N]**, which we have added, will stop the loop. After all, we have assigned the value x to that array element ourselves. This while-loop is shorter and faster than the former, since there is now no test i < N in it. The artificial array element **a[N]**, equal to the value we are looking for, is called a *sentinel*. Because of this artificial array element, we may regard this method as somewhat 'unnatural' or 'tricky', so we may call it a *trick*. At the same time, the method is very useful. This trick should be used whenever we use *linear search* (assuming speed to be an important factor, which is normally the case). It applies not only to arrays but also to linked lists, as we will see in Section 4.2.

1.3 Using Pointers as Arrays

The dimensions of arrays must be constants. For example, in the fragment[1]

```
#define N 1000
...
int a[N];
```

we cannot replace the constant N with a variable **n**, the value of which is computed in our program. However, we can declare **a** as a pointer, and, after assigning an appropriate address to it, use it as an array with dimension **n**. Here is a program to demonstrate this. After reading the value of **n**, it reads **n** integers and prints them in the reverse order:

---

[1] In C we must not replace **#define N 1000** with **const int** N=1000; in this example, because then N would technically be a *variable*. In C++, on the other hand, such a modification is possible and should even be recommended.

```
/* POINTER.C: Use a pointer as an array */
#include <stdio.h>
#include <stdlib.h>

main()
{  int n, i, *a;
   printf("Enter n, the size of the 'array': ");
   scanf("%d", &n);
   a = (int *)malloc(n * sizeof(int));
   if (a == NULL) puts("Memory problem"), exit(1);
   printf("Enter %d numbers:\n", n);
   for (i=0; i<n; i++) scanf("%d", a+i);
   puts("Here are the same numbers, in reverse order:");
   for (i=n-1; i>=0; i--) printf("%d\n", a[i]);
   return 0;
}
```

As you can see in this program, we can use **a[0]**, **a[1]**, ..., **a[n − 1]** in the same way that we would if **a** had been an array.

We can do something similar if a *matrix* with variable dimensions is required. For example, suppose we want to deal with double-precision floating-point numbers, arranged in a matrix with m rows and n columns, where m and n are not available until run time. This can be done by using the variable **matrix** of type pointer-to-pointer-to-**double**. We use **matrix** as an array of pointers, as shown in Fig. 1.1.

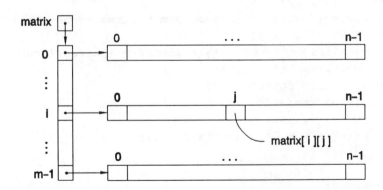

*Fig. 1.1. Pointer **matrix** used as a two-dimensional array*

In this case we first have to allocate memory once for m pointers. Then, in a loop, each of these m pointers is assigned the start address of a memory area for n values of type **double**. Program TWODIM.C shows how this is done. It also shows how **matrix** can be used as an argument in a function call.

```
/* TWODIM.C: A pointer to a pointer, used as a
             two-dimensional array.
*/
#include <stdio.h>
#include <stdlib.h>

void *getmemory(int n)
{   void *p=malloc(n);
    if (p == NULL) puts("Memory problem"), exit(1);
    return p;
}

void fillmatrix(double **table, int nrows, int ncolumns)
{   int i, j;
    for (i=0; i<nrows; i++)
    for (j=0; j<ncolumns; j++)
    table[i][j] = i + 0.01 * j;
}

main()
{   int i, j, m, n; /* m rows and n columns */
    double **matrix;
    printf("How many rows? ");
    scanf("%d", &m);
    printf("How many columns? ");
    scanf("%d", &n);
    matrix = (double **)getmemory(m * sizeof(double *));
    for (i=0; i<m; i++)
        matrix[i] = (double *)getmemory(n * sizeof(double));
    fillmatrix(matrix, m, n);
    puts("Matrix contents:");
    for (i=0; i<m; i++)
    {   for (j=0; j<n; j++)
        printf("% 5.2f", matrix[i][j]);
        puts("");
    }
    return 0;
}
```

Note the use of **matrix[i][j]** in function **main** and of **a[i][j]** in function **fillmatrix**. In each case a pointer works as a two-dimensional array. The advantage of this method is its flexibility: memory is allocated only as far as is needed. Here is a demonstration of this program:

```
How many rows? 3
How many columns? 5
Matrix contents:
 0.00 0.01 0.02 0.03 0.04
 1.00 1.01 1.02 1.03 1.04
 2.00 2.01 2.02 2.03 2.04
```

1.4 Global Variables and Side Effects

Suppose that we want to read some integers from the keyboard, to compute their sum. The integers are entered in their normal decimal form and they are separated by any number of white-space characters, that is, by spaces, tabs and newline characters. After the final integer, any nonnumeric string, such as **STOP**, **END**, **QUIT**, **EXIT**, should be allowed to signal the end of the input sequence. If numbers are expected in the input, the value returned by the function **scanf** tells us how many numbers have been successfully read, so it is zero if some nonnumeric string is entered instead of a number. (In case of end of file, **scanf** does not return 0 but **EOF** = −1.) Note that the value returned by **scanf** should not be confused with the actual values of the numbers that are read; the latter values are delivered through the arguments. Here is a program which detects the end of the number sequence in this way:

```
/* SUM.C: Compute the sum of a sequence of integers */
#include <stdio.h>

main()
{  int i, s;
   puts("Enter some integers followed by any "
        "nonnumerical character:");
   while (scanf("%d", &i) == 1) s += i;
   printf("\nThe sum is: %d\n", s);
   return 0;
}
```

This is a good program to introduce a somewhat controversial point. These days many students have to learn the language Pascal, which distinguishes between procedures and functions. They are often taught the following rules of thumb:

(1) The only thing a function should do is return a value; it should perform no input or output operations. For the latter, procedures rather than functions ought to be used. Functions should have only value parameters (without **var**).

(2) Neither procedures nor functions should access any global variables; they should deal with parameters and local variables only.

These rules of thumb are very instructive in elementary programming lessons. Without them, beginners might declare all variables at the global level and use only procedures without parameters, in other words, they might adopt the BASIC style of programming. When learning chess, we first have to master the elementary rules of the game. After this, it is a good idea to get familiar with some rules of thumb for the first moves. These rules are very useful recipes for beginners. More advanced chess players, though familiar with all elementary rules, know that there are very important exceptions to them. They are in a position to judge for themselves what is good style and what is not. With programming things are similar. At first sight, it seems that the above rules for Pascal do not apply to C, since in the latter language there is no distinction between procedures and functions. However, we can conceptually make this distinction, using functions returning a value (and with a type other than **void** at the beginning of their declarations) only as real functions, not as 'procedures'. In this way, we can still observe the above rules (1) and (2), if we wish. Anyone who switches from Pascal to C is inclined to make that conceptual distinction. For example, many people, including myself, have a tendency to use **scanf** in the same way as the Pascal procedure **read**, ignoring any return value. However, as the above program SUM.C shows, this value is very useful: it enables us to detect easily that no integer could be read, which means that the user has given the agreed signal (some nonnumeric string) for end of input. This way of using **scanf** as a genuine function, rather than as a 'procedure', is against the above rule of thumb (1) in two respects. First, it performs input, and, second, it passes information back through its parameters. (Although, formally, all parameters in C are value parameters, the pointer concept of C enables us to achieve the effect of passing information from a function back to its caller through parameters.) As in chess, we need not feel guilty about violating elementary rules of thumb, nor is the C language to blame for this. Although we could make a sharp distinction between procedures and functions, we won't! Incidentally, C functions that do not return a value are said to be **void** functions. They are similar to procedures in Pascal. More interesting, however, are functions that do return values. The fact that we can use or ignore these values as we like is a very elegant language aspect.

Rule of thumb (2) dissuades us from using global variables. This rule is more important than rule (1), and in most cases it is wise to observe it. Here is a very elementary example. The program is clumsy in several respects, but it is nevertheless instructive:

```
/* SIDE1.C: First program to demonstrate side effects
*/
#include <stdio.h>
int n;

int square(int x)
{   n = x * x;
    return n;
}
```

```
main()
{   int i, x;
    printf("Enter n: ");
    printf("Enter %d integers to be squared:\n", &n);
    for (i=0; i<n; i++)
    {   scanf("%d", &x);
        printf("Its square is: %d\n", square(x));
    }
    return 0;
}
```

The variable **n** is global. Its value is used in the for-loop, but, unfortunately, it is destroyed in the function **square**, which means that the program will not terminate correctly. We say that the function **square** has the side-effect of affecting the global variable **n**. In large programs errors like this one may be extremely hard to find.

There is another problem with side effects, which is due to the fact that in most cases the order in which the operands in an expression are evaluated is undefined. The following program illustrates this:

```
/* SIDE2.C: Second program to demonstrate side effects */
#include <stdio.h>
int i=5;

int f(void)
{   return ++i;
}

int g(void)
{   return i *= 10;
}

main()
{   printf("%d", f() + g());
    return 0;
}
```

If in the expression **f( ) + g( )** the first operand **f( )** is evaluated prior to the evaluation of the second operand **g( )**, the program computes 6 + 60, but if function **g** is evaluated first, the result is 51 + 50. Another odd point is that **f( ) + g( )** and **g( ) + f( )** will have different values. With bad habits, sometimes the best thing to do is to abolish them radically. Those who smoke too much know that the only good remedy is to stop smoking completely. In the same way we might consider forbidding any use of global variables. However, that would be unwise. After all, there is no scientific proof that global variables are bad for our health. Our rule of thumb (2), however useful, is not worth promoting to an absolute law. If we use global variables wisely, and only exceptionally, they may be very handy and not dangerous at all. Thanks to the fact that C allows us to split up a program into several modules (each of which is a file), we can restrict the scope of global variables to the file in which they are defined. We then add the keyword **static**, as, for example, in

```
static int Xcursor, Ycursor;

void left(int step)
{ removecursor(); Xcursor -= step; drawcursor();
}

void right(int step)
{ removecursor(); Xcursor += step; drawcursor();
}
```

In this example, all functions (such as **left** and **right**) defined in the same file as the variables **Xcursor** and **Ycursor** have access to these variables, but functions in other files (belonging to the same program!) have not. In this way we prevent **Xcursor** and **Ycursor** from being modified by unauthorized users, even though, in the above file, these variables are global.

As for *nonstatic* global variables, these can be defined in one module and used in another. For example, the following program consists of two modules, separated by a horizontal line. These modules can be compiled separately; their object modules ONE.OBJ and TWO.OBJ are then linked together. Variable **table** is defined in module ONE.C and used in module TWO.C:

```
/* ONE.C: Direct access to global variable.
         Not recommended.
*/
float table[1000];

void g(void)
{   void fun(void);
    fun();
}
```

```
/* TWO.C: */
extern float table[];
void fun(void)
{   int i;
    for (i=0; i<1000; i++) table[i] = 1/(1.0+i);
}
```

This way of using the same variable in several files can make programs more efficient in some cases, so it should not be absolutely forbidden. In most cases, however, we had better not follow this example, but rather restrict the use of the name **table** to one file (and make it **static**). Then in other files we can use **table** indirectly, in two ways.

First, we can use a function to which **table** is passed as an argument. This is done in the following example. Although array **table** does not occur in file PARAM_TWO.C, we assign values to it in that file:

```
/* PARAM_ONE.C: Parameter passing */
static float table[1000];

void g(void)
{   void parmfunction(float *t);
    parmfunction(table);
}
```

```
/* PARAM_TWO.C: */
void parmfunction(float *t)
{   int i;
    for (i=0; i<1000; i++) t[i] = 1/(1.0+i);
}
```

Second, we can use an *access function*, defined in the same file as the static variable in question:

```
/* ACCESS_ONE.C: Access function */
static float table[1000];

void accessfunction(void)
{   int i;
    for (i=0; i<1000; i++) table[i] = 1/(1.0+i);
}
```

```
/* ACCESS_TWO.C: */
void f(void)
{   void accessfunction(void);
    accessfunction();
}
```

Although array **table** does not occur in file ACCESS_TWO.C, the process of filling it is initiated in this file. Note that in our earlier example about cursor movements the functions **left** and **right** are also access functions, since they allow other program modules access to the **static** global variables **Xcursor** and **Ycursor**.

1.5 An Introduction to Recursion

A function that calls itself is said to be *recursive*. Recursion may be *indirect*. For example, function **f** may call function **g**, which in turn calls **f**. In Chapter 9 we will encounter quite useful applications of indirect recursion, but let us first deal with direct recursion, where only one function is involved. Program RECUR1.C, though useless for practical purposes, is instructive because of its simplicity:

```
/* RECUR1.C: First example of recursion
*/
#include <stdio.h>

void p(int n)
{  if (n>0) {p(n-2); printf("%3d", n); p(n-1);}
}

main()
{  p(4);
   return 0;
}
```

What does this program print? In spite of the very limited program size, this question turns out to be difficult for anyone who is unfamiliar with recursion. There are two ways of analyzing programs of this type, and we characterize these with the terms *top-down* and *bottom-up*. Using the top-down method, we begin with the call **p(4)** in the main program. The important point is that we immediately focus our attention on the three resulting actions, namely

```
p(2); printf("%3d", 4); p(3);
```

Thus, we have already found that the number 4 will occur somewhere in the output. Note that this way of program analysis is different from the usual one, where we follow the actions step by step in full detail. Here we have determined that the number 4 will be printed, although we have not yet fully analyzed the consequences of the call **p(2)**, which takes place earlier. The tree in Fig. 1.2 shows what happens. The node containing only 4 denotes the effect of **printf("%3d", 4)**; and so on. The tree does not branch further than the *leaves* **p(0)** and **p(-1)**, because these calls have no effect at all. The other leaves denote calls to **printf**, which produce the following output:

```
2   1   4   1   3   2   1
```

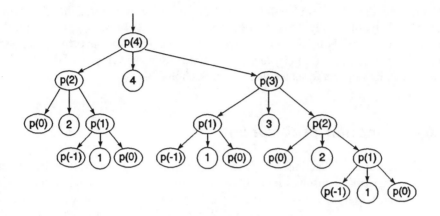

Fig. 1.2. Tree to analyze program RECUR1.C

This method of analysis usually leads to duplication of work. For example, the tree contains three identical subtrees that show the effect of the call **p(1)**. This observation leads to the 'bottom-up' method, which works as follows. After seeing that **p(n)** is effective only if **n** is positive, we begin with **p(1)**, even though this call does not occur in the program, and we can easily see that it results in printing the value 1. We then use this result in the second step, where we examine the effect of **p(2)**, and so on:

p(1):   1
p(2):   **p(0)** 2 **p(1)**, that is, 2 1
p(3):   **p(1)** 3 **p(2)**, that is, 1 3 2 1
p(4):   **p(2)** 4 **p(3)**, that is, 2 1 4 1 3 2 1

Although in this example the bottom-up method is more efficient than the top-down method, it is more difficult to use in other cases, as program RECUR2.C shows.

```
/* RECUR2.C: Second example of recursion
*/
#include <stdio.h>

void p(int n)
{  if (n>0) {p(n-40); printf("%3d", n); p(n-20);}
}

main()
{  p(80);
   return 0;
}
```

In this case the top-down method works as smoothly as before, but the bottom-up approach is feasible only if we discover that the analysis of **p(20)**, **p(40)**, **p(60)**, **p(80)** is all we need. Without this knowledge, we would have to have to go a long way, beginning with **p(1)**, then **p(2)**, and so on, until **p(80)**. Nevertheless, this possibility is fundamentally important, as we will see in Section 3.5.

1.6 Elimination of Recursion

In the programs of Section 1.5, function **p** calls itself recursively twice. Recursive functions that call themselves more than once are sometimes called *genuinely recursive*, to emphasize that usually we cannot easily replace them with equivalent iterative functions. This is different in program TAIL.C, which reads an unknown number of integers and prints their sum:

```
/* TAIL.C: Tail recursion
*/

#include <stdio.h>
int s=0;

void addnumbers(void)   /* Recursive version */
{  int x;
   if (scanf("%d", &x) == 1) {s += x; addnumbers();}
}

main()
{  puts("Enter some integers, followed by a "
        "nonnumeric character:");
   addnumbers();
   printf("\nThe sum is: %d\n", s);
   return 0;
}
```

This is an example of *tail recursion*. There is only one recursive call, which occurs at the end of the function **addnumbers**. This call is not much different from a jump to the beginning of the function. We can therefore replace the above function **addnumbers** with the following iterative version:

```
void addnumbers(void)     /* Iterative version */
{  int x;
   while (scanf("%d", &x) == 1) s += x;
}
```

With regard to efficiency, the latter version is to be preferred. If there are a great many numbers to be read, the recursive version may cause *stack overflow*. Since in principle a function may be used anywhere in the program, its return address, that is, the place to which it is to return, has to be stored somewhere. Because of the possibility of recursion, the only safe place to store it is a *stack*. The last item pushed on a stack is the first to be popped from it, which is just what we want. In addition to return addresses, local variables, such as x in our example, are also placed on the stack. Since the stack size may be limited to, say, several thousands of memory locations, there may be a problem if the same function is recursively called a great many times. Note that such problems will not occur if entering and leaving the function takes place alternately, no matter how often this occurs. The undesirable situation of stack overflow occurs only if the 'recursion depth' exceeds a certain value. Let us try to be more precise. We define the *recursion depth* of a function at a certain moment as the number of times that, from the beginning of program execution, this function has been called minus the number of times that it has returned to its caller. At any moment, each function has its own (current) recursion depth. There is a simple way of measuring the maximum recursion depth of a function experimentally, which is based on using two global variables, **depth** and **maxdepth**. For example, we can find the maximum recursion depth of a certain function **f** as follows:

```
int depth=0, maxdepth=0;

int f(int x)
{  if (++depth > maxdepth) maxdepth = depth;
   ...    /* Contents of recursive function f */
   depth--;
}
```

At the end of the **main** function, we have only to print the value of **maxdepth** to know the maximum recursion depth that has occurred. (Note that the value of **depth** will then be 0 again!)

We now go back to the general case and to a more theoretical approach. Immediately after program start, **main** has recursion depth 1 and all other functions have recursion depth 0. If we number the functions 1, 2, ..., k, then the amount of stack space used at a certain moment is equal to the sum

$$\mathbf{s} = d_1 n_1 + d_2 n_2 + ... + d_k \mathrm{n}_k$$

where d_i is the recursion depth and n_i is the amount of stack space involved by a single call to the ith function. The value of n_i includes space needed for the return address, all local variables, parameters and possibly the value to be returned, if any. Then clearly stack overflow will occur when the value of **s** exceeds some maximum stack size. We see that our second version of **addnumbers**, which is iterative, is absolutely safe, whereas the first, recursive version may cause stack overflow. Incidentally, even with the second function **addnumbers**, program TAIL.C would not be an example of good programming style, since the use of the global variable **s** is not justified here. See also the discussion about rule of thumb (2) in Section 1.4. However, it illustrates clearly that in certain cases we can replace recursion with iteration in a straightforward way. Speaking of rules of thumb, we can now add:

(3) A recursive function should call itself more than once, otherwise we should replace recursion with iteration.

Again, this is only a rule of thumb, not an exact law. Even if a recursive function calls itself only once, the elimination of recursion may be harder than in our last example. Also, a recursive function may be shorter and, in compiled form, occupy less memory than an equivalent iterative version. If at the same time the recursive version has no real disadvantages, it would be silly to obey rule (3) just because someone told us to do so. However, in many cases rule (3) applies. A well-known example of recursion is the computation of n-factorial, written:

$$n! = 1 \times 2 \times ... \times n$$

We can also write this definition of $n!$ as follows:

$$n! = 1 \qquad \text{if } n = 0 \text{ or } n = 1,$$
$$n! = n(n-1)! \quad \text{if } n > 1.$$

A translation of the latter definition to a recursive C function is straightforward. Already 8! does not fit into a 16-bit integer, so we use type **double** for reasons of generality:

```
double factorial(int n)      /* Recursive version */
{  return n > 1 ? n * factorial(n-1) : 1.0;
}
```

The return value is 1.0 if **n** is equal to 0 or to 1; for any **n** greater than 1, the return value is **n * factorial(n-1)**, in accordance with our second definition of $n!$. Note that the function assumes **n** to be zero or positive. If **n** is negative, **factorial** will simply return the value 1.0, while our mathematical definitions of $n!$ do not include this case. We could have checked if **n** is nonnegative, but that takes time. We often have to make the choice whether or not to include some time-consuming check in a function, only for the benefit of those who do not use that function properly. Most professionals are not fond of such tests: it is not fair that the wise should pay for the unwise. Incidentally, the absence of some run-time checks in C makes it doubtful if this language ought to be used in very elementary programming courses. Resuming our discussion about recursion, we see that in the function **factorial** the recursive call occurs only once. Indeed, this is a typical case where we should try to eliminate recursion. Here is an iterative version of this function:

```
double factorial(int n)        /* Iterative version */
{  double product=1.0;
   while (n > 1) product *= n--;
   return product;
}
```

Compared with our previous example, **addnumbers**, it is less straightforward to derive
the iterative function **factorial** from the recursive one. Since it is most unlikely for *n*!
to be computed for very large values of *n*, why replace recursion with iteration in this
case? It is often said that for a given problem its recursive solution will take more time
than the corresponding iterative solution. Before taking this for granted, we may as well
check this experimentally. Program TIMETEST.C can be used for this purpose:

```
/* TIMETEST.C: Computing time used by a recursive factorial
        function, compared with the time needed by an
        equivalent iterative version.
*/
#include <stdio.h>
#include <time.h>

double recfac(int n)        /* Recursive version  */
{  return n > 1 ? n * recfac(n-1) : 1.0;
}

double itfac(int n)         /* Iterative version  */
{  double product=1.0;
   while (n > 1) product *= n--;
   return product;
}

main()
{  clock_t t0, t1;
   int n, k, i;
   double f;
   printf("Enter the value of n, to compute n! : ");
   scanf("%d", &n);
   printf(
   "How many times do you want %d! to be computed? : ", n);
   scanf("%d", &k);
   t0 = clock();
   for (i=0; i<k; i++) f = recfac(n);
   t1 = clock();
   printf("Recursion: %d! = %1.0f    time = %7.2f s\n",
           n, f, (t1-t0)/(float)CLK_TCK);
```

```
    t0 = clock();
    for (i=0; i<k; i++) f = itfac(n);
    t1 = clock();
    printf("Iteration: %d! = %1.0f    time = %7.2f s\n",
          n, f, (t1-t0)/(float)CLK_TCK);
    return 0;
}
```

After this program was compiled by the C compiler that comes with Turbo C++, the following results were obtained on an IBM compatible PC with a 386 processor:

```
Enter the value of n, to compute n! : 7
How many times do you want 7! to be computed? : 30000
Recursion: 7! = 5040    time =    18.68 s
Iteration: 7! = 5040    time =    28.30 s
```

Curiously enough, as you can see, recursion turned out to be considerably faster than iteration in this example!

Most computers need much more time for floating-point arithmetic than for computing with integers. In an experiment with integer versions of our recursive and iterative functions, the time to compute the same result (7!), again 30000 times, was 1.10 s for recursion and 0.44 s for iteration. So in this case iteration is faster.

It should be noted that the figures for floating-point version are of a different order of magnitude from those for the integer version. Apparently, if speed is at stake, we should first look for ways of replacing floating-point with integer arithmetic.

1.7 Euclid's Algorithm for the Greatest Common Divisor

If x and y are integers, not both zero, we say that their *greatest common divisor*, $gcd(x, y)$, is the largest integer which evenly divides both x and y. For example,

$$gcd(1000, 600) = 200$$
$$gcd(-70, 90) = 10$$
$$gcd(0, 12) = 12$$

It is clear from this definition that for any pair x, y, we have

$$gcd(x, y) = gcd(y, x) \tag{1}$$

If d evenly divides the two positive integers x and y, it also evenly divides the two integers $x - y$ and y, and vice versa. This means that we have

$$gcd(x, y) = gcd(x - y, y) \tag{2}$$

If x is greater than y, the difference $x - y$ is less than x, so that replacing $gcd(x, y)$ with $gcd(x - y, y)$ means a simplification. If we now add the obvious fact that

$$gcd(x, 0) = x \tag{3}$$

then we have a simple means to compute the greatest common divisor of any two positive integers. For example, we have

$$gcd(1900, 700) = gcd(1200, 700)$$

We apply (2) once more, and write

$$gcd(1200, 700) = gcd(500, 700)$$

As the first argument is now less than the second in the right-hand side, we use (1):

$$gcd(500, 700) = gcd(700, 500)$$

We continue in the same way, each time applying either (2) or (1):

$$
\begin{aligned}
gcd(700, 500) &= gcd(200, 500) \\
&= gcd(500, 200) \\
&= gcd(300, 200) \\
&= gcd(100, 200) \\
&= gcd(200, 100) \\
&= gcd(100, 100) \\
&= gcd(0, 100) \\
&= gcd(100, 0)
\end{aligned}
$$

Applying (3), we obtain the desired result, 100, so we have found

$$gcd(1900, 700) = 100$$

If the difference between y and x is large, it is much more efficient to use the operator % instead of $-$. (Recall that $x \% y$ is the resulting remainder if x is evenly divided by y, for example, 1900 % 700 is equal to 500.) Since the remainder $x \% y$ is certainly less than y, we do not use

$$gcd(x, y) = gcd(x \% y, y)$$

followed by (1), as two separate steps, but we combine these into a single rule:

$$gcd(x, y) = gcd(y, x \% y) \tag{4}$$

In our example, we now find the answer in only five steps:

$$gcd(1900, 700) = gcd(700, 500)$$
$$= gcd(500, 200)$$
$$= gcd(200, 100)$$
$$= gcd(100, 0)$$
$$= 100$$

Surprisingly, we need not require that initially x be larger than y, since rule (4) will achieve this in the first step, if necessary. Not only by rule (1), but also by rule (4) we find

$$gcd(700, 1900) = gcd(1900, 700)$$

since 700 % 1900 gives 700.

This way of computing a gcd is called *Euclid's algorithm*. Here is our first version of it, written as a recursive C function:

```
int gcd(int x, int y)
{  return y ? gcd(y, x % y) : x;
}
```

Since this is a very short function, with only one recursive call, it is not difficult to replace it with the following iterative version, which also includes a provision for negative arguments:

```
/* EUCLID.C: Euclid's algorithm */
int gcd(int x, int y)
{  int r;
   if (x < 0) x = -x;
   if (y < 0) y = -y;
   while (y) {r = x % y; x = y; y = r;}
   return x;
}
```

1.8 Horner's Rule

Suppose that we are given the seven numbers

$$x, a_0, a_1, a_2, a_3, a_4, a_5$$

and that we have to compute the polynomial

$$P_5(x) = a_5 x^5 + a_4 x^4 + a_3 x^3 + a_2 x^2 + a_1 x + a_0$$

The most obvious way of doing this is to compute the individual terms of $P_5(x)$ and to add them up. However, it is much more efficient to apply *Horner's rule*, according to which $P_5(x)$ can be computed as follows:

$$P_5(x) = ((((a_5 x + a_4) x + a_3) x + a_2) x + a_1) x + a_0$$

Thanks to Horner's rule, only five multiplications and five additions are needed in this example. In general, we have to perform only n multiplications and n additions to compute a polynomial of degree n. Besides speed, Horner's rule also offers elegance and simplicity, and it may increase numerical accuracy. Here is a C function for $P_n(x)$, based on Horner's rule:

```
double P(double x, double *a, int n)
{   double s = a[n];
    while (--n >= 0) s = s * x + a[n];
    return s;
}
```

It is a good exercise to write also a recursive version:

```
double P(double x, double *a, int n)
{   return n ? x * P(x, a+1, n-1) + *a : *a;
}
```

The second and third parameters represent the sequence $a_0, a_1, ..., a_n$ of coefficients. If n is positive, there is a recursive call, which is applied to the shorter sequence $a_1, a_2, ..., a_n$. Using an obvious notation, we can express the way function **P** works as follows:

$$P(x, \{a_0, a_1, ..., a_n\}) = \begin{cases} x \cdot P(x, \{a_1, a_2, ..., a_n\}) + a_0 & \text{if } n > 0 \\ a_0 & \text{if } n = 0 \end{cases}$$

We can write this in more conventional notation as

$$a_n x^n + ... + a_0 = \begin{cases} x \cdot (a_n x^{n-1} + ... + a_1) + a_0 & \text{if } n > 0 \\ a_0 & \text{if } n = 0 \end{cases}$$

In order to compute

$$25 \times 0.5^2 + 15 \times 0.5 + 5.0 = 18.75$$

the following program can use either of the above functions **P**, with **x** = 0.5, **a[0]** = 5.0, **a[1]** = 15.0, **a[2]** = 25, **n** = 2:

```
#include <stdio.h>
main()
{  double a[3] = {5, 15, 25};
   double P(double x, double *a, int n);
   printf("%f", P(0.5, a, 2));
}
```

In an experiment with Turbo C, the recursive version was somewhat faster than the iterative one. It also leads to more compact object code. There is still the question about the stack, but it is most unlikely that with this application there should ever be any trouble. So the exercise of writing a recursive function for Horner's rule has yielded something quite useful!

Although we have seen two examples of recursive functions that are more efficient than their iterative counterparts, this is not a general rule. There are also situations in which the opposite is true. A striking example of this is provided by Exercise 1.14 at the end of this chapter.

1.9 Radix Conversion

In this section, we will use some program text to discuss algorithms; although this program text could really be used in C programs, it is not presented for that purpose. The C standard library offers very good ready-to-use facilities for input and output and for in-memory format conversion (such as **sscanf** and **sprintf**). It is therefore doubtful whether we will really need the functions discussed here. Yet this section is not superfluous. It is not intended as a software toolbox but rather as an explanation of algorithms and programming methods that will enable you to write similar but useful software yourself.

When, not necessarily in the C language, we are writing an input routine for integers, we are given a sequence of characters, mainly consisting of decimal digits, and we want to assemble these to an integer in the internal format of the computer. This is often called 'conversion from decimal to binary', since internally integers are usually in binary format. Thus reading an integer implies a conversion from radix 10 to radix 2. If the input routine is written in a high-level programming language, the fact that internally radix 2 is used is not essential. After all, we usually perform arithmetic operations ($+$, $-$, $*$, $/$, $\%$) on integers without bothering about their internal representation, and this is not different in an input routine. The only reason to be aware of the internal format is the possibility of *integer overflow*, a term used if the number entered is too large to fit into that format. Let us use an example to discuss how to use the decimal digits in the order they are given. The integer 5482 is entered as the four digits 5, 4, 8, 2. When only the first digit, 5, has been read, we do not yet know that it is to be multiplied by 1000. Therefore, instead of using the conventional form

$$5482 = 5 \times 10^3 + 4 \times 10^2 + 8 \times 10 + 2$$

we use Horner's rule:

$$5482 = ((5 \times 10 + 4) \times 10 + 8) \times 10 + 2$$

Successively, the numbers 5, 54, 548, 5482 are computed in this way. The function RDINT.C shows the program text for this.

```
/* RDINT.C: Function to read an integer
              (preliminary version)
*/
#include <stdio.h>
#include <ctype.h>
#include <stdlib.h>

int rdint(void)
{   int i, neg, d;
    char ch;
    do ch = getchar(); while (isspace(ch));
    /* We have now skipped any leading blanks */
    neg = ch == '-';
    if (neg || ch == '+') ch = getchar();
    if (!isdigit(ch)) puts("Invalid number"), exit(1);
    i = ch - '0';
    while (ch = getchar(), isdigit(ch))
    {   d = ch - '0';
        i = 10 * i + d;
    }
    ungetc(ch, stdin);
    return neg ? -i : i;
}
```

We begin by skipping any leading white-space characters (spaces, newline characters and tabs). Then we admit a plus or a minus sign with its usual meaning. After these leading characters, if any, we require a digit to follow; if not, we display an error message and stop program execution. The first character (say, '5') is then converted to the integer (5), by subtracting the character '0' from it. With this initial value, i, the while-loop is entered, where we apply Horner's rule.

The above version does not include a test for integer overflow. We now wish to include such a test; if integer overflow should take place, we will simply display an error message and stop program execution. (Of course, in practice we may replace this with a more sophisticated action, such as asking the user to retry.) Here we need some knowledge of the way integers are represented internally. Fortunately, ANSI C offers us this information in the form of some symbolic constants, defined in the header file *limits.h*. One of these is **INT_MAX**, which denotes the largest **int** value. For example, with 16-bit integers, this constant will be represented by the following bit sequence:

    0111 1111 1111 1111

the value of which is $2^{15} - 1 = 32767$. If we increase this by 1, we obtain

    1000 0000 0000 0000,

which is the 2's-complement notation for -32768. We see that the **unsigned** number 2^{15} = 32768 and the negative number -32768 have the same internal format. Similarly, (with 16-bit integers) the **unsigned** number 32769 has the same internal format as the negative number -32767, and so on. Consequently, integer overflow may give a negative result. If this were always the case, we could use the sign of an arithmetic result to test if there is integer overflow. However, this method would not work. For example, if we compute 10×9000, the resulting internal 16-bit value will be $90000 - 2^{16} = 24464$, which is positive! It is even greater than the original value, 9000, so even the fact that a multiplication $10 \times i$ gives an internal value greater than i does not guarantee the correctness of this value. The easiest way to solve this problem is based on using the constant **INT_MAX**, mentioned above. Similar to what we did in function **rdint**, we want to execute the statement

```
i1 = 10 * i + d;
```

Only if the theoretical value of **i1** is not greater than **INT_MAX** will the actual value of **i1** be correct. If we were prepared to use floating-point arithmetic, we could simply write

```
if (10.0 * i + d > INT_MAX) ... /* Overflow */
```

but it is better to restrict ourselves to integers wherever possible. Since type **long** may be identical with type **int**, it would not be a good idea to replace **10.0** with **10L** in this if-statement. The solution to our problem lies in testing the value of **i** *before* the multiplication takes place, as is done in

```
if (i > (INT_MAX - d)/10) ... /* Overflow */
```

Note that in this case the operator **/** performs integer division. For example, with **INT_MAX** = 32767 and **d** = 9, overflow will occur if (and only if) **i** is greater than 3275. With **d** = 7 or less, the corresponding value of **i** is 3276. We can check this by comparing the values of both **10 * i + d** and **10 * (i + 1) + d** with **INT_MAX** in these two cases.

If we simply modify function **rdint** by inserting the above test just before **i** is updated, we obtain a version that will probably do in practice, but we must realize that it is based on the assumption that the maximum **int** value is **INT_MAX** and that the minimum one is − **INT_MAX**. Unfortunately the latter need not be the case, and with most machines it is not! For example, with 16-bit integers and 2's-complement representation, the minimum **int** value is not −32767 but −32768. Since we want our input function to read −32768 correctly, we need a special way of dealing with negative integers. Besides **INT_MAX**, there is also the constant **INT_MIN**, denoting this minimum value.

If we want our input function to be generally applicable, we had better not restrict it to input from the stream **stdin**, that is, from the keyboard. Another undesirable aspect of our preliminary function **rdint** is that it may print an error message and terminate program execution. If an error occurs, we prefer the function to report this back to its caller. This is general practice in the C standard library. For example, the function **malloc** returns **NULL** if not enough memory is available, rather than printing an error message and terminating program execution. The advantage is twofold:

(1) The function that calls the standard function is problem oriented and can therefore supply an error message that is related to the application.
(2) It may be desirable not to terminate program execution but take other actions.

As is usual with many standard functions, such as **scanf**, for example, we will pass the value that has been read as a parameter, and use the return value for an error code. The declaration of our function will read as follows:

```
int readint(FILE *fp, int *p);
```

The second argument must be the address of an **int** variable into which the value that is read is to be written. The return value will be either **EOF**, defined as −1 in *stdio.h*, or one of the values defined in the following header file:

```
/* INTIO.H: A header file to be used in connection with the
            functions readint and writeint
*/
#define OK 1          /* Success                */
#define INVALID 0     /* Invalid character read */
#define OVFLOW  -2    /* Integer overflow       */
int readint(FILE *fp, int *p);
int writeint(FILE *fp, int w, int x);
```

The improved input function **readint** is listed below, along with a similar *output function* **writeint**. The latter is given here to show how radix conversion *from binary to decimal* can be done. It also shows how to use a given field width **w** in such a way that the output is right justified. This module can be compiled separately:

```
/* INTIO.C: Input and output of formatted integers.
            Function readint reads an integer from stream fp.
            It includes a test for integer overflow.
            The output function writeint writes integer x,
            using field width w.
            If reading or writing succeeds, return value is 1,
            otherwise it is zero or negative (see header file
            intio.h).
*/
#include <stdio.h>
#include <ctype.h>
#include <limits.h>
#include "intio.h"

int readint(FILE *fp, int *p)
{   int i, d, ch, neg;
    do ch = getc(fp); while (isspace(ch));
    if (ch == EOF) return EOF;
    /* We have now skipped any leading blanks */
    neg = ch == '-';
    if (neg || ch == '+') ch = getc(fp);
    if (ch == EOF) return EOF;
    if (!isdigit(ch)) return INVALID;
    i = ch - '0';
    if (neg) i = -i;
    while (ch = getc(fp), isdigit(ch))
    {   d = ch - '0';
        if (neg) d = -d;
        if ((!neg && i > (INT_MAX - d)/10) ||
            (neg && i < (INT_MIN - d)/10))
           return OVFLOW;
        i = 10 * i + d;
    }
    if (ch != EOF) ungetc(ch, stdin);
    *p = i;
    return OK;
}


#define CHARBUFSIZE 50
#define putchr(ch) if (putc(ch, fp) == EOF) return EOF

int writeint(FILE *fp, int w, int x)
{   int n = 0, i, r, neg = x < 0;
```

```
      char digs[CHARBUFSIZE];
      if (x == 0) { digs[0] = '0'; n = 1; } else
      do
      {  r = x % 10;
         digs[n++] = '0' + (neg ? -r : r);
         if (n == CHARBUFSIZE) return OVFLOW;
         /* This is extremely unlikely to happen
         */
         x /= 10;
      } while (x);
      i = w - n;
      if (neg) i--;
      while (i-- > 0) putchr(' ');
      if (neg) putchr('-');
      for (i = n-1; i >= 0; i--)
         putchr(digs[i]);
      return OK;
   }
```

Function **writeint** converts integers from the binary to the decimal format. Again, we can use Horner's rule to understand how it works. (As before, the external format, with radix 10, is more essential in our algorithm than the internal binary format.) For example, since

$$5482 = ((5 \times 10 + 4) \times 10 + 8) \times 10 + 2$$

we can obtain the least significant digit 2 as the remainder 5482 % 10. We also use the truncated quotient 5482/10 = 548. Since

$$548 = (5 \times 10 + 4) \times 10 + 8$$

we proceed by computing 548 % 10 = 8, 548 / 10 = 54, and so on, until the quotient is 0. In this way, we obtain the decimal digits of the given integer from right to left, but we need them from left to right. We therefore first store the digits in an array, and print them only when they have all been calculated. This also provides us with the possibility of printing leading spaces, using a given field width **w**. Note that the call **writeint(fp, w, x)** is almost equivalent to **fprintf(fp, "%*d", w, x)**. Both calls use more than **w** positions if needed.

Here is a simple demonstration program, which copies integers from an input file to an output file. It uses the status indicators returned by the functions **readint** and **writeint** to print error messages. After compiling this module, we must link it together with the object module resulting from compiling INTIO.C. Both modules include the header file INTIO.H, which must be in the current directory.

```
/* INTCOPY.C: This program demonstrates the use of readint
              and writeint. The names of input and output
              files are to be supplied as program
              arguments.
*/
#include <stdio.h>
#include <stdlib.h>
#include "intio.h"

main(int argc, char *argv[])
{  FILE *fpin, *fpout;
   int x, status;
   if (argc != 3)
   { puts("Usage: INTCOPY inputfile outputfile");
     exit(1);
   }
   if ((fpin = fopen(argv[1], "r")) == NULL)
   { puts("Cannot open input file"); exit(1);
   }
   if ((fpout = fopen(argv[2], "w")) == NULL)
   { puts("Cannot open output file"); exit(1);
   }
   while ((status = readint(fpin, &x)) == OK)
   {  if (writeint(fpout, 4, x) != OK)
      { puts("Output error"); exit(1);
      }
      fprintf(fpout, "\n");
   }
   if (status == OVFLOW) puts("Integer too large"); else
   if (status == INVALID) puts("Invalid character read");
   return 0;
}
```

If this program is executed on systems with **INT_MAX** = 32767 and **INT_MIN** = −32768, then with the input file

```
0   123   32767   −32768   32768
```

it produces the output file

```
    0
  123
32767
−32768
```

and then displays the message

```
Integer too large
```

The integers are not all right aligned, because the field width used in the call to **writeint** is 4. This program shows that **readint** accepts the minimum **int** value −32768 but rejects the corresponding positive value 32768 because it exceeds **INT_MAX**.

1.10 Powers with Integer Exponents

There are only four basic arithmetic operations, namely addition, subtraction, multiplication and division, in which any other arithmetic tasks must be expressed. However, we are not confined to these basic operations because the C language offers a set of standard mathematical functions (although, internally, at the machine level, only the four operations mentioned will take place). These standard functions include *pow*, which raises a number to a given power. For floating-point numbers x and y, where x is positive, we have

$$pow(x, y) = x^y$$

If this function had not been available, we could have defined:

```
#include <math.h>

double pow(double x, double y)
{  return exp(y * log(x));
}
```

Both this version and the standard function *pow* accept a floating-point exponent y. However, in many applications the given exponent is an integer, which means that the power in question can also be computed by repeated multiplication. Since in ANSI C the header file *math.h* contains a *function prototype* (that is, a complete declaration, including information about parameters) we can also use an integer n as an exponent and compute x^n by writing

```
pow(x, n)
```

However, there are three reasons to develop a special power function for this important special case:

(1) We want to admit negative values of x (or the value 0 if n is positive).
(2) We may find a faster algorithm.
(3) It is an instructive programming exercise.

Here is our first version:

```
double power1(double x, int n)
{   return n > 0 ? x * power1(x, n-1) :
            n < 0 ? 1.0/power1(x, -n)   : 1.0;
}
```

We wish to admit negative exponents n, but, unfortunately, the test to see if n is negative is performed a great many times if n is large, whereas only one such a test is actually needed. This is sometimes another drawback of recursive functions. It is due to the fact that the function is called both externally and internally. If we insist on using recursion, the only way to avoid this drawback is using two functions, namely a nonrecursive one, **power2**, for the external user, and a recursive one, **pw**, for internal use only:

```
static double pw(double x, int n)
{   return n ? x * pw(x, n-1) : 1.0;
}
```

```
double power2(double x, int n)
{   return n >= 0 ? pw(x, n) : 1.0/pw(x, -n);
}
```

(In cases like this, the nonrecursive function, available to the user, is sometimes called a *driver* function.) With an iterative solution, we have no such problems:

```
double power3(double x, int n)
{ double p = x;
  int negexp = n < 0;
  if (n == 0) return 1.0;
  if (negexp) n = -n;
  while (--n) p *= x;
  return negexp ? 1.0/p : p;
}
```

For the exponent values $-3 \leq n \leq 3$, this function is quite good because it does not perform any unnecessary multiplications. If $n = 4$, we see that three multiplications are carried out:

$$x^4 = x \cdot x \cdot x \cdot x$$

If we had to compute this by hand we would no doubt use

$$x^4 = (x^2)^2$$

which involves only two multiplications, and **power3** will be very inefficient for large values of n. As we have seen in previous sections, floating-point operations are very time-consuming, so we will try to find a faster solution. The following relationship provides a basis for this:

$$x^n = \begin{cases} 1/(x^{-n}) & \text{if } n < 0 \\ 1 & \text{if } n = 0 \\ x & \text{if } n = 1 \\ (x^h)^2 & \text{if } n \text{ is greater than 1 and even} \\ (x^h)^2 \cdot x & \text{if } n \text{ is greater than 1 and odd} \end{cases}$$

(where h is the truncated quotient $n/2$)

Again, we begin with a recursive version:

```
double power4(double x, int n)
{  if (n < 2)
       return (n == 0 ? 1.0 :
               n == 1 ? x : 1.0/power4(x, -n));
   else
   {  double y=power4(x, (n >> 1));
      y *= y;
      return n & 1 ? y * x : y;
   }
}
```

Remember, > > means *shift right* and & means *bitwise and*, so we have

```
(n >> 1) == (n / 2)
(n & 1)  == (n % 2)
```

A fast iterative power function

Replacing **power4** with an iterative function that is at least as fast is not a straight-forward task. It can be done by using the binary representation of the exponent. For example, we have

$$102 = (1100110)_2$$

Since the 1-bits in the positions 6, 5, 2, and 1 (with position 0 as the least significant bit) represent powers of 2, we also have

$$102 = 1 \times 2^6 + 1 \times 2^5 + 0 \times 2^4 + 0 \times 2^3 + 1 \times 2^2 + 1 \times 2^1 + 0 \times 2^0$$
$$= 64 + 32 + 4 + 2$$

and

$$x^{102} = x^{64} \times x^{32} \times x^4 \times x^2$$

In this right-hand side, we use a selection of the powers $x^1, x^2, x^4, x^8, x^{16}, x^{32}, x^{64}$, which we can compute very efficiently by repeated squaring. Note that the selection we want is based on the position of the 1-bits in the given exponent 102. This idea leads to our final power function:

```
/* POWER.C: Raising x to the power n
*/
double power(double x, int n)
{  int negexp = n<0;
   double y;
   if (n == 0) return 1.0;
   if (negexp) n = -n;
   while (!(n & 1)) {n >>= 1; x *= x;}
   y = x;
   while (n >>= 1)
   {  x *= x;
      if (n & 1) y *= x;
   }
   return negexp ? 1.0/y : y;
}
```

With a positive exponent n, we can use the binary representation of n to find the number of floating-point multiplications performed by the call **power(x, n)**:

(total number of bits in n) + (number of 1-bits in n) − 2

According to this, there are $7 + 4 - 2 = 9$ multiplications in our example, where

$$n = 102 = (1100110)_2$$

We can prove this as follows. Let us say that the binary representation of n consists of k bits, m of which are 1. In function **power**, there are two while-loops in which the squaring statement

```
x *= x;
```

is executed. Each time, this is immediately preceded by shifting **n** one bit to the right, and that statement is executed only as long as this shift operation gives a nonzero result. Since the result of the kth shift is zero, it follows that squaring takes place $k - 1$ times. The first while-loop detects the least significant 1-bit in n, and it terminates as soon as this is found. Except for this bit, the following statement is executed for all 1-bits, so it is executed $m - 1$ times:

```
y *= x;
```

Thus we have $k - 1$ squaring operations and $m - 1$ updates of y, so the total number of multiplications is

$$k + m - 2$$

We should not have the illusion that this 'binary' method of power evaluation should be optimal. There are cases where we can do better, as, for example, in the case $n = 15$. Since 15 is written 1111 in binary, our function **power** would perform $4 + 4 - 2 = 6$ multiplications, but only 5 are actually needed:

$$2^5 = (2^2)^2 \times 2 \qquad \text{(3 multiplications)}$$
$$2^{15} = 2^5 \times 2^5 \times 2^5 \qquad \text{(2 multiplications)}$$

This is only a theoretical remark, however. In general, it would be an extremely time-consuming task to find the least number of multiplications that are absolutely necessary for an exponentiation (even though such a task would be done with integers only)!

Some experiments with the above five power functions showed that for large exponents **power4** and **power** are much faster than **power1**, **power2** and **power3**. This is what we may expect, since in **power4** and **power** the number of multiplications is reduced dramatically by squaring intermediate results. It also turned out that there is very little difference in the speed of the three functions **power1**, **power2** and **power3**. Similarly, **power4** and **power** are about equally fast, so, in this example, it is hardly worthwhile to switch from recursion to iteration for reasons of efficiency. This illustrates that our rule of thumb (3) in Section 1.6 should not be taken too literally. Still, this rule may be useful in other cases. After all, in this section we have dealt with floating-point multiplication, which is a very time-consuming operation compared with recursive function calls. Replacing recursion with iteration is more likely to speed things up in applications with only integer arithmetic. More importantly, with recursion we always have to think of stack overflow, which is not the case with iteration.

Exercises

1.1 What is the output of the programs P1A.C and P1B.C, listed below?

```
/* P1A.C */
#include <stdio.h>
void f(int n)
{ if (n > 0) {f(n-3); printf("%3d\n", n); f(n-2);}
}
```

```
main()
{ f(6); return 0;
}


/* P1B.C */
#include <stdio.h>
f(int n)
{ if (n > 0)
    { f(n/10-100); printf("%6d\n", n); f(n/5-200);
    }
}
main()
{ f(10000); return 0;
}
```

1.2   Replace the following recursive functions **f, g,** and **h** with (more or less) equivalent
       iterative ones. In each case, compare the amount of memory space and computing
       time used by the two versions.

```
void f(void)
{ if (getchar() == ' ') f();
}

void g(int n)      /* You may assume:  n < 100  */
{ int i;
    if (n > 0)
    { scanf("%d", &i); g(n-1); printf("%d\n", i);
    }
}

int h(int n)
{ return n < 0 ? 0 :
         n == 0 ? 1 : h(n-1) + h(n-2);
}
```

1.3   Write a function with an integer argument, which returns the sum of the decimal
       digits of the argument. Compare a recursive and an iterative solution to this
       problem.

1.4   Write a program which reads a sequence of floating-point numbers and prints the
       sum of the 1st, 3rd, 6th, 10th, 15th, ... element of this sequence. Interpret any
       nonnumeric character as the end of the input sequence.

1.5 Write a program which reads a decimal digit d. Print all positive integers x less than 100 that have the characteristic that d occurs in the decimal representations of both x and the square of x.

1.6 Write a function with a floating-point argument x and an integer argument n, which returns the following approximation of e^x:

$$1 + x + \frac{x^2}{2!} + \frac{x^3}{3!} + \cdots + \frac{x^n}{n!}$$

1.7 Write the function **prime**, which has one integer argument n. The function returns 1 if n is a prime number (2, 3, 5, 7, 11, ...) and 0 if it is not.

1.8 Write a program which reads a positive integer and writes this as a product of primes. For example,

$$120 = 2 \times 2 \times 2 \times 3 \times 5$$

1.9 Write the function **trunc** with a floating-point argument **x** and a positive integer argument **n**. The function returns a floating-point value equal to **x** except for all fractional decimal positions after the nth, which are zero. For example,

```
trunc(-3.14159, 3) = -3.141
```

1.10 Write your own function **floor1**, similar to the standard function **floor**. It has one floating-point argument **x**. The floating-point value to be returned is obtained by truncating **x**. Use double-precision floating-point numbers, which may have a greater precision than long integers, so you cannot simply write

```
double floor1(x) double x;
{  return (double) (long) x;
}
```

1.11 Write your own function **cos1**, so that it can be used instead of the standard function **cos**. Use the following properties of the cosine function:

$$\cos x = 1 - \frac{x^2}{2!} + \frac{x^4}{4!} - \frac{x^6}{6!} + \cdots \tag{1}$$

$$\cos x = \cos(x - 2k\pi) \quad (k \text{ integer}) \tag{2}$$

$$\cos x = -\cos(\pi - x) \tag{3}$$

$$\cos x = 2 \cos^2(x/2) - 1 \tag{4}$$

With (2), (3), (4), you can reduce the argument of the function **cos1** to a value in some small domain, which will cause the series (1) to converge more rapidly.

1.12 Write the function **rdflo**, without parameters, which reads a number from the keyboard and returns this as a floating-point value. The function is to read integers and floating-point numbers in the usual notation, so that the two statements

```
scanf("%f", &x);
x = rdflo();
```

accept the same numerical input. In case of any leading nonnumeric characters, **rdflo** is to display a clear error message and to stop program execution. (In that case **scanf** would return the value 0.) Use **getchar** to read character by character.

1.13 Write the function **printflo** to print a floating-point number, so that we can write

```
printflo(w, d, x);
```

instead of

```
printf("%*.*f", w, d, x);
```

In ANSI C, the latter statement means that **x** is printed in **w** positions and with **d** digits after the decimal point. The expression **x** has floating-point type. Use **putchar** as the only output facility in this function.

1.14 Write two functions, one recursive and the other iterative, to compute the nth element of the Fibonacci sequence $F_0, F_1, F_2, ...$, defined by the rule that $F_0 = 0$, $F_1 = 1$ and every further term is the sum of the preceding two. Thus the sequence begins 0, 1, 1, 2, 3, 5, 8, 13, ... ; compare the efficiency of your functions, both analytically and experimentally.

1.15 As we will see in Section 3.3, a set of n objects has $C(n, k)$ distinct subsets of k objects, where $0 \le k \le n$ and

$$C(n, k) = \frac{n!}{k!\,(n - k)!} \tag{1}$$

Instead of computing $C(n, k)$ by using (1), we can use a recursive function, based on the following relation, which applies if n and k are both greater than zero:

$$C(n, k) = C(n-1, k-1) + C(n-1, k) \tag{2}$$

What if n and k are not both greater than zero?

Relation (2) is illustrated by *Pascal's triangle*, which consists of lines (numbered $n = 0, 1, ...$) of integers. Here are the first six lines of this triangle:

			1			$(n = 0)$
		1		1		$(n = 1)$
	1		2		1	$(n = 2)$

$$
\begin{array}{ccccccccccc}
 & & & & & 1 & & & & & (n=0)\\
 & & & & 1 & & 1 & & & & (n=1)\\
 & & & 1 & & 2 & & 1 & & & (n=2)\\
 & & 1 & & 3 & & 3 & & 1 & & (n=3)\\
 & 1 & & 4 & & 6 & & 4 & & 1 & (n=4)\\
1 & & 5 & & 10 & & 10 & & 5 & & 1 \quad (n=5)
\end{array}
$$

Except for the integers 1, each integer in this triangle is computed as the sum of the two nearest integers on the preceding line. The integers on line n are numbered $k = 0, 1, ..., n$, from left to right. We can find $C(n, k)$ in position k of line n. For example, we have $10 = 4 + 6$ for the first 10 on line $n = 5$. This can also be expressed as $C(5, 2) = C(4, 1) + C(4, 2)$, which is a special case of (2). Pascal's triangle enables us to compute $C(n, k)$ by means of a nonrecursive function, without using (1). Write C functions for $C(n, k)$ based on each of the three methods mentioned, and compare them, both analytically and experimentally.

1.16 Implement a structure similar to that shown in Fig. 1.1, but with rows of variable length. In each row i ($i > 0$), all positive divisors of i, other than 1 and i, are to be stored. These divisors are to be preceded by a number indicating how many there are. The situation is as shown in Fig. 1.3.

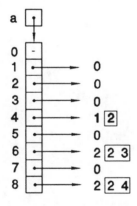

Fig. 1.3. Divisors stored in rows of variable length

Since all positive integers are divisors of 0, we set **a[0]** = **NULL**. For **i** > 0, there are n = **a[i][0]** nontrivial divisors of **i**, which are stored in **a[i][1]**, ..., **a[i][n]**. Let us write m for the greatest integer for which we store the divisors, so we have m = 8 in Fig. 1.3. Write a function to set up this data structure for a given m, and use a demonstration program to show that it works. This program reads m and uses this to store the divisors of all positive integers not greater than m, by means of the function just mentioned. Then, with some integer k (not greater than m) entered by the user, it displays all nontrivial divisors of k, found in the data structure.

2

Array and File Manipulation

In many applications, we have to re-arrange sets of objects in a specific order. An example of such a set is the data we would need to compile a telephone dictionary. Here each object is a 'record' consisting of three components, namely a name, an address and a telephone number. The process of placing objects in a specific order is called *sorting*. In the case of a telephone dictionary, the objects are sorted in alphabetic order of the names so that with a given name the corresponding telephone number can easily be found. We say that the name is used as a *key*. In general, we sort records in such a way that their keys will be in ascending (or, rarely, descending) order. As long as we are dealing with sorting methods themselves, rather than with their applications, we may as well use very simple objects such as numbers, which are, so to speak, their own keys.

2.1 Straight Sorting Methods

Let us use an example to discuss a simple sorting method. If the sequence

    109 75 200 25 38 19 150 11 20

is to be sorted, it is a good idea to exchange the smallest integer, 11, with the first, 109. We then obtain the new sequence

    <u>11</u> 75 200 25 38 19 150 109 20
    O.K.

The first element of the sequence is now O.K., so after this we can restrict ourselves to the remaining elements. We now apply the same procedure to the subsequence that

39

starts at the second integer, 75. Thus we select its smallest element, 19, and exchange it with 75, which gives:

<u>11   19</u>   200   25   38   75   150   11   20
   O.K.

We then proceed with the subsequence starting at the third element, 200, and so on, until we have dealt with a subsequence of only two elements. This sorting method is called *straight selection*. Here is a C function, which sorts an array **a** of *n* integers in this way:

```
/* SELSORT.C: Straight-selection sort, applied to an
              array of integers
*/
void selsort(int *a, int n)
{   int i, j, k, min;
    for (i=0; i<n-1; i++)
    {   k = i; min = a[k];
        for (j=i+1; j<n; j++)
        if (a[j] < min) {k = j; min = a[k];}
        /* Exchange a[k] ( = min) with a[i]: */
        a[k] = a[i]; a[i] = min;
    }
}
```

You may wonder why not replace the *i*-loop with the following one, which is slightly shorter:

```
for (i=0; i<n-1; i++)
{   k = i;
    for (j=i+1; j<n; j++)
        if (a[j] < a[k]) k = j;
    /* Exchange a[k] with a[i]:  */
    min = a[k]; a[k] = a[i]; a[i] = min;
}
```

However, if we modified **selsort** in this sense, the new version would be slightly slower, because in its inner loop we would perform the test **a[j] < a[k]**, instead of the simpler test **a[j] < min**. This test will often fail, so the higher speed of this test in the original version outweighs some extra work that is done only when the test succeeds (namely the work involved in assigning the value of **a[k]** to the variable **min**). Far more important than considering such subtle modifications is the observation that the running time of the straight-selection algorithm is $O(n^2)$. Recall that we discussed this 'big-oh' notation in Section 1.1. There are two nested loops in **selsort**; if we doubled the value of **n**, the range of the controlled variable **i**, in the outer loop, would approximately be doubled. (Actually, this range would increase by a factor $(2n-1)/(n-1)$ instead of 2, hence the word 'approximately', which from now on we will omit.) As for the inner loop, with controlled variable **j**, the average range would also be doubled, so as a result of increasing **n** by a factor 2, the total running time would increase by a factor 4, and, in general, increasing **n** by a factor k implies an increase in running time by a factor k^2. As we know, this is expressed very briefly by saying that the running time is $O(n^2)$, or equivalently, that the algorithm has time complexity n^2.

We will also consider a version of the straight-selection sorting algorithm for strings. When comparing two strings, we use the addresses of their first characters, because, technically, the value of a string is the address of its first character. Note that we use the term *string* either for that address or for the character sequence itself. This may seem confusing, but it is not in practice. For example, the value of ***"ABC"** is equal to **'A'**. This shows that the string **"ABC"** has type pointer-to-**char** and that its value is the address of its first character. On the other hand, we obviously refer to the actual sequence of characters when we are talking about the ith character of **"ABC"**. Recall that for strings **s** and **t**, we write

```
strcmp(s, t) < 0
```

for 'string **s** alphabetically precedes string **t**', and

```
strcpy(s, t)
```

for 'copy (the characters of) string **t** to **s**'. Should we instead write s < t and s = t, respectively, then this would manipulate addresses, not the character sequences starting at these addresses. We conclude this recapitulation of strings by recalling the essential role of the terminating null character, **'\0'**, in string handling routines such as **strcmp** and **strcpy**. This enables us to use a portion of a character array as a string, namely the portion that begins with a given address and ends with the first null character that follows.

In our first sorting function for strings, we will deal with strings of maximum length 20. To accommodate the terminating null character, each string will occupies 21 bytes. The following function sorts an array of n such strings:

```
/* CHSELSORT.C: Straight selection, applied to an array of
                fixed-length character strings
*/
void chselsort(char a[][21], int n)
{   char *p, min[21];
    int i, j;
    for (i=0; i<n-1; i++)
    {   p = a[i];
        for (j=i+1; j<n; j++)
```

```
            if (strcmp(a[j], p) < 0) p = a[j];
         /* Exchange the character sequence starting at p
            with that starting at a[i]:
         */
         strcpy(min, p);
         strcpy(p, a[i]);
         strcpy(a[i], min);
      }
   }
```

If the comparison **strcmp(a[j], p)** succeeds, we do not copy the characters themselves, but, instead, we store the value of **a[j]**, that is, the address of **a[j] [0]**, into the variable **p**. Copying the characters themselves to **min** at this stage would not lead to faster comparisons in the way copying integers did in **selsort**.

Since the functions **selsort** and **sort2** (both based on the straight-selection sorting method) have running time $O(n^2)$, they are suitable only for relatively small sequences. Besides straight selection, there are many other simple sorting methods which usually also have time complexity n^2. Collectively, we call them straight methods.

With straight selection, the number of comparisons does not depend on the initial order of the elements to be sorted. This is different in another straight sorting method, namely *shaker sort*. This method is even worse than straight selection if the elements are initially in random order. However, it is extremely fast if only a few elements are in a wrong position and all the others are in ascending order. Consider, for example, the following sequence:

10   21   <u>92</u>   35   50   69   80   83   90   95   100   120

The length of this sequence is $n = 12$. As usual in C, we number the positions of the elements 0, 1, ..., $n-1$. Only the underlined element, 92, is in a wrong position. If, starting at the left, we compare each two neighbor elements, and exchange them if the left one is greater than the right one, then 92 is exchanged with 35, then with 50, and so on, until it is in its correct position, between 90 and 95. In this example, all elements are then in ascending order, but in general this need not be the case. If we proceed from left to right, and if after exchanging the elements in the positions j and $j+1$ no other exchanges are carried out during this scan, then all elements in the positions $j+1$, $j+2$, ..., $n-1$ are in their correct places, so only elements in the positions 0, 1, ..., j may still be wrong. We could now deal with these, again starting at the left. We would then sort according to the method called *bubble sort*. However, we had better work from right to left this time, since there might be only one element that is too small for its position, so that it is to be shifted to the left. We therefore alternately proceed from left to right and from right to left, which explains the name *shaker sort*. If, after proceeding from right to left, the final exchanged elements are at the positions $j-1$ and j, the elements 0, 1, ..., $j-1$ are in their correct positions, so we can now restrict ourselves to the subsequence that starts at position j. The following function is based on this principle:

```
/* SHAKER.C: Shaker sort, applied to an array
                of integers
*/
void shaker(int *a, int n)
{  int *left=a, *right=a+n-1, *start=a, *p, *q, x;
   do
   {  for (p=left; p < right; p++)
      {  q = p + 1;
         if (*p > *q) {x = *q; *q = *p; *p = x; start = p;}
      }
      right = start;
      for (p=right; p > left; p--)
      {  q = p - 1;
         if (*q > *p) {x = *q; *q = *p; *p = x; start = p;}
      }
      left = start;
   }  while (left < right);
}
```

We have used pointer notation here, which turned out to be faster than the corresponding array notation. With shaker sort, there are usually more exchanges to be carried out than with straight-selection sort. It is therefore worthwhile to use two pointers **p** and **q** for the elements to be exchanged. With the more conventional array notation and integer variables **i**, **i1**, **left**, **right**, **j**, instead of pointers **p**, **q**, **left**, **right**, **start**, respectively, the first of the above two for-loops would have read

```
for (i=left; i<right; i++)
{  i1 = i + 1;
   if (a[i] > a[i1])
   {  x = a[i1]; a[i1] = a[i]; a[i] = x; j = i;
   }
}
```

which may be somewhat slower.

2.2 Quicksort

We will now discuss a sorting method which is very efficient for large sequences of objects. This method, called *quicksort* (C. A. R. Hoare, *Computer Journal*, April 1962), is based on partitioning the given sequence into two subsequences. For some rather arbitrarily chosen element x, called a *pivot*, all elements of the first resulting subsequence are not greater than x, and all elements of the second are not less than x.

Then the same method is applied to both subsequences, and so on. Here is a recursive function, which applies quicksort to a sequence of integers:

```
/* QSORT1.C: Quicksort applied to an array
            of integers; first version
*/
void qsort1(int *a, int n)
{  int i=0, j=n-1, x=a[j/2], w;
   do
   {  while (a[i] < x) i++;
      while (a[j] > x) j--;
      if (i < j) {w = a[i]; a[i] = a[j]; a[j] = w;}
   }  while (++i <= --j);
   if (i == j + 3) i--, j++;
   if (j > 0) qsort1(a, j+1);       /*  a[0], ..., a[j]    */
   if (i < n-1) qsort1(a+i, n-i); /*  a[i], ..., a[n-1] */
}
```

If, for example, we have defined

```
int a[8] = {23, 398, 34, 100, 57, 67, 55, 320};
```

then we can use **qsort1** as follows:

```
qsort1(a, 8);
```

In this example, we have $x = 100$, since $j = 7$ and $a[j/2] = a[3] = 100$. The integer variable i, starting with 0, is then incremented until $a[i] \geq x$, so in this example the first while-loop ends when with $i = 1$, because then $a[i] = 398 \geq 100$. Similarly, j is initially given the value $n - 1 = 7$, and is decremented until it has such a value that $a[j] \leq x$. This is the case when $j = 6$, since $a[6] = 55 \leq 100$. The two elements 398 and 55 are then exchanged, and, in the comparison

```
++i <= --j
```

the i and j are updated once again, which gives $i = 2$ and $j = 5$. The new situation is as follows:

		i				j	
0	1	2	3	4	5	6	7
23	55	34	100	57	67	398	320

$x = 100$

The first while-loop is executed again, so i is incremented until we have $a[i] = a[3] = 100$. In the second while-loop, j is not decremented this time, since 67 is not greater than x. So the elements 100 and 67 are now exchanged, and i and j are updated once again, which gives i = j = 4, as shown below:

```
           i j
   0   1   2   3  4   5    6    7
 ┌────┬────┬────┬────┬────┬─────┬─────┬─────┐
 │ 23 │ 55 │ 34 │ 67 │ 57 │ 100 │ 398 │ 320 │    x = 100
 └────┴────┴────┴────┴────┴─────┴─────┴─────┘
```

Since i is now equal to j, the test for continuation of the do-while-loop succeeds, and the first of the two inner while-loops is executed again; as 57 is less than x, the variable i is incremented. Then a[i] = 100, so this while-loop stops with i = 5. In the second while-loop, j is not decremented, since, with j = 4, element a[j] is not greater than x. The do-while-loop now ends with i = 5 and j = 4:

```
                       j    i
   0   1   2   3      4    5    6    7
 ┌────┬────┬────┬────┬────┐┌─────┬─────┬─────┐
 │ 23 │ 55 │ 34 │ 67 │ 57 ││ 100 │ 398 │ 320 │    x = 100
 └────┴────┴────┴────┴────┘└─────┴─────┴─────┘
   Left subsequence:        Right subsequence:
   j + 1 elements,          n − i elements,
   all ≤ x                  all ≥ x
```

This completes the partitioning process. To the left of the double vertical line no element is greater and to its right no element is less than x. It is interesting that this method will always work properly, even if x is unfortunately chosen. It would be ideal if x were the median, that is, if there were as many array elements less than x as there are elements greater than x. In less fortunate cases, the resulting subsequences have unequal lengths, as in the above example, where these lengths are 5 and 3. After partitioning the given sequence, it seems that we still have a long way to go before all elements are in ascending order. However, the only thing that remains to be done is to apply the same process to both the left and the right partitions, which have start addresses a and a + i, and lengths j + 1 and n − i, respectively. In qsort1 this is done recursively for both partitions, which is a very simple and elegant solution.

Because of the test at its end, the do-while-loop always ends with i > j. In our example, it ends with i = j + 1. There are two other possibilities, which we will consider now. First, it can end with i = j + 2. This occurs, for example, if the sequence {50, 40, 30, 20, 10} is given. In this case, we have i = 3 and j = 1 after the do-while-loop, and the element a[j+1] = x = 30 lies between a[i] and a[j], and is already in its correct position. As above, the left and right subsequences are {a[0], ..., a[j]} and {a[i], ..., a[n1]}, with a[j+1] in between.

Second, the do-while-loop can end with i = j + 3. This happens, for example, if the sequence to be sorted is {10, 20, 50, 30, 40}. We then have x = 50, and the first two elements to be exchanged are 50 and 40. After this, i and j are updated, which gives

```
           i j
   0   1   2   3   4
 ┌────┬────┬────┬────┬────┐
 │ 10 │ 20 │ 40 │ 30 │ 50 │    x = 50
 └────┴────┴────┴────┴────┘
```

Then the first while-loop increments **i** and the second leaves **j** unchanged, so we have **i** = 4 and **j** = 3. No elements are exchanged this time, and the test **++i <= --j** updates **i** and **j** once again, which gives **i** = 5, **j** = 2:

```
                 j                         i
     0     1     2     3     4       5
   ┌─────┬─────┬─────┬─────┬─────┐
   │ 10  │ 20  │ 40  │ 30  │ 50  │       x = 50
   └─────┴─────┴─────┴─────┴─────┘
```

It would now not be correct to restrict ourselves to the left subsequence **a[0]**, ..., **a[j]** (the right one **a[i]**, ..., **a[j]** being empty). We see that the last updates of **i** and **j** were undesirable, so we undo this by means of the conditional statement

```
if (i == j + 3) i--, j++;
```

After this, we have **i** = 4 and **j** = 3, so now we have the subsequence {10, 20, 30, 30} on the left, which is sorted recursively, and the short one {50} on the right. No recursive call is executed for the latter, because its length is less than 2. Instead of writing this possibly unaesthetic conditional statement after the do-while-loop, we could have written, for example,

```
if (i > j) break;
```

immediately after the second while-statement, but that would be slightly less efficient because it requires an additional test in the do-while-loop.[1] As discussed in Section 1.2, we always try to minimize the number of tests inside a loop, even if this requires some additional actions outside it. Besides, our version gave us a good opportunity to discuss the three cases **i** = **j** + 1, **i** = **j** + 2, and **i** = **j** + 3, so that we can clearly see how quicksort works.

Except for the worst-case situation, which in practice is extremely unlikely to occur, the running time of quicksort is $O(n \cdot \log n)$, so it will be approximately equal to $cn \cdot \log n$, where c is some constant. Note that the base of the logarithm only influences the value of c, and, since we leave the latter unspecified, that base is irrelevant in our discussion. Remember that for large arguments, logarithmic functions increase extremely slowly. For example, using base 10, we have

$$\log 1000 \quad = 3$$
$$\log 10000 \quad = 4$$

so if we switch from problem size n_1 = 1000 to problem size n_2 = 10000, the running time will increase by a factor

---

[1]   If we inserted this conditional break-statement in that way, we could omit the clause **if (i < j)** that follows. This would save a test, but it would cause the statements **w=a[i];** etc. to be executed unnecessarily if **i** is equal to **j**. The if-clause in question must not be omitted in our current version.

$$\frac{n_2 \cdot \log n_2}{n_1 \cdot \log n_1} = \frac{10000 \times 4}{1000 \times 3} \approx 13.3$$

whereas with a straight sorting method, that factor would be

$$\frac{n_2^{\,2}}{n_1^{\,2}} = \frac{10000^{\,2}}{1000^{\,2}} = 100$$

This example illustrates the significance of the concept of time complexity, as introduced in Section 1.1. For any algorithm with running time $O(n \cdot \log n)$ and any other algorithm with running time $O(n^2)$, there is a value of n beyond which the former algorithm will be faster than the latter. In practice we may work with values of n that will not exceed some limit, and we should be aware that we have not really shown that quicksort is faster than straight sorting methods, for, let us say, $n = 1000$, although we will probably expect that to be the case. Both analytic and experimental investigations have confirmed such expectations, that is, they have shown that quicksort is really a very fast sorting algorithm, even for rather small values of n, such as, say, 100.

It possible to eliminate one of the two recursive calls in **qsort1**. As discussed in Section 1.6, recursion is associated with the use of a stack, so it is reasonable to ask whether function **qsort1** might cause stack overflow if large arrays are to be sorted. In practice stack overflow is most unlikely to happen, but such a vague answer is not completely satisfactory. If each recursive call is applied to a subsequence that is almost as long as the current sequence, then, indeed, the recursion depth can be considerable and may even cause stack overflow. Although very improbable, this is not impossible. It would be nice if each recursive call were applied to a subsequence of at most half the size of the sequence under consideration. Fortunately, we can achieve this. In **qsort1**, one recursive call is at the very end of this function. As with *tail recursion* (where there is only one recursive call, as discussed in Section 1.6), that call at the end can be replaced with iteration. Instead of simply eliminating the second recursive call in **qsort1**, we actually want to eliminate the one that deals with the *longer subsequence*. That recursive call would always be the very last action in **qsort1** if the two program lines

```
if (j > 0) qsort1(a, j+1);      /*  a[0], ..., a[j]   */
if (i < n-1) qsort1(a+i, n-i); /*  a[i], ..., a[n-1] */
```

were replaced with

```
if (j + 1 < n - i)
{  if (j > 0) qsort1(a, j+1);      /* The shorter sequence */
   if (i < n-1) qsort1(a+i, n-i); /* The longer sequence  */
}
```

```
    else
    {  if (i < n-1) qsort1(a+i, n-i); /* The shorter sequence */
       if (j > 0) qsort1(a, j+1);      /* The longer sequence  */
    }
```

With this modification, the shorter subsequence is dealt with first, and the recursive call applied to the longer subsequence is executed as the final statement of the function. Then, in the **if** and the **else** branches, we can easily eliminate the final recursive calls, as function **q_sort** shows:

```
/* Q_SORT.C: Quicksort with limited recursion depth */
void q_sort(int *a, int n)
{  int i, j, x, w;
   do
   {  i=0; j=n-1;
      x = a[j/2];
      do
      {  while (a[i] < x) i++;
         while (a[j] > x) j--;
         if (i < j) {w = a[i]; a[i] = a[j]; a[j] = w;}
      }  while (++i <= --j);
      if (i == j + 3) {--i; ++j;}
      if (j+1 < n-i)
      {  if (j > 0) q_sort(a, j+1);
         a += i; n -= i;
      }  else
      {  if (i < n-1) q_sort(a+i, n-i);
         n = j + 1;
      }
   }  while (n > 1);
}
```

Since in each recursive call the sequence length is reduced by at least a factor 2, the recursion depth is not greater than the 2-logarithm of the original sequence length.

2.3 Sorting Strings of Variable Length

If *strings* instead of numbers are to be sorted, there is a problem, due to the variable length that strings usually have. An elegant and efficient solution to this problem is based on dynamic memory allocation and an array of pointers. Instead of exchanging the character sequences themselves, we simply exchange pointers to them, as shown in Fig. 2.1.

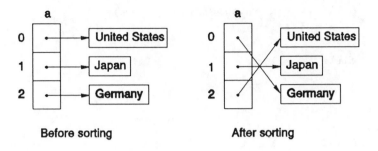

Fig. 2.1. *Sorting strings of variable length*

Program CHQSORT.C shows how this is done by function **chqsort**. Although this function is presented here in the same module as the main function, it can be compiled separately (including the line **#include <string.h>**) and linked later. This is especially useful if we want to use it for more than one application. This version is similar to our previous function, **q_sort**, in that it restricts recursion depth by performing only one recursive call, applied to the longer subsequence:

```
/* CHQSORT.C: This program sorts variable-length strings,
              using the quicksort method.
              The given strings can be read from any input
              file and are lines of that file.
*/
#include <stdio.h>
#include <stdlib.h>
#include <string.h>

void chqsort(char **a, int n)
{   int i, j;
    char *x, *w;
     do
      {   i=0; j=n-1;
          x = a[j/2];
          do
          {   while (strcmp(a[i], x) < 0) i++;
              while (strcmp(a[j], x) > 0) j--;
              if (i < j) {w = a[i]; a[i] = a[j]; a[j] = w;}
          } while (++i <= --j);
          if (i == j + 3) {--i; ++j;}
          if (j+1 < n-i)
          {   if (j > 0) chqsort(a, j+1);
              a += i; n -= i;
```

```
        } else
        {   if (i < n-1) chqsort(a+i, n-i);
            n = j + 1;
        }
    } while (n > 1);
}


main()
{   char **a, buf[101];
    unsigned n=0, length, i=0;
                        FILE *fpin, *fpout;
    printf("Input file:  "); scanf("%100s", buf);
    fpin = fopen(buf, "r");
    if (fpin == NULL) puts("File problem"), exit(1);
    /* Count how many lines there are: */
    while (fgets(buf, 100, fpin)) if (*buf != '\n') n++;
    rewind(fpin);
    a = (char **)malloc(n * sizeof(char *));
    if (a == NULL) puts("Memory problem"), exit(1);
    printf("Output file: "); scanf("%50s", buf);
    fpout = fopen(buf, "w");
    if (fpin == NULL) puts("File problem"), exit(1);
    while (fgets(buf, 100, fpin) != NULL)
    {   length = strlen(buf);
        if (*buf == '\n') continue;
        buf[length-1] = '\0'; /* Overwrite '\n' */
        a[i] = (char *)malloc(length);
        if (a[i] == NULL) puts("Memory problem"), exit(1);
        strcpy(a[i++], buf);
    }
    printf("%d strings will be sorted.\n", n);
    chqsort(a, n);
    puts("Sorting ready.");
    for (i=0; i<n; i++) fputs(a[i], fpout), putc('\n', fpout);
    return 0;
}
```

2.4 Sorting a File

So far, we have been discussing only internal sorting methods, with array elements as the objects to be sorted. Instead, we can sort *externally*, that is, re-arrange items in a file instead of in an array. Since on most computer systems files may be much larger than arrays, we need external sorting methods as soon as memory is insufficient for internal sorting. A good many years ago, internal sorting methods could hardly ever be used for data-processing applications, because of memory limitations. Now that we are accustomed to rather large amounts of internal memory, we should not reject internal sorting methods too soon. However, memory may still be insufficient to contain all data to be sorted, so we will also pay some attention to external sorting.

Note that the distinction between internal and external sorting methods is pragmatic rather than fundamental. Since in C we have random access to a disk file, we can adapt the methods of the preceding sections to files. To illustrate this, we will apply quicksort to a disk file, at the end of this section. On the other hand, sequential file access may be simulated with arrays. After all, it is not forbidden to use arrays purely sequentially. In practice, however, we should remember:

(1) With internal sorting methods, we normally use only one array, which only contains the data to be sorted. External methods, on the other hand, need not be so economical with space, but may use several files for the same data at the same time, if desirable for fast sorting.

(2) Sequential array access is not faster than random array access. This may be different for files, since with sequential file access large quantities of data can be buffered. So although random access is possible with a disk file, it might be faster to use sequential access if we sort externally. With tapes, we are limited to sequential access, which means that in this case quicksort is out of the question.

Let us now be more concrete. For convenience, we will again sort a sequence of integers. This time, they are not in an array but in a file. Since during the sorting process we have to read and to write them a great many times, we will read and write data in the *binary mode*. This means that the numbers are not converted from the external, decimal format to the internal, binary representation and vice versa. Instead, the numbers have the same format, both internally and externally. However, we will begin with a text file, which contains the unsorted data and is read only once. Similarly, our final action will be writing the sorted data to a text file. Thus, we will actually perform conversions from the external to the internal format and vice versa, but, as they are rather time-consuming, we will separate them from the sorting process, as Fig. 2.2 shows.

Natural merge sort, as its name says, is based on the principle of merging. We will deal with this principle first, and at the same time demonstrate the use of unformatted I/O. Suppose we have two ordered sequences of integers, in binary files, for example:

File *aaa*: 10 20 40 60 70 80
File *bbb*: 15 25 35 40 50 65 90

We want to form the following ordered sequence, consisting of all elements of the files *aaa* and *bbb*:

File *ccc*: 10 15 20 25 35 40 40 50 60 65 70 80 90

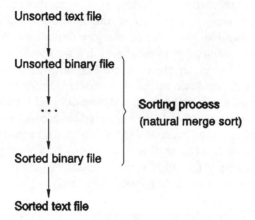

Fig. 2.2. Use of text files and binary files

Here is function **merge** to accomplish this:

```
/* MERGE.C: Merging two files  */
#include <stdio.h>
#include <stdlib.h>
#define in(fp, pbuf) fread(pbuf, sizeof(int), 1, fp)
#define out(fp, pbuf) fwrite(pbuf, sizeof(int), 1, fp)
FILE *fa, *fb, *f;

void merge(void)
{   int a, b;
    freopen("aaa", "rb", fa);
    freopen("bbb", "rb", fb);
    freopen("ccc", "wb", f);
    in(fa, &a);
    in(fb, &b);
    while (!feof(fa) && !feof(fb))
    {   if (a < b) out(f, &a), in(fa, &a);
             else out(f, &b), in(fb, &b);
    }
    while (!feof(fa)) out(f, &a), in(fa, &a);
    while (!feof(fb)) out(f, &b), in(fb, &b);
}

main()
{   int x;
    fa = fopen("aaa", "wb");
```

```
        fb = fopen("bbb", "wb");
        f = fopen("ccc", "wb");
        if (fa == NULL || fb == NULL || f == NULL)
            puts("File problem"), exit(1);
        puts(
        "Enter two monotonic nondecreasing sequences,");
        puts(
        "each followed by a zero as an end signal:\n");
        while (scanf("%d", &x), x) out(fa, &x);
        while (scanf("%d", &x), x) out(fb, &x);
        merge();                /* This is the function in question */
        freopen("ccc", "rb", f);
        puts("\nOutput:");
        while (in(f, &x) > 0) printf("%3d ", x);
        return 0;
    }
```

In function **merge**, the first while-loop compares two numbers, *a* and *b*, read from the files *aaa* and *bbb*, respectively. Each time, the smaller of these two numbers is written to file *ccc*, and then the next number is read from the file from which the number just written had been read, that is, if there is still a next number on that file. If not, the first while-loop ends, and either the second or the third deals with the remaining numbers in one of the two files *aaa* and *bbb*. Note that at this stage either file *aaa* or file *bbb* is exhausted, so indeed, only one of the last two while-loops is effective. So much for the merging process, which we will use now for sorting.

Natural merge sort is based on ordered subsequences, called *runs*. Suppose that file *f* contains the number sequence shown below:

f: <u>29 32 34</u> <u>21</u> <u>19 50</u> <u>10 43</u> <u>33 49 100</u> <u>60</u>

The underlined runs are now distributed onto the two other files *fa* and *fb*:

fa: <u>29 32 34</u> <u>19 50</u> <u>33 49 100</u>

fb: <u>21</u> <u>10 43</u> <u>60</u>

The first run of *f* has gone to *fa*, the second to *fb*, the third to *fa* again, and so on. Note that the fourth and the sixth runs of file *f* form spontaneously one single run (10, 43, 60) on file *fb*. This is no problem whatsoever; we even appreciate it, since the fewer runs there are the better. It is now time to use merging. In contrast to program MERGE.C, we will merge runs rather than files. Repeatedly, two runs are read, one from *fa* and the other from *fb*, and they are merged into one new run, written to file *f* again:

f: <u>21 29 32 34</u> <u>10 19 43 50 60</u> <u>33 49 100</u>

As soon as one of the two input files is exhausted, any remaining runs on the other are simply copied to *f*, as is done here with the final run (33, 49, 100) of *fa*. File *f* now contains the same numbers as it did originally, but in fewer and longer runs. We then repeat these two actions of distributing and merging, until there is only one run on file *f*. Sooner or later this will happen, and then we are ready with our sorting task.

Here is a complete program which reads integers from a text file, and writes them in ascending order to another text file. As illustrated by Fig. 2.2, binary files are used in the actual sorting process for reasons of efficiency:

```
/* NMSORT.C:
    This program demonstrates file sorting, using
    the Natural Merge Sort method.
    Both the input and output files are text files.
    Temporary binary files are used during sorting.
*/
#include <stdio.h>
#include <stdlib.h>
#include <time.h>

#define in(fp, pbuf) fread(pbuf, sizeof(int), 1, fp)
#define out(fp, pbuf) fwrite(pbuf, sizeof(int), 1, fp)

int number_of_runs;
FILE *f, *fa, *fb; /* Temporary files */
char  tmpfil[L_tmpnam], tmpfila[L_tmpnam], tmpfilb[L_tmpnam];

void copyarun(FILE *fin, FILE *fout, int *pnext)
{   int old;
    do
    {   out(fout, pnext);
        old = *pnext;
        in(fin, pnext);
    }  while (!(feof(fin) || *pnext < old));
    number_of_runs++;
}

void distribute(void)
{   int x;
    freopen(tmpfil, "rb", f);
    freopen(tmpfila, "wb", fa);
    freopen(tmpfilb, "wb", fb);
    in(f, &x);
```

```
       while (!feof(f))
       {  copyarun(f, fa, &x);
          if (feof(f)) break;
          copyarun(f, fb, &x);
       }
}

void merge(void)
{  int a, b, old;
   number_of_runs = 0;
   freopen(tmpfila, "rb", fa);
   freopen(tmpfilb, "rb", fb);
   freopen(tmpfil, "wb", f);
   in(fa, &a);
   in(fb, &b);
   while (!feof(fa) && !feof(fb))
   {  if (a < b)
      {  out(f, &a);
         old = a;
         in(fa, &a);
         if (feof(fa) || a < old) copyarun(fb, f, &b);
      } else
      {  out(f, &b);
         old = b;
         in(fb, &b);
         if (feof(fb) || b < old) copyarun(fa, f, &a);
      }
   }
   while (!feof(fa)) copyarun(fa, f, &a);
   while (!feof(fb)) copyarun(fb, f, &b);
}

void nmsort(void)
{  do
   {  distribute();
      merge();
   } while (number_of_runs > 1);
}

main()
{  char infil[41], outfil[41];
   FILE *fpin, *fpout;
   float dt;
   int count=0, x, i=0;
```

```
clock_t t0, t1;

/* Ask user for file names: */
printf("Name of input file:   "); scanf("%40s", infil);
printf("Name of output file: "); scanf("%40s", outfil);
tmpnam(tmpfil); tmpnam(tmpfila); tmpnam(tmpfilb);

/* Open input file fpin:    */
fpin = fopen(infil, "r");
if (fpin == NULL) puts("Cannot open input file"), exit(1);

/* Open temporary files:    */
f = fopen(tmpfil, "wb");
fa = fopen(tmpfila, "wb");
fb = fopen(tmpfilb, "wb");
if (f == NULL || fa == NULL || fb == NULL)
   puts("Cannot open temporary files"), exit(1);

/* Convert from text file to binary file: */
while (fscanf(fpin, "%d", &x) > 0) out(f, &x), count++;
fclose(fpin);

/* The actual sorting process, applied to file f: */
t0 = clock();
nmsort();
t1 = clock(); dt = t1 - t0;
printf("nmsort    n = %d,  computing time: %7.2f s\n",
        count, dt/CLK_TCK);
fclose(fa); remove(tmpfila);
fclose(fb); remove(tmpfilb);

/* Open output file: */
fpout = fopen(outfil, "w");
if (fpout == NULL) puts("Cannot open output file"), exit(1);

/* Convert from binary file to text file: */
freopen(tmpfil, "rb", f);
while (in(f, &x) > 0)
{ fprintf(fpout, "%5d ", x); i++;
   if (i == 10) fprintf(fpout, "\n"), i = 0;
}
fclose(f); remove(tmpfil);
return 0;
}
```

This program is somewhat complicated, which is mainly due to the fact that we can detect the end of a run only by reading the first element of the next run, if any. When **copyarun** is called, the first element to be copied has already been read. The address of the memory location in which this element has been stored is passed to **copyarun** as its third argument. Similarly, just before returning to its caller, this function has read one element too far (unless the end of the file has been reached), and this new element is stored in the memory location just mentioned. Recall that in C the function **feof** returns nonzero after a read attempt has failed, so we use it *after* a read attempt, not *before* (in the way **eof** is used in Pascal). We will discuss the performance of this program in connection with a competitive program, which we will write first.

Sorting by using random access

Traditionally, sequential access is used for external sorting. However, with a disk as background memory, we can instead use random access, originally applied to arrays. After all, random disk access is similar to the way we use arrays. Incidentally, not only the hardware but also the software may prohibit our using random file access, as (standard) Pascal does. In C, however, random access is a standard I/O facility, which we will now discuss briefly. After the call

```
fseek(fp, offset, code)
```

the next read or write operation for stream **fp** takes place at the position determined by **offset** and **code**. If **code** is equal to **SEEK_SET** (defined in *stdio.h* as 0), the **long int** argument **offset** is counted from the beginning, that is, for the very first byte of a file we have **offset** = 0. We also use **code** = **SEEK_END** (= 2), which means that we count from the position immediately after the file, so the following argument values apply to the final byte of a file:

```
offset = -1L, code = SEEK_END
```

(There is also the symbolic constant **SEEK_CUR** = 1, in case we want to count from the current position.) The position is expressed as a byte number. We can inquire the current position by using the call

```
ftell(fp)
```

which returns an absolute byte number, of type **long int**. Note that this call gives the file length (in bytes) if it is preceded by the call **fseek(fp, 0L, SEEK_END)**. We are now in a position to consider another file-sorting program for integers, which uses the method **quicksort**, discussed in Sections 2.2 and 2.3:

```
/* FQSORT.C: This program sorts integers, given in a text file.
          The resulting sorted file is also a text file.
          The user has to enter the names of these two files.
          During the sorting process, a temporary binary file is
          used. Method: quicksort.
*/
#include <stdio.h>
#include <stdlib.h>
#include <time.h>
#define SIZE sizeof(int)
#define in(fp, pbuf) fread(pbuf, SIZE, 1, fp)
#define out(fp, pbuf) fwrite(pbuf, SIZE, 1, fp)
FILE *f;
char tmpfil[L_tmpnam];

void fqsort(long start, long n)
{  long i, j, midpos;
   int x, xi, xj;
   do
   {  i = 0; j = n - 1; midpos = j/2;
      fseek(f, (start+midpos) * SIZE, SEEK_SET);
      in(f, &x);
      do
      {  while(
            fseek(f, (start+i) * SIZE, 0), in(f, &xi), xi < x)
              i++;
         while(
            fseek(f, (start+j) * SIZE, 0), in(f, &xj), xj > x)
              j--;
         if (i < j)
         {  fseek(f, (start+i) * SIZE, 0); out(f, &xj);
            fseek(f, (start+j) * SIZE, 0); out(f, &xi);
         }
      } while (++i <= --j);
      if (i == j + 3) {i--; j++;}
      if (j + 1 < n - i)
      {  if (j > 0) fqsort(start, j+1);
         start += i; n -= i;
      } else
      {  if (i < n-1) fqsort(start+i, n-i);
         n = j + 1;
      }
   } while (n > 1);
}
```

```
main()
{  char infil[51], outfil[51];
   FILE *fpin, *fpout;
   long t0, t1, n;
   int x;
   float dt;
   int i=0;
   /* Ask user for file names:    */
   printf("Name of input file:  "); scanf("%50s", infil);
   printf("Name of output file: "); scanf("%50s", outfil);
   fpin = fopen(infil, "r");
   if (fpin == NULL) puts("Cannot open input file"), exit(1);
   tmpnam(tmpfil); f = fopen(tmpfil, "w+b");
   if (f == NULL) puts("Cannot open temporary file"), exit(1);

   /* Convert from text file to binary file: */
   while (fscanf(fpin, "%d", &x) > 0) out(f, &x);
   fclose(fpin);

   /* The actual sorting process, applied to file f: */
   t0 = clock();
   fseek(f, 0, SEEK_END); n = ftell(f)/SIZE;
   fqsort(0L, n);
   t1 = clock(); dt = t1 - t0;
   printf(
   "Computing time for fqsort: %7.2f s\n", dt/CLK_TCK);

   /* Open output file:  */
   fpout = fopen(outfil, "w");
   if (fpout == NULL) puts("Cannot open output file"), exit(1);

   /* Convert from binary file to text file: */
   rewind(f);
   while (in(f, &x) > 0)
   {  fprintf(fpout, "%5d ", x); i++;
      if (i == 10) fprintf(fpout, "\n"), i = 0;
   }
   fclose(f); remove(tmpfil);
   return 0;
}
```

Note that function **fqsort** is similar to function **q_sort**, discussed in Section 2.2. Again, only the smaller partition is dealt with recursively, so that the recursion depth will not exceed the 2-logarithm of the number of objects to be sorted.

It is interesting to compare the two programs NMSORT.C and FQSORT.C. The running time for either program is $O(n \cdot \log n)$, so both programs can be used for large files. In an experiment with a personal computer, FQSORT.C turned out to be faster than NMSORT.C, that is, when applied to real files on a hard disk. Instead of the latter, the experiment was also carried out with 'virtual disk', also called 'ramdisk', which means that input and output operations are simulated in main memory. With virtual disk, NMSORT.C did much better than FQSORT.C. Curiously enough, FQSORT.C was relatively slow on a virtual disk. (Of course, this slowness is not due to the method quicksort itself, but rather to our way of using it. Originally, quicksort was meant for internal memory, see Sections 2.2 and 2.3. We then wrote FQSORT.C, which runs fast with real files on disk, but, with virtual disk, we are using this version to sort in internal memory again, which is hardly a sensible thing to do!) Anyway, we see that much depends on the circumstances, that is, on the hardware and software that is available. The above two programs are easy to use, so if you are interested in their performances on a particular machine, the best thing to do is to experiment with them yourself. As to NMSORT.C, we must remember that this program uses much more file space than FQSORT.C. The following points are worth remembering:

(1) Natural merge sort uses temporary files, while quicksort does not.
(2) Since quicksort is based on random access, we cannot apply it to sort a tape instead of a disk. There is no such problem with natural merge sort, since this method is based on sequential file access.
(3) If the file happens to be in ascending order already, NMSORT.C is faster than FQSORT.C.
(4) Natural merge sort is a stable method, while quicksort is not, see below.
(5) The number of key comparisons with quicksort is considerably less than that number with natural merge sort.

Point (4) deserves some explanation. Usually we do not sort just numbers but rather records, as mentioned at the beginning of this chapter. For example, let us assume that we have records with a number and a name, and that the number is the key, so that we are comparing the numbers. If two records have identical keys, we may require the old order of these two records to be maintained. This implies that sorting

```
345    Patterson
289    Taylor
345    Johnson
```

where **Patterson** and **Johnson** have identical keys, should not alter the order of these two names, so that after sorting we have

```
289    Taylor
345    Patterson
345    Johnson
```

With a stable sorting method, this will indeed happen. If the method is not stable, the following result may appear:

```
289    Taylor
345    Johnson
345    Patterson
```

In most applications the sorting method need not be stable, either because we have unique keys, or (more rarely) because the order of elements with identical keys is irrelevant. In particular, if the objects to be sorted have no other fields than their keys, then obviously their order is irrelevant. This is the case if we sort either a sequence of numbers, as in most of our sample programs, or a sequence of strings, as in Section 2.3.

2.5 The qsort Library Function and Generic Code

Most functions discussed so far can be used only for one particular purpose. For example, function **q_sort** of Section 2.2 can be applied to arrays of integers; if we want to sort an array of float numbers, we have to modify this function. It is possible to write a *generic* sorting function, which is applicable to any array. Actually, we need not do this ourselves, since there is a library function **qsort**, declared in the header file *stdlib.h*, which we can use immediately. There are some reasons why we have paid attention to several quicksort functions of our own:

(1) We not only want to *use* sorting functions, but we also want to *understand* them.
(2) The library function **qsort** can only sort arrays, while we have also applied the quicksort method to a file.
(3) Due to their generality, generic functions, such as **qsort**, are not always the most efficient, and their use is more complicated than one might expect. The latter is true in particular if we want our program to be correct not only in C but also in C++.

The following program, QSORT.C, uses **qsort** to sort an array of **float** values, read from an input file. The resulting sorted array is written to an output file. The names of these two files can be entered on the keyboard.

```
/* QSORT.C: The library function qsort applied to
            a float array.
*/
#include <stdlib.h>
#include <stdio.h>
#ifdef __cplusplus
extern "C"
#endif
```

```
int compare(const void *p, const void *q)
{  return *(float *)p < *(float *)q ? -1 :
          *(float *)p > *(float *)q ? +1 : 0;
}


main()
{  FILE *fpin, *fpout;
   char infile[51], outfile[51];
   int n=0, i;
   float x, *a;
   printf("Input file:  "); scanf("%50s", infile);
   printf("Output file: "); scanf("%50s", outfile);
   fpin = fopen(infile, "r"); fpout = fopen(outfile, "w");
   if (fpin == NULL || fpout == NULL)
      puts("File problem"), exit(1);
   /* Find out how many numbers are to be sorted: */
   while (fscanf(fpin, "%f", &x) == 1) n++;
   rewind(fpin);
   printf("n = %d\n", n);
   /* Allocate memory: */
   a = (float *)malloc(n * sizeof(float));
   if (a == NULL) puts("Memory problem"), exit(1);
   /* Read numbers into 'array' a: */
   for (i=0; i<n; i++) fscanf(fpin, "%f", a + i);
   /* Sort array a: */
   puts("Sorting ... ");
   qsort(a, n, sizeof(float), compare);
   puts("Sorted");
   /* Write result to output file: */
   for (i=0; i<n; i++)
   { fprintf(fpout, "%6.2f ", a[i]);
     if (i % 10 == 9) fprintf(fpout, "\n");
   }
   return 0;
}
```

Since **qsort** is a very general function, we must specify how to compare two array elements. This is done by means of its fourth argument, which is the name of a compare function. This function, **compare**, is very similar to the well-known function **strcmp**: it returns an integer that is positive, zero, or negative as codes for *greater than*, *equal to*, and *less than*, respectively. The version of **compare** shown here is written in such a way that it is correct both in C and in C++. Because of (relatively) strong type checking in C++, we must specify the parameters of this function as **const void** pointers; writing **float*** instead of **const void*** would contradict the way **qsort** is declared in *stdlib.h*:

```
void qsort(void *base, size_t n, size_t width,
           int (*fcmp)(const void*, const void*));
```

On the other hand, we need **float** values in the actual comparisons, so here some casts of the form **(float*)** are used to convert **void** pointers to **float** pointers. Another complication is that for some C++ compilers it may be required to use the prefix

```
extern "C"
```

for functions that are passed as arguments to C library functions. In our example this applies to the function **compare**, which is passed as an argument to the C library function **qsort**. On the other hand, this prefix must not be used if our program is compiled by a plain C compiler. We can solve this problem by using conditional compilation: the constant __**cplusplus** (with two leading underscores) is defined if and only if we are using a C++ compiler. C++ compilers will therefore compile the above prefix, while C compilers will ignore it.

Generic functions of our own

Instead of the library function **qsort**, let us use a simpler example of a function that can be applied to any array. The function **maxelement** in the following program can find the 'largest' element of an array, with elements of any type. The relation *less than* can be defined arbitrarily for these elements:

```
/* GENCOMP.C: A generic function to find the address of the
              maximum element of any array
*/
#include <stdio.h>
#include <string.h>

void *maxelement(void* a, int n, int width,
                 int (*fcmp)(void*, void*))
{  int i;
   void *p=a, *pmax=a;
   for (i=1; i<n; i++)
   {  p = (void*)((char*)p + width);
      if (fcmp(p, pmax) > 0) pmax = p;
   }
   return pmax;
}
```

```
int comparefloat(void* p, void* q)
{  return *(float*)p < *(float*)q ? -1 :
           *(float*)p > *(float*)q ? +1 : 0;
}


typedef struct{int nr; char name[30];} person;

int compareperson(void *p, void *q)
{ return strcmp(((person*)p)->name, ((person*)q)->name);
}

main()
{  float *p_float, table[5] = {10, 50, 25, 15, 30};
   person *p_person, list[3] =
   {{1945, "Johnson"},
   {1947, "Wood"},
   {1950, "Blake"}};
   p_float = (float*)maxelement(table, 5, sizeof(float),
           comparefloat);
   p_person = (person*)maxelement(list, 3, sizeof(person),
           compareperson);
   printf("Maximum float number: %6.2f\n", *p_float);
   printf("Last person according to alphabetic order: %s\n",
           p_person->name);
   return 0;
}
```

There are two calls to **maxelement** in the **main** function, one applied to an array of **float** numbers and the other to an array of structures. In the latter case, it is not immediately clear what is meant by the 'maximum element'. Therefore the function **compareperson** is used as an argument in the second call to **maxelement**. It says that the **name** members of the given structures must be compared. Since these names are stored as character arrays with trailing null characters, we use the library function **strcmp** for this purpose. We cannot directly use the given **void** pointers **p** and **q** to select the **name** members, but we first have to convert them to type pointer-to-**person**, hence the cast (**person***), applied to **p** and **q**. For example, instead of **p->name**, we write

```
((person*)p)->name
```

Because of the high precedence of the operator **->**, the extra pair of parentheses must not be omitted. Note that **maxelement** does not return the maximum array element itself but a pointer to it. This gives us access to that element, so that we can place new data in it if we like. Besides, the generic nature of this function makes it essential to use **void** pointers. Instead of **void** pointers, the term *generic pointers* is sometimes used. We also say that generic program elements make our software *reusable*. Yet another term used to express that one pointer can be used for data of different types is *polymorphism*. As we can see in this example, aiming at reusability may have a negative effect on the *readability* of our source code. In this book, program text is therefore not always presented in its most reusable form. Most algorithms are easier to explain with concrete data types, such as **int**, than with generic pointers and casts to other pointer types. Remember, however, in practice we must sometimes accept reduced readability to make our software generic and therefore reusable. A good example of a reusable function is **qsort**, which should be recommended in many practical situations.

2.6 Binary Search

This section deals with searching ordered sequences. Similar to our introduction to sorting algorithms in Section 2.1, we shall be dealing with sequences of numbers, keeping in mind that in practice we normally have records with keys and data. The records will have unique keys, so in our case all numbers in the given sequence are different from each other. Besides, the sequence is increasing, so that, with array elements **a[i]** ($i = 0, 1, ..., n-1$) we have:

$$a[0] < a[1] < ... < a[n-1]$$

Let us declare

```
int a[M], x;
```

where **M** is greater than or equal to n. The value x (of the program variable **x**) is a given integer, for which array **a** is to be searched. We can benefit from the fact that the sequence is in increasing order, and search it very efficiently. The method to be discussed is widely known as *binary search*. We begin with an element in the middle of the sequence, and, if this is not the one we are looking for, we proceed by searching either the left or the right half of the original sequence, depending on whether x is less or greater than the element in the middle, and so on. This description of the method is inaccurate and incomplete, since x may be unequal to all elements **a[i]**, and when writing a function for binary search, we have to provide a means to enable the user of the function to know whether or not x has been found. One solution would be to make the function return either -1 if x is not found, or i if x is found and equal to **a[i]**. We will go a step further and, in case x is not found, provide the user with information about where it logically belongs in the sequence. Our function **binsearch** will therefore return the integer value i, determined as follows:

$$i = \begin{cases} 0 & \text{if } x \le a[0] \\ n & \text{if } x > a[n-1] \\ j & \text{if } a[j-1] < x \le a[j] \text{ for some } j \ (1 \le j \le n-1) \end{cases}$$

In Chapter 6 we will apply binary search to B-trees, and we will then really need such a value i, both if the value x occurs in the array that is searched and if it does not. The first line of **binsearch** will be

```
int binsearch(int x, int *a, int n)
```

Before we proceed with binary search, we observe that we can also obtain the desired value i by using the following function for *linear* search:

```
int linsearch(int x, int *a, int n)
{   int i=0;
    while (i < n && x > a[i]) i++;
    return i;
}
```

Note that, for all possible values x, function **linsearch** returns the correct value. However, linear search is relatively slow, since its running time is $O(n)$. As we are given an ordered array, using linear search here is as foolish as searching a dictionary for a word without using the fact that the words are listed in alphabetic order. We therefore want to replace the latter function with **binsearch**, which gives the same result as **linsearch**, but runs in $O(\log n)$ time. If the range to be searched is exactly twice as small each time, then we need k steps, where

$$2^k = n$$

so

$$k = {}^2\!\log n$$

which explains the logarithmic time complexity.

Writing a function for binary search is a well-known and instructive programming exercise. We have to be cautious to avoid both a wrong result and an endless loop. If we test for the two cases $x \le a[0]$ and $x > a[n-1]$ in advance, the remaining case to be considered is

$$a[0] < x \le a[n-1]$$

We then have to reduce this condition to

$$a[j-1] < x \le a[j]$$

and we note that both conditions are special cases of

$$a[\text{left}] < x \le a[\text{right}] \tag{1}$$

so we begin with **left** = 0, **right** = $n-1$, and all we have to do is to halve the range **left**, ..., **right** in such a way that (1) also holds for the reduced range, and to repeat this until we have

$$\text{right} - \text{left} = 1 \tag{2}$$

At this moment, both (1) and (2) are true, which means that **right** is the desired value *i*. Here is a function **binsearch** that works in this way:

```
/* BINSEARCH.C: Function for binary search.
       Array a[0], a[1], ..., a[n-1] is searched for x.
       Returned value:  0 if x <= a[0], or
                        n if x > a[n-1], or
                        i, where  a[i-1] < x <= a[i].
*/
int binsearch(int x, int *a, int n)
{  int middle, left=0, right=n-1;
   if (x <= a[left]) return 0;
   if (x > a[right]) return n;
   while (right - left > 1)
   {  middle = (right + left)/2;
      if (x <= a[middle]) right = middle;
                    else left = middle;
   }
   return right;
}
```

In function **binsearch**, we assign the value of **middle** to the variable **right** if

$$x \le a[\text{middle}]$$

so that afterwards we have

$$x \le a[\text{right}]$$

Similarly, if

$$a[\text{middle}] < x$$

we assign the value of **middle** to **left**, so that

a[left] $< x$

holds after this assignment. Since there are no other assignments to the variables **left** and **right** in the loop, condition (1) will always be satisfied. We also have to verify that the loop terminates. This is rather simple, since, each time, the inner part of the loop is entered only for a subrange

left, ..., right

of at least three elements, which means that the computed value of **middle** satisfies

left < middle < right

This implies that either **left** will increase or **right** will decrease, so it is guaranteed that the length of the subrange under consideration really decreases each time. When discussing condition (2) for loop termination, we implicitly assumed the sequence to consist of at least two elements. However, function **binsearch** also allows the sequence length 1. In that case, the loop is not entered at all, since then **a[n−1]** is in fact **a[0]**, so we have either $x \le$ **a[0]** or $x >$ **a[n−1]**. The return value is 0 in the former case and 1 (that is, n) in the latter, as it should be. The case $n = 1$ may seem far-fetched, but it is not. It will actually occur in Section 6.1, and, in general, when dealing with a sequence of length n, we ought to know which values for n are allowed. For our binary-search algorithm, n may be any positive integer, including 1. Binary search is notorious for its pitfalls when programmed sloppily, and it is one of the rare cases in programming in which a more or less formal correctness proof is both worthwhile and feasible.

It may not be superfluous to point out how **binsearch** should be used. If **i** is an **int** variable and, coincidentally, the actual arguments have the same names as the formal parameters of **binsearch**, we can write

```
i = binsearch(x, a, n);
if (i < n && x == a[i])
{   /* Found.
        The given integer x is equal to a[i].
    */
    ...
} else
{   /* Not found.
        Either a[i] is the first element
        that is greater than x (and i < n),
        or  x > a[n-1] (and i = n).
    */
    ...
}
```

The test **i < n** after the call is essential, since otherwise the memory location following the final element **a[n−1]** would be inspected if x happened to be greater than that final element. First, this would be fundamentally incorrect because we may have no access to that memory location. Note that the operator **&&** guarantees the second operand not to be evaluated if the first is 0, so in our function the case that i should be equal to n causes no such problems. Second, that memory location might contain a value equal to x, so if our computer system allows us to inspect it (which is the more probable case), the test **x = = a[i]** may succeed, and our program would behave as if x had been found.

There is also a standard *library function* **bsearch** for binary search. Except for its first parameter, denoting the address of the key to be searched for, it has the same parameters as the **qsort** library function. Its declaration in *stdlib.h* is as follows:

```
void *bsearch(const void *key, const void *base,
              size_t n, size_t width,
              int (*fcmp)(const void*, const void*));
```

In contrast to **qsort, bsearch** returns a value, which is the address of the array element with the given key value or **NULL** if there is no such element. Note that in the latter case **bsearch** does not give us any information about the position where that element belongs. There will therefore be applications in which we had better use our own function **binsearch**, which does give us such information. If the array to be searched has elements of a type other than **int**, we must adapt **binsearch**, which is a simple task because of the compactness of this function.

2.7 Hashing

We will now discuss a well-known technique, called *hashing*, to store and retrieve objects very efficiently. We shall call these objects *records* and assume each of them to contain a unique key which, as usual, serves as a means to search the set of all stored records. It would be nice if we could derive the position of each record from its key. If the keys were natural numbers lying in a range that is small enough, we could indeed store each record in the position given by its key, so that we would know its place when we needed it later. Unfortunately, that is not the case in most practical situations. If the keys are natural numbers, their range is usually much larger than the amount of space available. If the keys are strings, we can transform them into natural numbers, but the requirement that unequal strings should give unequal numbers would lead to very large numbers, so again, their range would be too large. However, the idea of transforming keys into a reasonable range of natural numbers is useful, both with numbers and with strings as keys. We will assume storage space to be available for at most N records, numbered

$$0, 1, ..., N-1$$

and we will apply a so-called *hash function* to the keys to obtain a *primary index value*, which is a nonnegative integer i, less than N. Although a one-to-one mapping remains desirable, we shall not require this. Thus we do not require our hashing function to transform any two distinct keys $k1$ and $k2$ into two distinct integers $i1$ and $i2$. This means that with hash function h, the situation

$$h(k1) = h(k2) = i$$

which we call a *collision*, may occur. We will base our discussion on type **rectype** and array **a**, declared as

```
typedef struct {char k[21]; int d;} rectype;
rectype a[N];
```

with character strings **k** as keys and data **d** of type **int**. Then, for example, the following hash function may be used:

```
int hash(char *key)
{  int strlength = strlen(key);
   return (101 * key[0] + 103 * key[strlength-1]
          + 107 * strlength) % N;
}
```

This function has been chosen rather arbitrarily. It is based only on the first and the final character and on the length of the key. This makes it easy to find an example of a collision. With $N = 1000$ and ASCII values **'A'** = 65, **'B'** = 66, and so on we have

$$\textbf{hash("ABC")} = (101 * 65 + 103 * 67 + 107 * 3) \% 1000 = 787$$

but, unfortunately, **hash("ARC")** is also equal to 787.

This does not mean that this hash function is a bad one, because collisions will appear anyway. It is not a particularly good one either, since we can easily replace it by others that are equally good. The multiplication factors were introduced to give all locations a reasonable chance to be chosen. For example, if we had written

```
return key[0] + key[strlength-1] + strlength;
```

then all primary index values would apply to the lower part of the hash table. On the other hand, we could use a more sophisticated hash function, based on all characters of the string, but such a function would be slower. The choice of the numbers 101, 103, 107 in our hash function was quite arbitrary.

There are several methods to deal with *collisions*. So far, we have assumed all data to be stored in the given array. This principle, to be discussed in a moment, is called *open addressing*. An essentially different, and more elegant way of collision handling, called *chaining*, is based on an array of pointers pointing to linked lists. Once we are familiar with linked lists, discussed in Chapter 4, collision handling by chaining is very easy to implement. You can verify this by solving Exercise 4.5. At the moment, we have not yet discussed linked lists, so we will restrict ourselves to open addressing, based on an array in which all items are stored.

A very simple way to cope with collisions is known as *linear probing*. It works as follows. When we are storing objects, we distinguish between occupied and empty locations. If we want to store a record with key k, and the location computed as $i = h(k)$ happens to be already occupied, we simply try the next one, that is, location

$$
\begin{array}{ll}
i + 1 & \text{if } i < N - 1, \text{ or} \\
0 & \text{if } i = N - 1
\end{array}
$$

If that location is also occupied already, we again try the next one, and so on. When, later, we want to find that record, we simply use the same procedure, that is, we compute $i = h(k)$, and check whether the key of the record stored in location i is the given key k. If not, we try the next location, and so on, until, if we keep finding other keys than the given one, we have either tried N locations or found an empty location. A function, based on linear probing, to store **rectype** object ***p** in array **a** can be written as follows:

```
/* Linear probing
*/
int store(rectype *p)
{   int i, count=0;
    i = hash(p->k);
    while (strlen(a[i].k))          /* Location i occupied?  */
    {   if (strcmp(a[i].k, p->k) == 0    /* Duplicate key      */
        || ++count == N) return 0;       /* or table full?     */
        if (++i == N) i = 0;
    }
    a[i] = *p;                      /* Use empty location */
    return 1;
}
```

Function **hash** is applied to the given string **p->k**, which gives position **i** in array **a**. Then we test to see if **a[i]** is still 'empty'. Remember, global variables such as array **a** are implicitly initialized to zero, so initially the first character of each string **a[i].k** is the null character, and **strlen(a[i].k)** is zero. In that case the inner part of the while-loop is not executed, and the given record ***p** is copied to **a[i]**. If **a[i]** is already occupied, we normally only increase **i** by one and repeat the test just mentioned. However, if we find that the same key value is already in the table, we will not store the given data once again, but rather return zero as a status code. We must also think of the possibility of the entire array being full. This is the case if our **count** variable, indicating how often we have found an occupied table entry, becomes equal to the table length N. Finally, incrementing **i** is done cyclically: after the final position **i** = N − 1 of array **a**, we continue with position **i** = 0. Function **store** returns 1 after its task has successfully been completed.

Finding an element in array **a** on the basis of the given key can be done by means of the following function:

```
int lookup(rectype *p)    /* p->k is the given key */
{  int i, count=0;
   i = hash(p->k);
   while (strcmp(a[i].k, p->k))      /* Strings unequal?    */
   {  if (strlen(a[i].k) == 0        /* Empty location      */
      || ++count == N) return 0;     /* or table exhausted? */
      if (++i == N) i = 0;
   }
   *p = a[i];                        /* Found!              */
   return 1;
}
```

Although linear probing looks attractive because of its simplicity, it is not very efficient, because it leads to clusters. There are several more advanced methods, of which we will consider one, namely *double hashing*. According to this method, we use another function to compute some increment to be applied to the subscript *i*, instead of using the increment 1 as we did with linear probing. This increment is also derived from the key, and we again count cyclically, so position $N-1$ is followed by position 0. In a complete program, HASH2.C, we will use the functions **store2** and **lookup2**, based on double hashing. In addition to **hash**, there will be another hash function, **incrhash**, to compute increment values.

Since double hashing is based on increment values other than 1, it is most desirable that the table length N should now be some prime number, say, 1009, instead of 1000. If we used 1000, as before, and the increment were 50, for example, then after 20 steps we would be back at the location where we started, and most locations would not be visited. This is because 1000 is a multiple of 50. We now see that we can avoid such situations by using a prime number for the table length, for a prime number N is not a multiple of any other integer between 1 and N. So much for preventing N from being a multiple of the increment, called **inc** in the program. However, we must also prevent **inc** from being a multiple of N. If for some positive integer k, the value of **inc** were equal to kN, an attempt to increment **i** by means of the statement pair

```
i += inc; i %= N;
```

would fail, as you can easily verify. There will be no such problem if **inc** is less than (prime number) N. This is the case if, with $N = 1009$, we compute **inc** as follows from the key stored in character array **key**:

```
        key[0] + 2 * key[1]
```

Program HASH.C demonstrates double hashing. It assumes that there is an input file *data* from which the pairs consisting of a string and an integer can be read. After all data read from this file has been stored in array **a** the user can enter a string, which is then looked up in the array. The integer stored together with the given string is then displayed:

```
/* HASH2.C: Double hashing. This demonstration program reads
      file 'data' with pairs of names and integers. The names
      may consist of at most 20 characters (excluding '\0').
*/
#include <stdio.h>
#include <string.h>
#include <stdlib.h>
#define N 1009

typedef struct {char k[21]; int d;} rectype;
rectype a[N]; /* Members k initialized with null strings */

int hash(char *key)
{  int strlength = strlen(key);
   return (101 * key[0] + 103 * key[strlength-1]
         + 107 * strlength) % N;
}

int incrhash(char *key)
{  return key[0] + 2 * key[1];
}

int store2(rectype *p)
{  int i, inc, count=0;
   i = hash(p->k);
   if (strlen(a[i].k))
   {  inc = incrhash(p->k);
      do
      {  if (strcmp(a[i].k, p->k) == 0    /* Duplicate key   */
         || ++count == N) return 0;       /* or table full   */
         i += inc; i %= N;
      } while (strlen(a[i].k));  /* Location i occupied?  */
   }
   a[i] = *p;                             /* Empty location  */
   return 1;
}
```

```
int lookup2(rectype *p)
{  int i, inc, count=0;
   i = hash(p->k);
   if (strcmp(a[i].k, p->k))              /* Strings unequal? */
   {  inc = incrhash(p->k);
      do
      {  if (strlen(a[i].k) == 0          /* Empty location or*/
         || ++count == N) return 0;       /* table exhausted? */
         i += inc; i %= N;
      } while (strcmp(a[i].k, p->k));      /* Strings unequal? */
   }
   *p = a[i];                             /* Found!           */
   return 1;
}


main()
{  FILE *fp;
   rectype r;
   fp = fopen("data", "r");
   if (fp == NULL) puts("File 'data' not available"), exit(1);
   while (fscanf(fp, "%20s %d", r.k, &r.d) == 2)
   {  if (store2(&r) == 0)
      {  printf(
         "Table full or duplicate key, (%s, %d) not stored\n",
         r.k, r.d);
      }
   }
   fclose(fp);
   for ( ; ; )
   {  printf("\nEnter a string, or ! to stop: ");
      scanf("%20s", r.k);
      if (strcmp(r.k, "!") == 0) break;   /* 0 if equal */
      if (lookup2(&r))
          printf("Data field:%6d\n", r.d);
      else puts("Key not stored in hash table");
   }
   return 0;
}
```

We could have written the functions **store2** and **lookup2** in a somewhat simpler form by computing the value of **inc** unconditionally at the beginning of these functions. After this, we could have used a while-statement, as we did in the linear-probing functions **store** and **lookup**. However, the primary index value **i**, returned by the function **hash**, may quite frequently be the subscript that actually will be used. Then no collision handling is needed, and it would be a waste of time to call the function **incrhash** in this important special case. We therefore compute **inc** only if there is really a collision. Again, the given function **incrhash** is only an example. It will work satisfactorily, but the peculiar way of computing its returned value, like most examples, is based on no scientific theory whatsoever.

It is obvious that searching a hash table will be slow if the table is almost full. Therefore it is recommended that the table length **N** should be a good deal greater than the number of records actually stored. Ordinarily we do not know in advance how many records are to be stored, so whenever we store things in a table, it is quite usual that only a small portion of its space is actually in use. In the most primitive way of storing and searching, we would fill a table consecutively as far as we need, starting at the top, and use linear search (see Section 1.2) to look things up. Compared with this, hashing is more sophisticated in that it makes use of the whole table straightaway. If we use only a small fraction of all locations available, we are rewarded with fast access, so with hashing we immediately benefit from what we have paid.

If you are somewhat familiar with assembly language, note that the ideas used in program HASH2.C can also be applied to an assembler to translate 'symbols' into addresses. Then our key **k** denotes a such a symbol, that is, a symbolic notation for an address, and our data field **d** is the numerical value of that address. In the first scan, the assembler stores symbols and addresses, and in the second it generates object code with concrete addresses, found in the symbol table and corresponding to the symbols it encounters. As an assembler usually consults the symbol table a great many times, it is a good illustration of the fact that speed may be an important factor, even if the table has only a moderate size.

Exercises

2.1   We have been discussing four sorting methods, namely straight selection, shaker sort, quicksort and natural merge sort. Which of these methods are stable? Use records with at least one data field besides the key, to give a demonstration.

2.2   Rewrite **q_sort** in Section 2.2, replacing array notation with pointers. This makes it less suitable for a subsequent translation into another high-level language. On the other hand, if it had to be rewritten into assembly language, your pointer version would be at least as easy to use as the original array version.

2.3   Use the sorting method natural merge sort for internal sorting. Use three arrays instead of three files. Compare the speed of the resulting function with that of **qsort3** in Section 2.2.

2.4   Use the shaker sort method for external sorting. Although this will be slow in general, it may be useful in applications where almost all elements in the given file are already in increasing order.

2.5 Our versions of quicksort chose the element in the middle of the subsequence under consideration, to compare other elements with. Ideally, the chosen element should be the median of that subsequence. To improve the choice, use three elements in the middle of the subsequence, and choose the median of these three elements to compare all other elements of the subsequence with. (The median of a sequence is the element that would be in the middle if the sequence were sorted.)

2.6 Apply the binary search method to a file of which all elements are in increasing order.

2.7 Apply the hashing method to a file, and compare linear probing with double hashing in an experiment. (Linear probing might be faster in this case, since a sequence of adjacent locations to be searched may be located in a buffer in main memory, so that, after dealing with some location, examining the next may not involve real disk access.)

3

Some Combinatorial Algorithms

3.1 A Variable Number of Nested Loops

Suppose that we have an integer array **r**, say, of length 3, and that we want some action, such as printing the contents of **r**, to be performed for all possible values of **r[0]**, **r[1]**, **r[2]**, where each **r[i]** ranges from a given lower bound **lower[i]** to a given upper bound **upper[i]**. For example, let us use global variables for these arrays, defined as

```
int r[3],
    lower[3] = {5, 2, 8},
    upper[3] = {7, 2, 9};
```

Then we want array **r** to obtain the following values, in this order:

r[0]	r[1]	r[2]
5	2	8
5	2	9
6	2	8
6	2	9
7	2	8
7	2	9

Obviously, we can achieve this by means of three nested loops:

```
for (r[0] = lower[0]; r[0] <= upper[0]; r[0]++)
for (r[1] = lower[1]; r[1] <= upper[1]; r[1]++)
for (r[2] = lower[2]; r[2] <= upper[2]; r[2]++) print_r();
```

Although in function **print_r** the contents of array **r** can be used for any purpose, let us simply display a line with the integer values **r[0]**, **r[1]**, **r[2]**, in that order:

```
void print_r(void)
{ int i;
  for (i=0; i<n; i++) printf("%6d", r[i]);
  puts("");
}
```

Note that there will be no call to **print_r** at all if for some value of **i** the value **lower[i]** is greater than **upper[i]**.

So far, everything is extremely simple. We now wish to generalize these three nested loops to n nested loops, where n is variable. Again, we will use the three arrays **r**, **lower**, **upper**, but we will now distinguish between their physical length **LEN** and their logical length n which is not greater than **LEN**. Only the first n elements of both **lower** and **upper** will now be used, and it is our task to achieve the effect that we can write in pseudo-code as follows:

```
for (r[0] = lower[0]; r[0] <= upper[0]; r[0]++)
for (r[1] = lower[1]; r[1] <= upper[1]; r[1]++)
               . . .
for (r[n-1] = lower[n-1]; r[n-1] <= upper[n-1]; r[n-1]++)
  print_r();
```

We are now faced with the problem that we cannot write a variable number of nested for-loops. However, with recursion there is a simple and elegant solution to this problem. We will use a function **f**, with one integer argument, **k**. Its effect can be described as

```
for (r[k] = lower[k]; r[k] <= upper[k]; r[k]++)
for (r[k+1] = lower[k+1]; r[k+1] <= upper[k+1]; r[k+1]++)
               . . .
for (r[n-1] = lower[n-1]; r[n-1] <= upper[n-1]; r[n-1]++)
  print_r();
```

Here we have $n-k$ nested loops. With $k = 0$, we have our original n nested loops. If we make the call **f(n)** result in the call **print_r( )**, then we can describe the effect of **f(k)** for k less than n as follows:

```
    for (r[k] = lower[k]; r[k] <= upper[k]; r[k]++)
       f(k+1);
```

If this is fully understood, the following program should also be clear:

```
/* NESTED.C: A variable number of nested loops
*/
#include <stdio.h>
#define LEN 10
int n, r[LEN], lower[LEN], upper[LEN];

void print_r(void)
{  int i;
   for (i=0; i<n; i++) printf("%6d", r[i]);
   puts("");
}

void f(int k)
{  if (k == n) print_r(); else
   for (r[k] = lower[k]; r[k] <= upper[k]; r[k]++)
       f(k+1);
}

main()
{  int i;
   printf("Enter n (not greater than %d): ", LEN);
   scanf("%d", &n);
   puts("Enter n pairs (lower, upper):");
   for (i=0; i<n; i++)
       scanf("%d %d", lower + i, upper + i);
   puts("\nOutput:\n");
   for (i=0; i<n; i++) printf("  r[%d]", i);
   puts("");
   f(0);
   return 0;
}
```

Here is a demonstration of this program:

```
Enter n (not greater than 10): 3
Enter n pairs (lower, upper):
5   7
2   2
8   9
```

Output:

r[0]	r[1]	r[2]
5	2	8
5	2	9
6	2	8
6	2	9
7	2	8
7	2	9

Although statically there is only one occurrence of a recursive call in function **f**, this call will normally be executed more than once, so dynamically there are several recursive calls. We can analyze the effect of **f(0)** by means of a tree, as discussed in Section 1.5 and shown in Fig. 3.1 for the above example. There is a node in this tree for each call to **f**. Calls with the same argument are on the same level. There is one call **f(0)**, which leads to successively storing the values 5, 6 and 7 in array element **r[0]**. For each value of **r[0]** there is a call **f(1)**. In general, for each value of **r[k]** there is a call **f(k+1)**. In Fig. 3.1, the *leaves* of the tree (at the bottom) show the values of **r[2]**. Each corresponding call **f(3)** results in a call **print_r( )**, which prints the values stored in **r[0]**, **r[1]** and **r[2]**. In many recursive programming problems it will be helpful to imagine a tree similar to this one.

It is instructive to compare our recursive function **f** with an iterative one. In **f**, the argument **k** was necessary because we used the function both in the main program and recursively, and all calls had to be distinguished from one another. With a nonrecursive version there is only one function call, say **f_it( )**, and no argument is needed. We begin by copying the values of **lower[0]**, ..., **lower[n−1]** into **r[0]**, ..., **r[n−1]**. At the same

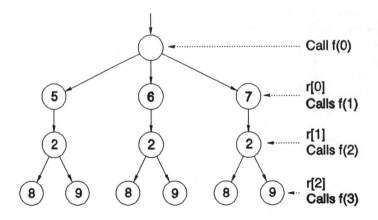

Fig. 3.1. Nested loops represented by a tree

time we check to see if each of these values is less than or equal to the corresponding element of array **upper**, since otherwise no further actions are to be performed and we can return to the main program. After copying **lower** into **r**, we enter a loop in which we immediately perform the call **print_r( )**. In the same loop, we then update array **r**. Since the final element, **r[n−1]**, changes most frequently, it is this element that is incremented. Only when it is equal to **upper[n−1]** do we have both to reset it to the value of **lower[n−1]** and to go back to **r[n−2]**. If this is less than **upper[n−2]** we increment it, otherwise we reset it to the value **lower[n−2]** and go back to **r[n−3]**, and so on:

```
void f_it(void)
{   int i, n1=n-1;
    for (i=0; i<n; i++)
        if (lower[i] > upper[i]) return;
        else r[i] = lower[i];
    for (;;)
    {   print_r();
        i = n1;
        for (;;)
        {   if (r[i] < upper[i])
            {   r[i]++; break;
            }
            r[i] = lower[i];
            if (--i < 0) return;
        }
    }
}
```

Function **f_it** is longer and may be harder to understand than the elegant recursive version **f**, but it will be somewhat faster. In **f**, a recursive call takes place each time **r[n−1]** is incremented, which happens quite frequently. In the same situation, **f_it** executes the break-statement, which has the effect of jumping back to the call to **print_r**. However, with our function **print_r**, which takes comparatively much time, the difference in speed between **f_it** and **f** will be negligible.

There is, however, another argument in favor of an iterative solution. On the basis of the iterative function **f_it**, we can easily write a function, say, **nextsequence**, which generates the next sequence **r[0]**, ..., **r[n−1]**, each time we call it. In our example, with {5, 2, 8} as initial contents of **r**, the first call to **nextsequence** would replace these contents with {5, 2, 9}, and after the second call the contents of **r** would be {6, 2, 8}, and so on. This way of generating sequences is required if we want to generate these sequences on the basis of certain decisions, made elsewhere in our program. A recursive function, such as **f**, can only generate these sequences 'under its own control', which is not always what we want. We will discuss this point in more detail at the end of the next section.

3.2 Permutations

With n (distinct) objects, we can form

$$n! = 1 \times 2 \times ... \times n$$

distinct sequences. We verify this as follows. We can choose n objects as the first element of the sequence. Then for the second element, we have to choose out of the $n-1$ remaining objects. Since such a choice of $n-1$ elements can be made after each of the n previous choices for the first element, we have

$$n \times (n-1)$$

possible choices for the first two elements of the sequence. Now there are only $n-2$ objects left, out of which we choose the third element, so for the first three elements we have

$$n \times (n-1) \times (n-2)$$

possible choices, and so on. Continuing in this way until there is only one object left, we find that altogether the number of choices (that is, the number of possible sequences) is

$$n \times (n-1) \times (n-2) \times ... \times 2 \times 1$$

which is written as $n!$. We call each sequence a *permutation*, so there are $n!$ permutations of n distinct objects. Without loss of generality, we will use the numbers

$$1, 2, ..., n$$

for these objects. (In case of other objects, we can use their positions in an array to identify them.) We now want to write a program which reads n, and generates all permutations of those n numbers. Each of these permutations can be regarded as a (long) integer in the number system with base m, where m can be any number greater than n. Quite simply, if n is less than 10, we can associate each sequence with an integer written as n decimal digits. For example, with $n = 6$, the permutation

    3 6 1 5 4 2

corresponds to the integer 361542. With this association of permutations and integers, we can order the permutations according to the *less than* relation for integers. For example, if $n = 3$, our program is to generate the following six permutations:

```
1   2   3
1   3   2
2   1   3
2   3   1
3   1   2
3   2   1
```

We will write function **permut**, which in the array elements **r[1]**, ..., **r[n]**, generates all permutations of the integers 1, ..., n, as shown above for $n = 3$. This function is based on induction. Using its parameter k, we divide the relevant elements of array **r** into a left and a right partition, the latter starting at position k:

```
r[1]   ...   r[k-1]        |      r[k]   ...   r[n]
(k − 1 elements)           |      (n − k + 1 elements)
```

Instead of demanding that all n array elements be used in our permutation-generating process, we keep those in the left partition constant. In other words, the call **permut(k)** will print all $(n − k + 1)!$ permutations of the right-hand partition, in ascending order, each preceded by the constant partition of length $k − 1$. It follows that in the **main** function we can write **permut(1)** to print all $n!$ permutations of the given array elements, because $k = 1$ implies that the left partition is empty and that the right one has length n. As you may expect, function **permut** is recursive, and any call **permut(k)** (with $k \leq n$) gives rise to $n − k + 1$ calls **permut(k+1)**. Remember, the higher k is, the simpler the problem. In particular, we simply print the current values of **r[1]**, ..., **r[n]** if $k = n + 1$. We now assume that **permut(k+1)** works properly, and we use this to construct the actions required for the call **permut(k)**. In other words, we assume that we know how to generate all permutations of the final $n − k$ elements, and we use this to generate all permutations of the final $n − k + 1$ elements (of the right-hand partition). Each of the elements **r[i]** ($i = k, ..., n$) of this partition must in turn appear in position k. For example, with $n = 6$ and $k = 3$, there are $6 − 3 + 1 = 4$ elements in the right partition, which gives $4! = 24$ permutations of this partition. These can be divided into four groups of six permutations. The first of these groups is

```
1     2     3     4     5     6                                          (P₃)
1     2     3     4     6     5
1     2     3     5     4     6
1     2     3     5     6     4
1     2     3     6     4     5
1     2     3     6     5     4
```
$$(P_3)$$

Only the first permutation of each of the other three groups is listed below:

```
1     2     4     3     5     6                                          (P₄)
1     2     5     3     4     6                                          (P₅)
1     2     6     3     4     5                                          (P₆)
```
$$(P_4)$$
$$(P_5)$$
$$(P_6)$$

Each of these four group is characterized by its kth position, printed here in boldface. For each group, we use its first permutation to construct the others by means of recursive calls **permut(k+1)**. The first permutation (P_3) of the first group is given. The only remaining problem is to derive the first permutations (P_4), (P_5), (P_6) of the other groups from it. We do this by means of *rotations*. For example, we find (P_5) as follows: in (P_3) we shift the contents of **r[3]** and **r[4]** one position to the right and place the old contents of **r[5]** into **r[3]**. In general, with a given initial permutation (P_k) (such as (P_3) in our example), we find (P_i) $(i = k+1, ..., n)$ as follows:

```
tmp = r[i];
for (j=i; j>k; j--) r[j] = r[j-1];
r[k] = tmp;
```

Here is a complete demonstration program, including function **permut**, in which all this is realized:

```
/* PERM.C: Generation of permutations in natural order
*/
#include <stdio.h>
#include <stdlib.h>

#define LEN 11
int n, r[LEN];

void permut(int k)
/* The call permut(k) prints a group of (n-k+1)! lines, each
   with the n integers r[1], ..., r[k-1], r[k], ..., r[n] in
   which r[1], ..., r[k-1] do not change but in which
   r[k], ..., r[n] assume all permutations of these n-k+1
   elements on the right. It follows that the call permut(1)
   prints all n! permutations of r[1], ..., r[n]. The
   permutations are printed in ascending order.
*/
{ int i, j, tmp;
  if (k <= n)
  for (i=k; i<=n; i++)
  { /* For each i, element r[i] is moved to
       position k and the (old) elements
       r[k], ..., r[i-1] are shifted one
       position to the right:
    */
    tmp = r[i];
    for (j=i; j>k; j--) r[j] = r[j-1];
    r[k] = tmp;
```

```
                 /* Without altering r[k], a recursive call
                    is applied to r[k+1], ..., r[n]:
                 */
                 permut(k+1);
                 /* Restore old situation:
                 */
                 for (j=k; j<i; j++) r[j] = r[j+1];
                 r[i] = tmp;
           } else
           {  /* If k == n, the group consists of only one
                  permutation, which is now printed:
              */
              for (i=1; i<=n; i++) printf("%3d", r[i]);
              puts("");
           }
     }


     main()
     {  int i;
        printf("Enter n: "); scanf("%d", &n);
        if (n >= LEN) puts("Too large"), exit(1);
        for (i=1; i<=n; i++) r[i] = i;
        puts("\nOutput:\n");
        permut(1);
        return 0;
     }
```

As in the previous section, a tree may be helpful to understand how this program works. For *n* = 3, this tree is shown in Fig. 3.2. Each node shows the contents of array **r** just before a call to **permut** indicated by a dotted arrow on the right. For example, the node in the center of the tree says that we have **r[1]** = 2, **r[2]** = 1, **r[3]** = 3 immediately before a call **permut(2)**. The argument **2** of this call expresses that only the partition {**r[2]**, **r[3]**} is permuted in the two descendant nodes, shown in the middle at the bottom, with contents 2, 1, 3 and 2, 3, 1.

Generating one permutation at a time

In program PERM.C the generation process is controlled by the recursive function **permut**. This is undesirable or even unacceptable if our program, with a flow of control dictated by our application, simply contains a loop in which repeatedly the next permutation of the sequence 1, 2, ..., *n* is required. We could of course generate all permutations beforehand, store them in a file, and read them one by one later. However, it is more elegant and more efficient not to generate a new permutation until

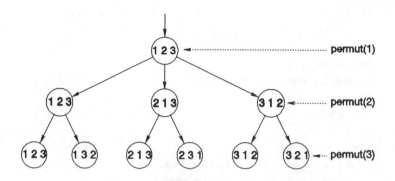

Fig. 3.2. Tree illustrating the generation of permutations

we need it. The idea of generating permutations in ascending order is now very helpful. Initially we fill array **r** in the same way as before, that is, with 1 in **r[1]**, 2 in **r[2]**, ..., n in **r[n]**. Then we can derive each new permutation from the previous one. For example, suppose that $n = 4$ and that, at some moment, the current permutation is

$$2 \qquad 3 \qquad 1 \qquad 4 \tag{1}$$

Since $1 < 4$, the next permutation is obtained by swapping 1 and 4, which gives

$$2 \qquad 3 \qquad 4 \qquad 1 \tag{2}$$

Now that the two final elements, 4 and 1, are in decreasing order, finding the next permutation is somewhat trickier. We must not simply use (2) to swap 3 and 4, because that does not lead to the result

$$2 \qquad 4 \qquad 1 \qquad 3 \tag{3}$$

which we need. We can, however, swap 3 and 4 in (1) to obtain (3). If we use some more concrete examples, we soon find that we should proceed as follows:

1. Find the longest decreasing subsequence (possibly of length 1) at the end of the current permutation. Let us say that this sequence starts at position $k + 1$. The process terminates if $k = 0$, for then all elements of **r** are in decreasing order and all permutations have been generated.
2. Convert this subsequence into an increasing one.
3. There is at least one element in this subsequence that is greater than **r[k]**. Out of these elements greater than **r[k]**, select the smallest one, say, **r[i]**.
4. Swap **r[k]** and **r[i]**.

This algorithm is remarkably simple. It is implemented as function **nextperm** in the following program. This function is called each time the user enters 1 on the keyboard.

```
/* NEXTPERM.C: Find the next permutation
*/
#include <stdio.h>
#include <stdlib.h>
#define LEN 11
int r[LEN], n;

void nextperm(void)
/* This function replaces r[1], ..., r[n],
   containing a permutation of 1, ..., n,
   with the next permutation.
*/
{  int i, k, tmp, left, right;
   /* Find longest decreasing subsequence
       r[k+1], ..., r[n] on the right:
   */
   k = n-1;
   while (k > 0 && r[k] > r[k+1]) k--;
   left = k+1; right = n;
   /* Convert that subsequence into an
       increasing one:
   */
   while (left < right)
   { tmp = r[left]; r[left++] = r[right]; r[right--] = tmp;
   }
   if (k == 0) return; /* No element to the left of r[k+1] */
   /* The subsequence mentioned above is increasing.
      Out of this subsequence, select the smallest
      element r[i] that is greater than r[k]. Swap r[i] and
      r[k]:
   */
   i = k+1;
   while (r[i] < r[k]) i++;
   tmp = r[i]; r[i] = r[k]; r[k] = tmp;
}

main()
{  int i, code, j=0;
   puts("Iterative permutation generator");
   puts("for 1, 2, ..., n.");
   printf("Enter n: "); scanf("%d", &n);
   if (n >= LEN) puts("Too large"), exit(1);
   for (i=1; i<=n; i++) r[i] = i;
   for (;;)
```

```
    {  puts("Enter 1 to display the next permutation");
       printf("or 0 to stop: ");
       scanf("%d", &code);
       if (code == 0) return 0;
       printf("Permutation %3d: ", ++j);
       for (i=1; i<=n; i++) printf(" %d", r[i]);
       puts("");
       nextperm();
    }
}
```

3.3 Combinations

If we are given both a set of n objects, say, the numbers 1, 2, ..., n, and an integer k ($0 \le k \le n$), we may be interested in all possible subsets of k objects. There are

$$\binom{n}{k} = \frac{n\,(n-1)(n-2)\,\ldots\,(n-k+1)}{k!} = \frac{n!}{k!\,(n-k)!}$$

such subsets, each of which is called a *combination*. For example, if $n = 5$ and $k = 3$, we have the following 10 combinations:

```
1 2 3
1 2 4
1 2 5
1 3 4
1 3 5
1 4 5
2 3 4
2 3 5
2 4 5
3 4 5
```

Since each combination is a subset, the order of the elements in it is irrelevant, as the order of the elements in any set is irrelevant. For example, the triple

```
3 2 1
```

is not included in these ten lines, since it would represent the same combination as

```
1 2 3
```

Let us write each combination as an increasing sequence. We now want to write a program to generate all combinations of k elements out of n objects, where n and k are given. Besides representing each combination by an increasing sequence, we also want these representations to appear in ascending order, in the same way as the permutations were ordered in the previous section. Note that the ten combinations listed above are in this order. This time, we begin with a tree for the above example with $n = 5$ and $k = 3$, as Fig. 3.3 shows.

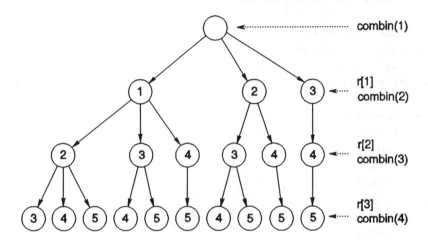

Fig. 3.3. Tree illustrating the generation of combinations

The numbers in the nodes are placed in $r[1]$, $r[2]$, or $r[3]$, as mentioned in the column on the right. Each path from the root to a leaf represents a combination. For the first element, $r[1]$, we can choose 1, 2, or 3; not 4 or 5, for then not enough greater numbers would be available to follow $r[1]$. In general, $r[1]$ ranges from 1 to $n - k + 1$. Depending on $r[1]$, we can make one or more choices for $r[2]$. More precisely, $r[2]$ ranges from $r[1] + 1$ to $n - k + 2$. In the same way, $r[3]$ ranges from $r[2] + 1$ to $n - k + 3$, and so on. So conceptually we need the following nested for-statement:

```
for (r[1] = 1; r[1] <= n - k + 1; r[1]++)
for (r[2] = r[1] + 1; r[2] <= n - k + 2; r[2]++)
                    . . .
for (r[k] = r[k-1] + 1; r[k] <= n; r[k]++)
   print r[1], r[2], ..., r[n]
```

This problem is similar to our subject of Section 3.1. Again we can implement this variable number of loops by means of a recursive function. The above nested loops can be given a more homogeneous appearance if we define **r[0]** = 0, since then the first line can be replaced with

```
for (r[1] = r[0] + 1; r[1] <= n - k + 1; r[1]++)
```

which makes it more similar to the other lines. The complete program for the rather complex task is surprisingly small:

```
/* COMB.C: Generate combinations
*/
#include <stdio.h>
#include <stdlib.h>
#define LEN 100
int n, k, r[LEN];

void combin(int m)
{   int i;
    if (m <= k)
    for (i=r[m-1]+1; i <= n-k+m; i++)
    {   r[m]=i; combin(m+1);
    } else
    {   for (i=1; i<=k; i++) printf("%3d", r[i]);
        puts("");
    }
}

main()
{   printf("Enter n ( < %d): ", LEN);
    scanf("%d", &n);
    if (n >= LEN) puts("Too large"), exit(1);
    printf("Enter k ( < %d): ", n+1); scanf("%d", &k);
    if (k > n) puts("Too large"), exit(1);
    puts("\nOutput:\n");
    combin(1);
    return 0;
}
```

Like permutations, combinations may be required one by one. We can therefore also write an iterative function **nextcomb**, based on the same array elements r[1], ..., r[k] containing a combination of 1, 2, ..., *n*. This function simply replaces the contents of this array with the next combination (according to the way we have ordered them). Function **nextcomb** is part of the following demonstration program. An explanation of how it works is given in the form of comments:

```
/* NEXTCOMB.C: Find the next combination
*/
#include <stdio.h>
#include <stdlib.h>
#define LEN 11
int r[LEN], n, k;

int nextcomb(void)
/* If another a new combination can be generated, this is
   placed in r[1], ..., r[k], and the return value is 1.
   Otherwise, the return value is 0.
*/
{  int i=k, j;
   /* Find the greatest i for which r[i] can be increased:
   */
   while (i > 0 && r[i] == n - k + i) i--;
   if (i == 0) return 0; /* No new combination */
   /* Increase r[i], and reset r[i+1], ..., r[k]
      to their lowest possible values:
   */
   r[i]++;
   for (j=i+1; j<=k; j++) r[j] = r[j-1] + 1;
   return 1; /* New combination in array r */
}

main()
{  int i, code, j=0;
   puts("Iterative combination generator");
   puts("for k elements out of 1, 2, ..., n.");
   printf("Enter n: "); scanf("%d", &n);
   if (n >= LEN) puts("Too large"), exit(1);
   printf("Enter k: "); scanf("%d", &k);
   if (k > n) puts("Too large"), exit(1);
   for (i=1; i<=k; i++) r[i] = i;
   do
   {  puts("Enter 1 to display the next combination");
      printf("or 0 to stop: "); scanf("%d", &code);
      if (code == 0) break;
      printf("Combination %3d: ", ++j);
      for (i=1; i<=k; i++) printf(" %d", r[i]);
      puts("");
   } while (nextcomb());
   return 0;
}
```

3.4 The Knapsack Problem

The combination problem in the last section was essentially about finding subsets of a given set. This is also the case in the classic *knapsack problem*. Suppose we have to choose out of several items, to be carried on our back. Each item has both a weight and a utility value, and a choice must be made such that the total weight of the selected items does not exceed some limit (the maximum load that can be carried). At the same time, the total utility of the chosen items should be maximized. We will simplify this problem in two respects. First, we will require the total weight to be exactly equal to the given limit, and, second, we will assume the utility values of the items to be proportional to their weights. This means that, if possible, we have to find a subset consisting of items with a total weight equal to the maximum weight that can be carried. It will be clear that we can think of many similar problems, for example, how to choose a subset of the coins and banknotes that are in our purse, to pay some amount of money. In general, we are given both a sum s and n positive integers

$$d_0, d_1, ..., d_{n-1}$$

and we are to find a subset of these integers (each occurring at most once) whose sum is s. To solve this problem, we will develop a function **exactsum**, called in the main program as follows:

```
if (exactsum(s, 0))
    puts("\nThe problem has been solved"); else
    puts("\nNo solution");
```

In general, the call **exactsum(t, i)** is to examine if the target t can be formed as the sum of some integers chosen out of the sequence

$$d_i, d_{i+1}, ..., d_{n-1}$$

If this is possible, the chosen integers are to be printed and the value to be returned is 1; if not, the value 0 is to be returned. Function **exactsum** is recursive; as usual with recursion, we have an 'escape clause' to prevent the function from calling itself forever. If $t = 0$, the problem is solved by using an empty subset, and the problem cannot be solved if $t < 0$ or $i = n$. If t is positive and i is less than n, **exactsum** (with arguments t and i) finds out if the target $t - d_i$ can be formed as the sum of some integers chosen out of the sequence

$$d_{i+1}, d_{i+2}, ..., d_{n-1}$$

For this, we use the recursive call

```
exactsum(t - d[i], i + 1)
```

If its value is 1, we know that there is a solution, and we print the value of d_i, which is included in the solution. If it returns 0, we perform the call

```
exactsum(t, i + 1)
```

to examine if there is a solution that does not include d_i. If this is not the case either, there is no solution. Program KNAPSACK.C shows both the definition of function **exactsum** and the way this function can be used.

```
/* KNAPSACK.C:
      This program solves the (simplified) knapsack problem:
      given a sum s and a set of positive integers, it finds
      a subset whose elements have sum s, if this is possible.
*/
#include <stdio.h>
#include <stdlib.h>

int *d, n;

int exactsum(int t, int i)
{  return
   t == 0 ? 1 :
   t < 0 || i == n ? 0 :
   exactsum(t - d[i], i+1) ? (printf("%d ", d[i]), 1) :
   exactsum(t, i+1);
}

main()
{  int s, i;
   printf("Enter the desired sum: ");
   scanf("%d", &s);
   puts("Enter n, followed by the n given "
        "integers themselves:");
   scanf("%d", &n);
   d = (int *)malloc(n * sizeof(int));
   if (d == NULL) puts("Not enough memory"), exit(1);
   for (i=0; i<n; i++) scanf("%d", d+i);
   puts("\nOutput:");
   if (exactsum(s, 0))
      puts("\nThe problem has been solved"); else
      puts("\nNo solution");
   return 0;
}
```

Here is a demonstration of this program:

```
Enter the desired sum: 18
Enter n, followed by the n given integers themselves:
7
2  2  2  5  5  9  11

Output:
9 5 2 2
The problem has been solved
```

We see that program KNAPSACK.C simply gives the first solution it finds. Instead, we may want to select the best, or *optimal*, solution in some particular sense. In our example, we may require the sum s to consist of as few terms as is possible. We see that besides the computed solution

$$18 = 9 + 5 + 2 + 2$$

there is also the solution

$$18 = 11 + 5 + 2$$

which, according to the above requirement, would be required instead, because this sum consists of only three terms instead of four. Program KNAPSACK.C would actually have found the latter solution if we had entered the numbers d_i in the reverse order, that is, as the sequence

11 9 5 5 2 2 2

We could, of course, sort the numbers d_i in the program itself, and use them in decreasing order, no matter in what order they are entered. However, a decreasing sequence does not guarantee finding the 'shortest' solution either, as the following demonstration shows:

```
Enter the desired sum: 18
Enter n, followed by the n given integers themselves:
7
7  7  6  6  6  2  2

Output:
2 2 7 7
The problem has been solved
```

Unfortunately, the shorter solution

$$18 = 6 + 6 + 6$$

is not found. Although in most cases it is a good strategy to use the largest number available, there are exceptions. An algorithm based on the strategy of selecting what 'looks best' is called *greedy*. (For some problems, there are greedy algorithms that always lead to an optimal solution, so 'greedy' is not necessarily a bad qualification, as far as algorithms are concerned.) In the next section, we will find an optimal solution for a problem for which we cannot use a greedy algorithm.

3.5 Dynamic Programming

We will now deal with a problem similar to the previous one. Again, an integer sum s is given, along with n positive integers

$$d_0, d_1, ..., d_{n-1}$$

In contrast to the knapsack problem, solved in Section 3.4, each integer d_i may now occur more than once as a term in the solution. A more interesting new point is that we will now insist on using as few terms as possible in forming sum s. For example, if we have

$$s = 18$$
$$n = 3$$
$$d_0 = 2, d_1 = 6, d_2 = 7$$

then we want the sum s to be formed as

$$18 = 6 + 6 + 6,$$

but not as, for example,

$$18 = 7 + 7 + 2 + 2$$

or as

$$18 = 6 + 2 + 2 + 2 + 2 + 2 + 2$$

Recall that there was no such requirement with the knapsack problem in the previous section. As you can see, 6 occurs three times in the desired solution, although it is given only once in the input data. This, too, was different in our discussion of the knapsack problem. An application of this is making change in a shop, assuming that we have plenty of coins and banknotes. If, for example, we have coins with values of 1c, 5c, 10c, 25c, and we have to pay 42c, we immediately compute

$42 = 25 + 10 + 5 + 1 + 1,$

if we want to use as few coins as possible. With the coin values mentioned, we always obtain the optimal solution by using a *greedy* algorithm. As mentioned in Section 3.4, this means that, each time, we simply use the largest coin that does not exceed the remaining amount to be paid. However, we will use a more general algorithm, which gives an optimal solution even in cases where a greedy algorithm does not. We really need such an algorithm if there are no coins of 5c available. With

$s = 42,$
$n = 3,$
$d_0 = 1, d_1 = 10, d_2 = 25,$

a greedy algorithm would yield

$42 = 25 + 10 + 1 + 1 + 1 + 1 + 1 + 1 + 1$

instead of the optimal solution

$42 = 10 + 10 + 10 + 10 + 1 + 1$

In cases like this (and many others) we can use a tabular technique, called *dynamic programming*. Explaining this important technique in full generality would be beyond the scope of this book, so we will discuss it only in connection with our problem. We define function $F(x)$ as the minimum number of terms (or coins) needed to form the sum x. It follows that F is defined only for those values x for which there is a solution. So if the smallest value d_i is greater than 1, then, for example, $F(1)$ is undefined. Dynamic programming, applied to our application, is based on the equation

$$F(x) = 1 + \min_{0 \le i < n} F(x - d_i)$$

for certain positive integers x (see below) and on

$$F(0) = 0$$

If, with the given range of i, some values $F(x - d_i)$ exist, we select the minimum of them, and add 1 to this minimum to obtain the value $F(x)$. If no such values $F(x - d_i)$ exist, then $F(x)$ does not exist either. Although the above formula suggests recursion, we had better take the 'bottom-up' approach this time (see also Section 1.5, where we analyzed a simple recursive function in a similar way). Thus, we will not begin with the given sum s, but rather try to compute $F(1), F(2), ..., F(s)$, in that order. The resulting program would be very simple if only the value $F(s)$ were needed, since then we would only have to use an array of integers to store the computed values $F(x)$. As we are also interested in the selected values d_i, we will instead use an array **p** of pointers. If $F(x)$

is undefined, then **p[x]** is equal to the special pointer value **NULL**. Otherwise, **p[x]** will point to a sequence of integers; the first of these is the value $F(x)$, and it is followed by $F(x)$ selected values d_i, which sum to exactly x. Again we will benefit from the possibility of allocating a block of memory, using the standard function **malloc**, as program DYNPRO.C shows.

```c
/* DYNPRO.C: An application of dynamic programming.
      With a given integer s and a set of positive
      integers, we try to write s as a minimal sum
      using these integers zero or more times.
*/
#include <stdio.h>
#include <stdlib.h>
#include <limits.h>

typedef int *pint;
int n, *d;
pint *p;

int *getints(int n)
{   int *q;
    q = (int *)malloc(n * sizeof(int));
    if (q == NULL) puts("Not enough memory"), exit(1);
    return q;
}

int *solution(int s)
{   int x, u, i, j, min, imin, *destin, *source;
    p[0] = getints(1); p[0][0] = 0; /* = F(0) */
    for (x=1; x<=s; x++)
    {   min = INT_MAX;
        for (i=0; i<n; i++)
        {   u = x - d[i];
            if (u >= 0 && p[u] != NULL && p[u][0] < min)
            {   min = p[u][0]; imin = i;
            }
        }
        if (min < INT_MAX)
        {   p[x] = destin = getints(min + 2);
            source = p[x-d[imin]];
            destin[0] = min + 1;
            for (j=1; j<=min; j++) destin[j] = source[j];
            destin[min+1] = d[imin];
        }
```

```
        else p[x] = NULL;
    }
    return p[s];
}


main()
{   int s, i, j, m, *row;
    printf("Enter the desired sum: ");
    scanf("%d", &s);
    puts("Enter n, followed by the n given "
        "integers themselves:");
    scanf("%d", &n);
    d = getints(n);
    p = (pint *)malloc((s+1)*sizeof(pint));
    if (p == NULL) puts("Not enough memory"), exit(1);
    for (i=0; i<n; i++) scanf("%d", d+i);
    row = solution(s);
    if (row == NULL) puts("No solution");
    else
    {   printf("Solution:\n    %d = ", s);
        m = row[0];
        for (j=1; j<=m; j++)
            printf("%d %s", row[j], j<m ? "+ " : "\n");
    }
    return 0;
}
```

Here are three demonstrations of this program:

```
Enter the desired sum: 42
Enter n, followed by the n given integers themselves:
3
1  10  25
Solution:
    42 = 10 + 10 + 10 + 10 + 1 + 1



Enter the desired sum: 11
Enter n, followed by the n given integers themselves:
3
5  7  9
No solution
```

```
Enter the desired sum: 18
Enter n, followed by the n given integers themselves:
3
2   6   7
Solution:
    18 = 6 + 6 + 6
```

It may be instructive to see what actually is computed in a relatively simple case, as in the last example:

x	$F(x)$	Selected integers
0	0	
1	-	
2	1	2
3	-	
4	2	2 + 2
5	-	
6	1	6
7	1	7
8	2	6 + 2
9	2	7 + 2
10	3	6 + 2 + 2
11	3	7 + 2 + 2
12	2	6 + 6
13	2	7 + 6
14	2	7 + 7
15	3	7 + 6 + 2
16	3	7 + 7 + 2
17	4	7 + 6 + 2 + 2
18	3	6 + 6 + 6

To find the final value, $F(18)$, the minimum of the three values

$$F(18 - 2) = F(16) = 3$$
$$F(18 - 6) = F(12) = 2$$
$$F(18 - 7) = F(11) = 3$$

is chosen and increased by 1, so we have

$$F(18) = F(18 - 6) + 1 = 3$$

Exercises

3.1   Write a program to generate 'words'. The program is to read the word length n and, for each of the n positions, the letters that are allowed in that position. For example, with $n = 3$, the following letters may be given:

Position 1: **B, L, N, R**
Position 2: **A, E, O, U**
Position 3: **L, M, N, S, T**

This should lead to $4 \times 4 \times 5 = 80$ words:

BAL
BAM
• • •
RUS
RUT

(It may disappoint you that only few of such generated 'words' have a meaning. It shows that if we need an unused letter combination for a new word, there are plenty, even if we want the word to be very short!)

3.2   In Section 3.2, we were generating permutations in a certain order. To achieve this, each recursive call was preceded by a rotation to the right. If the order in which the permutations appear is irrelevant, it is faster to exchange two elements instead. The inverse operation is to be performed after the recursive call. Write a program that uses this faster method.

3.3   Write a program which reads a positive integer n, followed by n distinct capital letters. The program is to generate all words that are permutations of the given n letters, except for words with more than two successive vowels and words with more than two successive consonants. The five letters A, E, I, O, U are vowels, the 21 others are to be regarded as consonants.

3.4   Write a program which reads the positive integers n and k ($k \leq n$), followed by n names. Generate all combinations of k names out of the given n names. This program may be useful if for some game we want a list of all possible teams of k persons, to be formed out of a population of n persons.

4

Linked Lists

4.1 Introduction

In this chapter we will use blocks of memory locations which are linked together. Each of these blocks contains at least one component that may refer to another block. If each block (except the final one) contains a pointer to the next block, so that they form a chain, then the entire collection of linked blocks, together with a pointer to the initial block, is called a *linked list*, also known as a *linear list* or even a *linear linked list*. Sometimes we simply speak of a *list* if it clear from the context what type of list is meant. The blocks of memory locations of a linked list are usually called the *elements* or *nodes* of the list. They are *structures* (in some other languages called *records*), and for a given list they all have the same type and size. Every node of a linked list, except the final one, contains a pointer to its (immediate) *successor*, and every node except the first one is pointed to by its (immediate) *predecessor*.

Figure 4.1 shows an example of a linked list, each node of which contains an integer and a pointer. Let us call these the *members* of the node. There is an additional pointer variable, **start**, pointing to the first node. The first and the final nodes are called *head* and *tail*, respectively. The pointer member of the tail has the value **NULL**; all other pointer members point to the next node in the list. If the list is empty, there is neither a head nor a tail and the variable **start** has the value **NULL**. If the list consists of only one node, this node is both head and tail at the same time.

Program LIST.C reads integers from the keyboard and builds a linked list to store them. Any special character (such as #) may be used to end the number sequence. If we enter the numbers 24, 20, 71, 19, 38, in that order, they are stored in the list as shown in Fig. 4.1. Note that the last number, 38, is stored in the head of the list. The output of the program consists of the numbers 38, 19, 71, 20, 24, in that order.

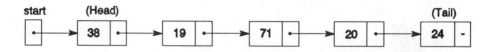

Fig. 4.1. Linked list

```
/* LIST.C: Read numbers from the keyboard, and build a
            linked list to store them.
*/
#include <stdio.h>
#include <stdlib.h>
typedef struct Node{int num; struct Node *next;} node;
node *start=NULL;

void ins(int x)   /* Insert x */
{   node *p=start;
    start = (node *)malloc(sizeof(node));
    if (start == NULL) puts("Not enough memory"), exit(1);
    start->num = x;
    start->next = p;
}

main()
{   int x;
    node *p;
    puts("Enter a sequence of integers, followed "
    "by a nonnumeric character:");
    while (scanf("%d", &x) == 1) ins(x);
    puts("\nIn reverse order, the following numbers have "
         "been read:");
    for (p = start; p != NULL; p = p->next)
       printf("%5d\n", p->num);
    return 0;
}
```

Besides or instead of an integer, used in our example, there there may be other
information members in the nodes. Extending the above type **node** to a more realistic
structure type is obvious and simple. From a programmer's point of view, however, it
is more interesting to extend our subject in another direction, as the next section will
show.

4.2 Manipulating Linked Lists

In many applications linked lists are searched. Not surprisingly, the search method involved is linear search, so we can benefit from a *sentinel*, in a way similar to our array search in Section 1.2. In a linked list, a sentinel is an extra node at the end, as shown in Fig. 4.2.

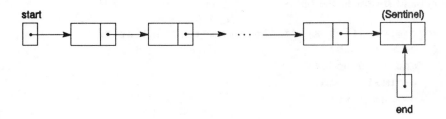

Fig. 4.2. Linked list with a sentinel

If we define

```
typedef struct Node{int num; struct Node *next;} node;
node *start, *end;

node *getnode(void)
{   node *p;
    p = (node *)malloc(sizeof(node));
    if (p == NULL) puts("Not enough memory"), exit(1);
    return p;
}
```

we can set up an empty list, that is, a list with a sentinel as its only node, by calling the following function:

```
void initlist(void)
{   start = end = getnode();
}
```

The contents of the sentinel are irrelevant. We can use the pointer variable **end** to distinguish the sentinel from all other nodes, so there is no need for the value **NULL** to be stored in the sentinel. As we will see in Section 4.4, a list in which nodes are inserted and deleted at the front is also known as a *stack*, and we say that we *push* an item onto a stack. This can be done by means of the following function:

```
void push(int x) /* Insert x at the head of the list */
{   node *p = start;
    start = getnode();
    start->next = p;
    start->num = x;
}
```

Instead, we can place *x* in a new node at the tail of the list. We then create a new sentinel and store *x* in the old one:

```
void append(int x) /*  Append x to the list */
{   node *p=end;
    end = getnode();
    p->next = end;
    p->num = x;
}
```

Searching a linked list

Assuming some integer *x* to be given, we will now search the list for it. The list may not contain *x*; in particular, the list may be empty. If *x* is found in some node, function **searchlist** returns the address of that node. If *x* cannot be found, it returns **NULL**:

```
node *searchlist(int x)
{   /* Search a linked list for x  */
    node *p=start;
    end->num = x;   /* Sentinel */
    while (p->num != x) p = p->next;
    return p == end ? NULL : p;
}
```

If the integers stored in the list are in ascending order, we can stop as soon as we encounter a node with an integer not less than *x*. If *x* cannot be found, we will not return **NULL**, but rather the address of the first node whose **num** value is not less than *x*. This can be very useful as we will see in a moment:

```
node *searchorderedlist(int x)
{   /* Search an ordered linked list for x  */
    node *p=start;
    end->num = x;   /* Sentinel */
    while (p->num < x) p = p->next;
    return p;
}
```

With this function, we need a more complicated test to see if x could be found, as shown by the if-clause in the following program fragment:

```
node *p;
int x;

...   /* Here x is given some value */

p = searchorderedlist(x);
if (p->num == x  &&  p != end)
{   /* x found in node *p */
    ...
}   else
{   /* x not found */
    ...
}
```

Clearly, $p->num == x$ is not sufficient as a test to see if x has been found, since there is the possibility that x was found in the sentinel. In that case, the simple test just mentioned would succeed although x was not present in the original list. This explains the full test $p->num == x \ \&\& \ p \ != end$.

List insertion

Suppose that we are given pointer **p**, pointing to some node of the list, and that a new node, say, with a given integer x in its **num** member, is to be inserted just before the node pointed to by **p**. Figure 4.3 shows such a situation. A new node is to be inserted such that 25 will occur between 20 and 30.

This seems a difficult problem, since **p** does not enable us to find the preceding node, that is, the node whose **next** member has the same value as **p**. To solve this problem, we use a trick, the first part of which is shown in Fig. 4.4.

We create a new node and fill it with the contents of the node pointed to by **p**. The latter node is then used to store the given integer x, and we make its pointer member point to the newly created node, as shown in Fig. 4.5.

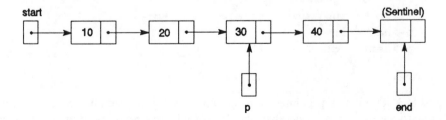

Fig. 4.3. A list in which a new node (with contents 25) is to be inserted

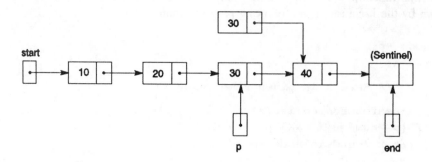

Fig. 4.4. Creating a copy of the node pointed to by p

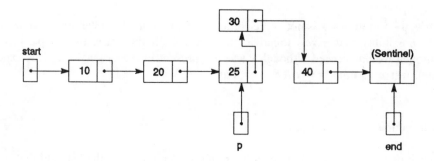

Fig. 4.5. List after insertion

The program text that corresponds to Figs. 4.3–4.5 is very short:

```
void insert(node *p, int x)
/* Insert a new node with a given value x in its
   information member, just before the node pointed
   to by p, see Fig. 4.3.
*/
{  node *q = getnode();
   if (p == end) end = q; else *q = *p;
   p->num = x;
   p->next = q;
}
```

In Figs. 4.3–4.5, pointer **p** pointed to a real node, not to the sentinel. Since we want a method to insert a new node that should precede the node pointed to by **p**, it is reasonable to admit **p** to point to the sentinel, for otherwise we would not be able to insert a node just before the sentinel. Thus we also have to consider the case that the pointer values of **p** and **end** are equal. In this case, we need not copy the contents of the sentinel, since those contents are irrelevant. On the other hand, we should realize that the newly generated node will be the new sentinel, so this is the node that the pointer **end** is to point to. This explains the above if-statement.

If we begin with an empty list and we combine the last two program fragments, we obtain a useful algorithm to build an ordered list. We will demonstrate this by a program that reads integers from the keyboard to store them in an ordered linked list. Then the contents of the list are printed. The effect is that the integers that are read appear in ascending order, so we can say that this program *sorts* them:

```
/* SORTLIST.C: This program reads integers and stores them
               in ascending order in a linked list.
*/
#include <stdio.h>
#include <stdlib.h>
typedef struct Node{int num; struct Node *next;}node;
node *start, *end;

node *getnode(void)
{   node *p;
    p = (node *)malloc(sizeof(node));
    if (p == NULL) puts("Not enough memory"), exit(1);
    return p;
}

void initlist(void)
{   start = end = getnode();
}

node *searchorderedlist(int x)
{   /* Search an ordered list for the given integer x:   */
    node *p=start;
    end->num = x;   /* Sentinel */
    while (p->num < x) p = p->next;
    return p;
}

void insert(node *p, int x)
/* Insert a new node with a given value x in its
   information member, just before the node pointed
   to by p, see Fig. 4.3.
*/
```

```
{   node *q = getnode();
    if (p == end) end = q; else *q = *p;
    p->num = x;
    p->next = q;
}

void printlist(void)
{   node *p;
    for (p=start; p!=end; p=p->next)
        printf(" %3d", p->num);
}

main()
{   int x;
    node *p;
    initlist();
    puts("Enter integers, followed by a nonnumeric character:");
    while (scanf("%d", &x) == 1)
    {   p = searchorderedlist(x);
        insert(p, x);
    }
    puts("Here are the same integers in ascending order:");
    printlist();
    putchar('\n');
    return 0;
}
```

Node deletion

Finally, we want also be able to *delete* a node pointed to by a given pointer **p**, as shown in Fig. 4.6.

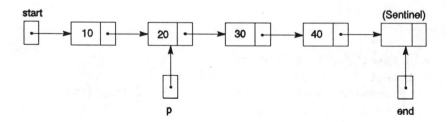

*Fig. 4.6. Node *p is to be deleted*

Again we use the trick of copying an entire node. We first make an auxiliary pointer **q** point to the successor of ***p**. Then we copy the contents of ***q** to ***p**. (Recall that in C the notation ***p** is used for the node pointed to by **p**.) This gives the situation of Fig. 4.7.

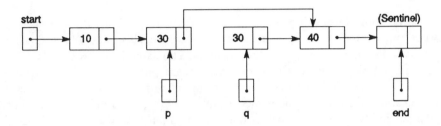

*Fig. 4.7. Situation after copying *q to *p*

Now the only thing that remains to be done is deleting node ***q**. We do this by calling the standard function **free**, which is the opposite of **malloc** because it returns memory space to the operating system. Function **deletenode** puts all this into practice:

```
void deletenode(node *p)
{   node *q=p->next;
    if (q == end) end = p; else   /* See explanation below */
    *p = *q;                       /* See Fig. 4.7          */
    free(q);
}
```

Again, we have taken a special measure for the node at the end of the list. If ***p** is the node that immediately precedes the sentinel, ***q** is the (old) sentinel. In this case ***p** will be the new sentinel and ***q** will be returned to the operating system by means of **free**. We need not then copy the contents of the old sentinel, so in this special case the statement to be executed is **end** = **p**; instead of ***p** = ***q**;.

4.3 Linked Lists and Variable-length Strings

We will now use a linked list which contains some more information than only integers. This list will occur in a complete program, which can be used, for example, to build and maintain a telephone directory. Every node of the list will have the two data members **name** and **num** and also a pointer member **next**. Data member **name** contains a pointer to a sequence of nonnumeric characters representing a name, and data member **num** contains a long integer. The nodes of the list will be in alphabetic order of the names. For example, the list may contain, in this order, the following data:

```
Atherton,P.R.   600312
Atkinson,J.     551288
Ellis,F.        371103
Miller,B.       300611
Wood,E.G.       600228
```

Lines of the above form will be entered on the keyboard, with at least one space or tab between the number and the name. As this example illustrates, blank space is not allowed within a name, not even after a comma. The name length will be limited to 40 characters, but only as many characters as there are (including a null character at the end) will be stored. The data may be entered in any order. In the linked list, the nodes will be in ascending order of the names. Besides adding new items, we will also provide for the possibility of deleting existing ones. For this purpose, we will use the slash (/), to be used instead of a number in the input. Also, it will be possible to change the stored number. If there is already a list element with the given name, the new number will overwrite the old one. If the list is as shown above and we supply the data

```
Miller,B.       /
Ellis,F.        371104
Atherton,P.R.   /
Armstrong,M.    301205
```

then the new list will be as follows:

```
Armstrong,M.    301205
Atkinson,J.     551288
Ellis,F.        371104
Wood,E.G.       600228
```

To obtain a person's number, we enter his or her name, followed by a question mark. For example, if we enter

```
Ellis, F.    ?
```

we obtain the answer

```
Ellis, F.       371104
```

Finally, we introduce the following four commands:

.L   Load all data stored in a permanent file to build a new linked list.
.P   Print the contents of the entire list.
.S   Save the contents of the list in a permanent file.
.Q   Quit.

(Lower-case letters **l**, **p**, **s**, **q** may be used instead of the corresponding capital letters.) After **.S** and **.L** the system asks us to enter a file name, as program INFSYS1.C shows.

```
/* INFSYS1.C: An information system based on a linked list.
*/
#include <stdio.h>
#include <stdlib.h>
#include <string.h>
#include <ctype.h>
typedef
struct Node {char *name; long num; struct Node *next;} node;
node *start, *end;

void *getmemory(int n)
{  void *p=malloc(n);
   if (p == NULL) puts("Not enough memory\n"), exit(1);
   return p;
}

node *getnode(void)
{  return (node *)getmemory(sizeof(node));
}

void printlist(void)
{  node *p;
   puts("Contents:");
   p = start;
   while (p != end)
   {  printf("%-40s %8ld\n", p->name, p->num);
      p = p->next;
   }
}

void append(char *str, long ii)
{  node *p=end;
   end = getnode();
   p->next = end;
   p->name = (char *)getmemory(strlen(str) + 1);
   strcpy(p->name, str);
   p->num = ii;
}

void loadlist(void)
{  char buf[41]; /* General input buffer */
```

```
      long ii;
      FILE *fp;
      if (start != end)
      { puts("List is not empty"); return;
      }
      printf("File name: "); scanf("%40s", buf);
      fp = fopen(buf, "r");
      if (fp == NULL) {puts("Unknown file"); return;}
      while (fscanf(fp, "%40s %ld", buf, &ii) == 2)
         append(buf, ii);
      fclose(fp);
   }


   void savelist(void)
   { node *p;
      char filnam[51];
      FILE *fp;
      printf("File name: "); scanf("%50s", filnam);
      fp = fopen(filnam, "w");
      p = start;
      while (p != end)
      { fprintf(fp, "%s %ld\n", p->name, p->num);
         p = p->next;
      }
      fclose(fp);
   }


   void insertnode(node *p, char *str, long ii)
   { node *q;
      q = getnode();
      if (p == end) end = q; else *q = *p;
      p->next = q;
      p->name = (char *)getmemory(strlen(str) + 1);
      strcpy(p->name, str);
      p->num = ii;
   }


   void deletenode(node *p)
   { node *q;
      free(p->name);
      q = p->next;
      if (q == end) end = p; else *p = *q;
      free(q);
   }
```

```
node *searchlist(char *str, int *pstatus)
{  node *p=start;
   int code;
   end->name=str;  /* Sentinel */
   while ((code = strcmp(str, p->name)) > 0)
     p = p->next;
   *pstatus = (p != end && code == 0);
   /* Status = 1 if str has been found */
   return p;
}

void skiprestline(void)
{ while (getchar() != '\n') ;
}

main()
{  char ch, str[41];
   long ii;
   int found, busy=1;
   node *p;
   puts("Enter a name and a number, or");
   puts("a name followed either by / or by ?, or");
   puts("one of the commands .Load, .Print, .Save, .Quit");
   puts("There must be blank space after a name, "
        "not within it.");
   /* Install empty list: */
   start = end = getnode();
   /* Load, save, print or update the list:  */
   while (busy)
   {  printf(">>");
      scanf("%40s", str);
      ch = getchar(); ungetc(ch, stdin);
      if (!isspace(ch)) puts("Name too long"); else
      if (str[0] == '.')
      switch (toupper(str[1]))
      {  case 'L': loadlist(); break;
         case 'P': printlist(); break;
         case 'S': savelist(); break;
         case 'Q': busy=0; break;
         default: puts("Wrong command. "
         "Use .Load, .Print, .Save, or .Quit");
      } else
      {  p = searchlist(str, &found);
         if (scanf("%ld", &ii) == 1)
```

```
            {  if (found) p->num = ii;
               else insertnode(p, str, ii);
            }  else
            {  ch = getchar();
               if (ch == '/' || ch == '?')
               {  if (!found) puts("Unknown name"); else
                  {  if (ch == '/') deletenode(p); else
                        printf("%-40s %8ld\n", p->name, p->num);
                  }
               }  else puts("A name must be followed by a "
                  "number, a question mark, or a slash.");
            }
         }
         skiprestline();
      }
      return 0;
}
```

Note that in this example we use **malloc** to allocate memory space not only for nodes but also for strings. In each node the member called **name** is a pointer to the first character of a name which is stored elsewhere. For example, as a result of the .L command, function **main** calls **loadlist** to read data from a file and to build a linked list. Function **loadlist** in turn calls **append**. We can depict the relationship between these and some other function calls as follows:

main → **loadlist** → **append** → **getmemory** → **malloc**   (allocates memory
                          ↓   for a string)
                     getnode
                          ↓
                     getmemory
                          ↓
                     malloc   (allocates memory for a node)

We also use the standard function **free** for two purposes, as the function **deletenode** shows.

Our 'information system' INFSYS1.C works reasonably as long as the *heap* is large enough. (For our purposes, we can define a *heap* as a large area of memory of which portions become available when we call the standard function **malloc**.) If we search a linked list for some item, the time this takes depends on the position of that item in the list: if the item is at the end of the list, we have to traverse the entire list to reach that item. Remember that we are doing linear search, with running time $O(n)$. This may be a real drawback if we have to search the list very frequently. However, when using program INFSYS1.C for a list of, say, a thousand elements, we will find the program quick enough, because searching the list is a very fast operation compared with the repeated entry of input lines.

4.4 Stacks and Queues

In Section 4.1, we inserted new nodes at the head of the list. If we insert nodes only in this way and also delete nodes only at the head, we say that we are using the list as a *stack*, based on the principle *Last In First Out* (LIFO). Implementing a stack by means of a linked list is not always the best solution; in many cases it has no real advantages over the more usual method, that is, with an array. In the latter case, we use an integer variable as a stack pointer, which is incremented when an element is pushed onto the stack and decremented when it is popped from the stack, as the following program fragment shows:

```
#define STSIZE 1000
int stack[STSIZE], stptr=0;
/* stack[stptr] is the first free stack location */

void push(int x)
{  if (stptr == STSIZE) error("Stack overflow"); else
   stack[stptr++] = x;
}

int pop(void)
{  if (stptr == 0) error("Pop attempt with empty stack");
   else return stack[--stptr];
}
```

Note that our stack pointer **stptr** points to the free location next to the last occupied location. Instead, we can make the stack pointer point to the last occupied location. Both solutions are correct, but we must always carefully realize which choice we have made, and be consistent. For C programmers, our choice is perhaps the more natural, since we often use n elements

a[0], a[1], ..., a[n−1]

Here, too, a[n] is the first array element following those which are actually in use, so we may regard n as 'pointing to' the first free location.

For many applications, an array is a good means to implement a stack. Note, however, that a maximum stack size must be specified in advance (although we can solve this problem by using the standard functions **malloc** and **realloc** as we will see shortly). We have no such problems with a linked list, as the following program fragment shows:

```
typedef struct Node {int num; struct Node *link;} node;
node *start=NULL, *p;

void push(int x)
{  p = (node *)malloc(sizeof(node));
   if (p == NULL) error("Stack overflow");
   else
   {  p->link = start;
      p->num = x;
      start = p;
   }
}

int pop(void)
{  int x;
   if (start == NULL) error("Pop from empty stack");
   else
   {  x = start->num;
      p = start;
      start = start->link;
      free(p);
      return x;
   }
}
```

Note that in both stack implementations we perform tests to prevent misusing an *empty* stack. These tests take time, so we should remove them in applications where we know them to be superfluous. This is often the case, since all we have to do is take care that we do not try to fetch more items from the stack than we have stored on it.

Tests for stack *overflow*, also included in the above program fragments, are usually not superfluous. It is wise to perform them whenever there is the slightest chance of the stack growing larger than permitted by the amount of available memory. In our last stack implementation (by means of a linked list), a considerable amount of memory is used for pointers. It seems therefore that a stack in the form of a linked list is less economical with memory space than one in the form of an array. However, with an array of a fixed size, we will normally allocate more memory for the stack than we actually need, which is not efficient either. If we use a conventional array declaration, the array size will often be some compromise, based on the amount of memory that is available. If we use a very large array, there may be trouble with small computer systems; a small array, on the other hand, may make the program unnecessarily restrictive. Fortunately, the C language offers a better solution. As we have done several times, we can benefit from the possibility of allocating a block of memory, pointed to by a pointer variable, and then use this pointer as an array. With memory space allocated by **malloc** rather than by an array declaration, we can cope with 'stack overflow' by enlarging the allocated amount of memory space, using **realloc**. We may then obtain an entirely new block of memory to which the old stack contents are automatically copied. As this will take some time, we had better not use **realloc** for each new item to be placed on the stack, but rather increase the stack size by a block of, say, 50 items (or by, say, 10 per cent of the current size). See also Exercise 4.6, at the end of this chapter.

A linked list is more elegant in this regard: on a large machine, the function **malloc** will simply supply more memory than on a small one if we call this function a great many times. Apart from testing the pointer value returned by **malloc**, we need no special provisions in our program. Also, when items are popped from the stack, their memory locations are immediately returned by **free** to the operating system in the case of a linked list, while with an array they will normally remain allocated. Thus, there may be good reasons for implementing stacks as linked lists. In Sections 8.3 and 8.4 we will actually use such stacks, and refer to them as *linked stacks*.

Queues

Instead of the LIFO principle, on which a stack is based, we may want to use the idea of *First In First Out* (FIFO), which applies to a *queue*. In this case, a linked list is certainly easier to use than an array. In Fig. 4.8, we have a queue in the form of a linked list, with two special pointer variables **frontptr** and **rearptr**. New nodes are inserted at the *rear*, pointed to by **rearptr**, and old nodes are deleted from the *front*, pointed to by **frontptr**. Note that the arrows point from the front to the rear: if node A points to node B then A was inserted before B.

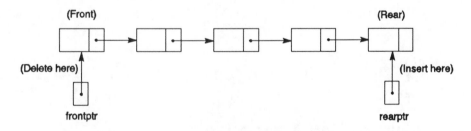

Fig. 4.8. A queue

Program QUEUE.C uses a queue. Repeatedly, it reads an integer, preceded by an exclamation mark, from the keyboard, and stores it in a newly created node; this node is then inserted at the rear of the list. Instead of an exclamation mark and an integer, we can enter a question mark, as a signal to print the integer stored at the front of the queue and to delete that node. A dollar sign will stop program execution.

```
/* QUEUE.C: Demonstration of a queue   */
#include <stdio.h>
#include <stdlib.h>
typedef struct Node {int num; struct Node *link;} node;
node *frontptr, *rearptr=NULL;

int empty_queue(void)
{ return rearptr == NULL;
}

node *insert_rear(int x)
{  node *p = (node *)malloc(sizeof(node));
   if (p != NULL)
   {  if (empty_queue()) frontptr = p;
      else rearptr->link = p;
      p->num = x;
   }
   return p;
}

int delete_front(void)
{  int x;
   node *p=frontptr;
   x = frontptr->num;
   if (frontptr == rearptr) rearptr = NULL;
   else frontptr = p->link;
   free(p);
   return x;
}

main()
{  int x;
   node *p;
   char ch;
   puts("Each time, enter:\n");
   puts("  !   followed by an integer to be stored");
   puts(
      "  ?  (to print the oldest integer in the queue)");
   puts("  $  (to stop program execution)\n");
   for ( ; ; )
   {  do  ch = getchar(); while (ch != '!' && ch != '?'
                            && ch != '$');
      if (ch == '!')  /* Node to be inserted */
      {  if (scanf("%d", &x) == 1)
```

```
           {  p = insert_rear(x);
              if (p == NULL)
              puts("No memory available; "
                   "use ? first to delete nodes");
              else rearptr = p;
           } else puts("Integer expected");
        } else
        if (ch == '?')  /* Node to be deleted */
        { if (empty_queue())
          puts("Use  !...  first, or use $\n"); else
          x = delete_front();
          printf("%30d\n", x);
        } else break; /* ch == '$' */
     }
     return 0;
}
```

Here is a demonstration of this program:

```
Each time, enter:

    !  followed by an integer to be stored
    ?  (to print the oldest integer in the queue)
    $  (to stop program execution)


!  1492
!  1945
?
                            1492
!  1813
?
                            1945

?
                            1813

?
Use  !...  first, or use $
$
```

The numbers in the left column are input data and those in the right column form the output. Since in both columns we find the same number in the same order, this demonstration clearly shows the FIFO principle. In this example, the length of the queue was successively 0, 1, 2, 1, 2, 1, 0.

4.5 Circular, Doubly-linked Lists

A list is called *circular* if its tail contains a pointer to its head, as shown in Fig. 4.9.

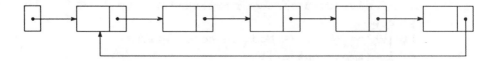

Fig. 4.9. A circular list

We obtain a more interesting extension of the simple linked list if we supply each node with two pointers, such that one, as usual, points to its successor and the other to its predecessor. The resulting data structure is called a *doubly-linked list*, an example of which is shown in Fig. 4.10.

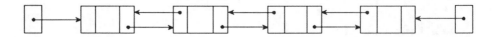

Fig. 4.10. A doubly-linked list

Finally, we can combine both concepts to obtain a circular, doubly-linked list, as Fig. 4.11 illustrates.

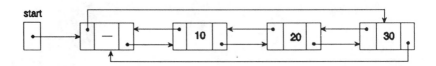

Fig. 4.11. A circular, doubly-linked list

The node on the left, pointed to by **start**, is a *dummy header node*. It is useful as a sentinel, and it makes dealing with an empty list easier. For example, let us assume that each information member consists of an integer, as shown in Fig. 4.11. Then we set up a circular doubly-linked list that is empty by calling function **setup_cdl_list**, shown below. It returns either the address of the dummy header node or **NULL** in case no memory is available:

```
typedef struct Node {int num; struct Node *left, *right;} node;

node *setup_cdl_list(void)
{   node *p = (node *)malloc(sizeof(node));
    if (p != NULL)
    {   p->right = p->left = start;
    }
    return p;
}
```

We can call this function as follows:

```
node *start;
...
start = setup_cdl_list();
if (start == NULL) puts("Not enough memory"), exit(1);
```

If this call is successful, the situation is as shown in Fig. 4.12.

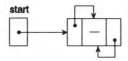

Fig. 4.12. An empty circular doubly-linked list

Starting with this empty list, we can insert new nodes by calling the following function:

```
int insert_cdl_list(int x)
{   node *q, *p = (node *)malloc(sizeof(node));
    if (p == NULL) return 0; /* Failure */
    p->num = x;
    q = start->left;
    start->left = p;
    p->right = start;
    q->right = p;
    p->left = q;
    return 1;    /* Success */
}
```

For example, if we call this function three times, with 10, 20, and 30, in that order, as arguments, we obtain the list of Fig. 4.11.

With a given pointer **p**, pointing to some node, we can insert a new node either to the right or to the left of **p**, without copying an entire node as we did with the simple linked list. The following function inserts a node immediately to the left of the node pointed to by argument **p** and stores argument **x** in it. The return value is 0 if no free memory is available; normally the return value will be 1:

```
int insert_left(node *p, int x)
/* Insert x in a new node of a circular doubly-linked
   list, immediately to the left of *p
*/
{  node *q = (node *)malloc(sizeof(node));
   if (q == NULL) return 0; /* Failure */
   q->left = p->left;
   q->num = x;
   q->right = p;
   p->left->right = q;
   p->left = q;
   return 1;
}
```

Here **q** is an auxiliary pointer, pointing to the newly created node (see Fig. 4.13).

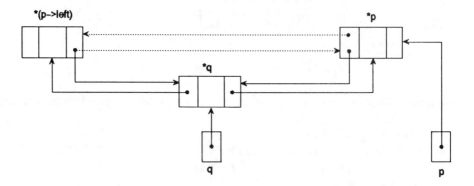

Fig. 4.13. Inserting a node (···· = old; — = new)

We can delete the node pointed to by a given pointer **p** in an elegant and efficient way by calling this function:

```
void nodedelete(node *p)
{  p->left->right = p->right;
   p->right->left = p->left;
   free(p);
}
```

Verifying this in a diagram is left as an exercise for the reader. Note that in some applications it may be wise to include a test in this program fragment. If the given pointer **p** depends on possibly incorrect input data, we ought to verify that **p** is unequal to **start**, see Figs. 4.11 and 4.12. Should **p** and **start** have equal values, then **p** points to the dummy header node, which should always be present, even in an empty list.

Interesting as our last two program fragments are, a more important new aspect is that we can traverse (and search) a circular doubly-linked list in two directions. In either case, we can use the dummy header node as a sentinel. There are many applications where collections of data are to be traversed both forward and backward. An example is a *text editor*. In this case, the data member in each node would not be a character sequence itself but rather a pointer to it, so that the amount of memory allocated for each text line depends on the length of that line. This is illustrated in Fig. 4.14.

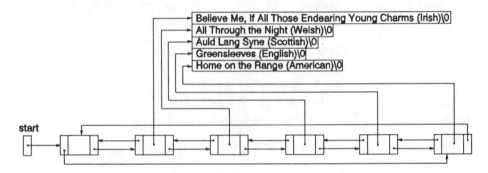

Fig. 4.14. Data structure used by text editor

Adopting the convention that **&&&** at the beginning of an input line denotes end-of-input, we can enter the five lines shown in Fig. 4.14 (followed by **&&&**) on the keyboard and place them in a circular doubly-linked list, by using the following program fragment:

```
#include <stdio.h>
#include <stdlib.h>
char buf[200];

typedef
struct Node {char *line; struct Node *left, *right;} node;
node *start, *current, *p;
...
for (;;)
{  if (fgets(buf, 200, stdin) == NULL) break;
   buf[strlen(buf)-1] = '\0'; /* Remove trailing '\n' */
   if (strcmp(buf, "&&&") == 0) break;
```

```
        p = insertline(current, buf);
        if (p == NULL)
        {  puts("Not enough memory"); break;
        } else current = p;
    }
```

Suppose, for example, that we enter the three letters **ABC** and press the Enter key. Then the standard function **fgets** fills array **buf** as follows

i	→	0	1	2	3	4
buf[i]	→	A	B	C	'\n'	'\0'

In this case we have **strlen(buf)** = 4. We remove '**\n**' by replacing it with '**\0**', hence the statement

```
buf(strlen(buf)-1] = '\0';
```

The pointer variable **current** is to point to the current line, that is, the line under consideration. There may be an edit command **TOP**, which means that the first line is to be the current line. Then the statement to be executed is

```
current = start->right;
```

Thanks to the circular nature of the list, we need an equally simple statement for an edit command **BOTTOM**, to go to the final line:

```
current = start->left;
```

Once the above data structure exists, we can print all text lines stored in the list as follows:

```
current = start->right;
while (current != start)
{  printf("%s\n", current->line);
   current = current->right;
}
```

Obviously, an editor must have the possibility to store all data on disk. We can do this with almost the same program fragment as the last one, using **fprintf(fp, ...)** instead of **printf(...)**. It might be noted that a very simple (though possibly not useful) change in the last program fragment would cause the file to be listed in the reverse order, that is, the bottom line first and the top line last. Replacing **right** with **left** twice is all that would be needed.

If the variable **current** has a value different from **start**, there is a current line and we can implement a command to go to the next line, so that the latter becomes the current line. This command is to be ignored if the current line should be the bottom line, because then there is no next line:

```
p = current->right;   /* Go to next line, if any */
if (p != start) current = p;
```

The if-statement alters the variable **current** only if there is a next line.

Analogously, a command to go back to the previous line, if there is one, is implemented as follows:

```
p = current->left;    /* Go to previous line, if any */
if (p != start) current = p;
```

The above operations assume that the circular doubly-linked list exists. However, we have not yet discussed the function **insertline**, which we used (when discussing Fig. 4.14) to build such a list. There is one thing, though, that must be done in advance, namely creating an empty list, that is, a list with only a dummy header node:

```
start = (node *)malloc(sizeof(node));
start->left = start->right = current = start;
```

Note that initially **current** is equal to **start**. The following function, **insertline**, can handle this situation as well. In general, it inserts a new node, immediately after the node pointed to by its first argument. Its second argument is the start address of a buffer area, containing the actual characters in question. Since we want to use the same buffer for all lines that are read, these characters will be copied to a new area, where they are safe. Function **insertline** returns a pointer to the inserted node. We can use this return value to make the inserted node the new current node. In this way, we can easily insert more than one line so that the lines appear in the list in the same order as they are given:

```
node *insertline(node *pcur, char *buf)
{  node *pnode, *pline;
   pnode = (node *)malloc(sizeof(node));
   pline = (char *)malloc(strlen(buf)+1);
   if (pnode == NULL || pline == NULL) return NULL;
   strcpy(pnode->line, buf);
   pnode->left = pcur; pnode->right = pcur->right;
   pcur->right->left = pnew; pcur->right = pnew;
   return pnode;
}
```

Note that in **insertline** there are two calls to the standard function **malloc**, namely both for the node to be created and for the actual line of text to be stored.

Analogously, deleting the current line involves two calls of the standard function **free**. We call the function **deleteline** as follows:

```
current = deleteline(current);
```

This function returns the node representing the new current line, that is, the line that follows the deleted line:

```
node *delete(node *pcur)
{   node *pnext;
    if (pcur == start) return start;
    pnext = pcur->right;
    free(pcur->line);
    pcur->left->right = pnext;
    pnext->left = pcur->left;
    free(pcur);
    return pnext;
}
```

The if-statement takes care that we maintain a correct empty list, with a dummy header node, in case the function should be applied to an empty list.

Exercises

In the following exercises, the contents of the data structures under consideration are to be printed wherever this is necessary to show that the program in question works properly.

4.1 Write a program which reads a sequence of integers and builds a linked list to store these integers. The order of the stored integers, from head to tail, is to be the same as the order in which the numbers are read.

4.2 Extend the program of Exercise 1, and delete all even integers (2, 4, ...) from the list. Use the standard function **free** to release the nodes that contain the even integers.

4.3 Write a program which reads text from a file. Let us define *words* as strings separated by one or more white-space characters. Each word read from the file is to be stored in some memory locations obtained by a call to the standard function **malloc**, but if a word is read several times it is to be stored only once. Build a linked list with a node for each word that is read. Each node has two members, a pointer to the stored word and a pointer to the next node. The order of the nodes in the list must be the same as the order of the corresponding words in the file.

4.4 Write a program that reads two positive integers n and k. Build a circular list (as shown in Fig. 4.9) in which the numbers 1, 2, ..., n, in that order, are stored. Starting at the node with number 1, delete each kth node from the list, going round, until all nodes have been deleted. After deleting a node, the next one in the circle is counted as number 1 and so on. For example, if $n = 8$ and $k = 3$, we delete the nodes with the integers

    3, 6, 1, 5, 2, 8, 4, 7,

in that order. (This process, illustrated by initially having n persons arranged in a circle and by repeatedly eliminating the kth of those who are still present, is known as the *Josephus* problem).

4.5 Instead of using only one linked list to store data, we can have a great many of them, each starting in an element **p[i]** of an array of pointer elements. Use this principle to implement *hashing with chaining*, mentioned in Section 2.7 and illustrated by Fig. 4.15. As with open addressing, the keys are used to compute a primary index i. All records with keys resulting in the same value i are stored in the list starting at **p[i]**. Compare chaining with open addressing, discussed in Section 2.7. With either hashing method, investigate the possibility of deleting items.

4.6 In Section 4.4, we observed that to implement a stack as an array we have to specify a fixed maximum size in advance, unless we allocate memory by using the standard functions **malloc** and **realloc**. Write a program to implement such a more flexible stack.

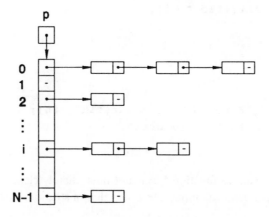

Fig. 4.15. Hashing with chaining, used in Exercise 4.5

4.7 Use a fixed-size array to implement a queue. The first array element should be considered the successor of the final one, so that we regard the array as a circle. A certain portion of the circle represents the queue; it continually grows at one end and shrinks at the other. Obviously, the number of elements in the queue must not exceed the array length.

4.8 Write a simple text editor, based on a doubly-linked circular list and on program fragments listed in Section 4.5.

4.9 Recall that *natural merge sort*, discussed in Section 2.4, is based on sequential access. This fact enables us to apply this sorting method to linked lists. Write a program to demonstrate this. While sorting, use three linked lists instead of three files.

4.10 Write and demonstrate a function **reverse**, which accepts a start pointer of a linked list as an argument and returns a start pointer of a new linked list with the same nodes as the given list but reversed: the head of the new list contains the same data as the tail of the original one, and so on.

4.11 Consider the following program:

```
#include <stdio.h>

void f(int i)
{  if (i > 0)
   {  f(i/4 - 37);
      f(i/3 - 41);
      f(i/2 - 43);
      printf("%d ", i);
   }
}

main()
{ int n;
  printf("Enter n: "); scanf("%d", &n);
  f(n); puts(""); return 0;
}
```

Due to the recursive function **f**, it is not immediately clear how the output of this program depends on its input. Here is a demonstration:

```
Enter n: 500
1 88 19 125 14 28 60 207 500
```

Let us assume that the order of the integers in the output is irrelevant. Replace the recursive function **f** with a nonrecursive one **g**, in such a way that the same integers appear in the output (although possibly in a different order). Use a *stack* to accomplish this. Initially this stack is empty. In your function **g**, deal with any integers that are on the stack in the same way as with its argument. For each i, which is either the argument or an integer popped from the stack, print i and push $i/4-37$, $i/3-41$ and $i/2-43$ onto the stack, that is, if i is positive. We may say that we *defer recursive calls* by pushing their arguments onto a stack.

4.12 Write a nonrecursive version of our function **q_sort**, listed in Section 2.2. Use a stack for deferred recursive calls, in the same way as in Exercise 4.11.

4.13 Store the coefficients and the exponents of a polynomial in a linked list. For example, the list shown in Fig. 4.16 represents the polynomial $5x^4 - 3x + 2$. Then evaluate this polynomial for a given value x. Use at least two functions in your program: one to build the list on the basis of the coefficients and exponents, entered on the keyboard, and the other to evaluate the polynomial for the value x, also read from the keyboard. Use x and the start pointer of the linked list as arguments for the latter function.

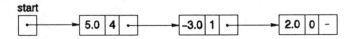

Fig. 4.16. Linked list for a polynomial

5

Binary Trees

5.1 Basic Operations on Binary Search Trees

As we saw in Chapter 4, searching a linked list is done by means of linear search, which is slow compared with binary search, discussed in Section 2.5. We now want to apply the latter search method to dynamic data structures. A *binary tree*, as shown in Fig. 5.1, enables us to do this. It consists of a pointer variable, the so-called *root*, and (zero or more) nodes. The tree is said to be *empty* if there are no such nodes; in that case the root has the value **NULL**. Let us use the term *root node* for the node pointed to by the root (in a nonempty tree). Each node has one or more information members and has always two pointer members, each of which acts as a root, either pointing to another node or having the value **NULL**. If a node contains any pointers to other nodes, these latter nodes are said to be the *children* of the former, and we distinguish between a *left* and a *right* child. A node that has children is said to be the *parent* of these children. Unlike a traditional family situation, every child has only one parent; in other words, any two distinct pointers point to distinct nodes. Each pointer is in fact the root of a subtree, so each node has a left and a right subtree. This holds even if a pointer member has the value **NULL**, since a subtree may be empty. A *leaf* is defined as a node that has no children, which means that a leaf has two pointer members whose values are **NULL**. With each node we can associate a *level*. The root node is said to be at level 1, and if a node at level i has any children then these are at level $i + 1$. In addition to this, we say that the root of a tree is at level 0. Thus, the level of a node is in fact the number of branches to be traversed if we follow the path from the root of the tree to that node. The highest level that occurs in a binary tree is called the *height* of that tree. For example, the binary tree shown in Fig. 5.1 has height 6. (The reader should be aware that there are books that give other definitions. What we are calling a 'root node'

131

is sometimes termed a 'root'; some authors define that node to be at level 0, and, if it is the only node of the tree, they sometimes define the height of that tree to be 0. Our definitions, with a root being a special pointer variable, and with an empty tree having height 0, are very convenient from a programmer's point of view.)

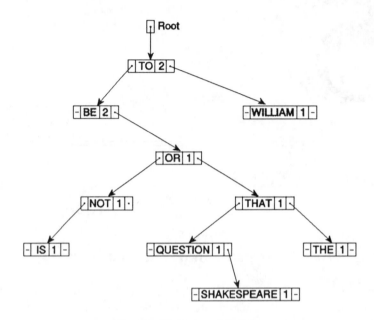

Fig. 5.1. Binary search tree

Let us now develop a useful program, which performs a *frequency count* for words read from a text file. It lists all words in alphabetic order, together with its frequency. After this, we can enter a word to display its frequency once again. This program can be used to analyze text. For example, very frequent use of the same word may indicate bad style.

We will store the words in a binary tree. We want to store the words in such a way that we can quickly search the tree for a given word. If a word is read more than once, we will store it only once in the tree, but it will be accompanied by a word count, which says how often the word has been read. Besides the two pointers to its children, if any, each node will contain both a pointer to a word, stored somewhere else, and the (integer) word count just mentioned. We will use each word as a key, which implies that it will be used when we search the tree. In general, each node of a binary tree may contain several data items, one of which, the key, is used in search operations. In each node, the key is both greater than the key in the left child and less than the key in the right child, that is, as far as the node in question has a left and a right child. As this enables us to use the binary search method, we call this type of a binary tree a *binary search tree*. In our example, every key is a string, and we will use the words *greater* and *less* in the sense of string comparison, referring to the usual alphabetic order. Consider, for example, the following text fragment:

```
"To be or not to be,
that is the question".
William Shakespeare.
```

Since we do not want to distinguish between capital and small letters, we will convert any small letters into the corresponding capital letters. Any sequence of nonalphabetic characters, such as blanks, newline characters, punctuation characters and digits, will act as word separators. In other respects they are ignored, so for our purpose the above fragment is equivalent to

TO BE OR NOT TO BE THAT IS THE
QUESTION WILLIAM SHAKESPEARE

With either fragment as input, our program will build the tree shown in Fig. 5.1.

We sometimes call a binary tree a *recursive* data structure, because it can be expressed in terms of smaller binary trees. Since each nonempty binary tree has two subtrees, we are dealing with 'genuine' recursion (see Section 1.6). It will therefore not surprise us that in this context recursive functions are extremely useful. For example, if we have to print all information stored in a binary tree, then we can express this task in terms of printing all information stored in its subtrees (which are also binary trees); all we have to do is:

If the tree is empty, nothing is to be printed.
If the tree is not empty, we are to perform the following three tasks, in this order:
-    Print all information stored in the left subtree.
-    Print the information members in the node pointed to by the given root.
-    Print all information stored in the right subtree.

As follows from the definition of a binary search tree, this procedure leads to an output sequence in ascending order.

Searching a binary search tree can be done either by recursion or by iteration. In a recursive solution, only one recursive call would be executed. As we know, this makes it doubtful whether recursion is really advantageous here. An iterative solution is indeed rather simple. Initially we make pointer **p** equal to the root of the whole tree. Then, in a loop, we perform the following actions:

-    If **p** is equal to **NULL**, the key cannot be found, so we return **NULL**.
-    If the given key is found in the node pointed to by **p**, we return **p**.
-    If the given key is less than the key value of the node pointed to by **p**, we assign the root of the left subtree to **p**; otherwise, we assign the root of the right subtree to **p**.

To add new data, including a key, to a binary search tree, we first search the tree for that key. If we find the given key, we increment the count member (that is, if the application so requires, as in our example). If the key is not found, we create a new node in which we store the given data. The address of the new node (returned by **malloc**) is then placed in the pointer member (with the old value **NULL**) that we have reached during searching, as program BINTREE.C shows.

```c
/* BINTREE.C:
       This program builds and searches a binary search
       tree and prints its contents.
       The program produces a frequency distribution of
       words read from a text file.
       We can also search the tree for a given word, to
       inquire how often that word occurs.
*/
#include <stdio.h>
#include <ctype.h>
#include <stdlib.h>
#include <string.h>

typedef struct Node
    {char *pword; int count; struct Node *left, *right;} node;
char buffer[101];

int readword(FILE *fp)
/* This function reads a word from stream fp.
   It skips any leading nonalphabetic characters.
   Then the longest possible string of letters is
   read and placed in 'buffer'.
   Return value:
       1 = success,
       0 = failure (due to end of file)
*/
{   int ch, i;
    do
    {   ch = getc(fp);
        if (ch == EOF) return 0;
    }   while (!isalpha(ch));
    for (i=0; i<100; )
    {   buffer[i++] = toupper(ch);
        ch = getc(fp);
        if (!isalpha(ch)) break;
    }
    buffer[i] = '\0';
    return 1;
}
```

```
void *getmemory(int n)
{   void *p=malloc(n);
    if (p == NULL)
    {   puts("Not enough memory"); exit(1);
    }
    return p;
}


node *addnode(node *p)
{   int code;
    if (p == NULL)
    {   p = (node *)getmemory(sizeof(node));
        p->pword = (char *)getmemory(strlen(buffer) + 1);
        strcpy(p->pword, buffer);
        p->count = 1;   p->left = p->right = NULL;
    } else
    {   code = strcmp(buffer, p->pword);
        if (code < 0) p->left = addnode(p->left); else
        if (code > 0) p->right = addnode(p->right); else
        p->count ++;
    }
    return p;
}


void printtree(node *p)
{   if (p != NULL)
    {   printtree(p->left);
        printf("%5d %s\n", p->count, p->pword);
        printtree(p->right);
    }
}


node *search(node *p)
/* This function searches the tree with root p
   for the word stored in 'buffer'.
*/
{   int code;
    for ( ; ; )
    {   if (p == NULL) return NULL;
        code = strcmp(buffer, p->pword);
        if (code == 0) return p;
        p = (code < 0 ? p->left : p->right);
    }
}
```

```
node *buildtree(node *root)
{ char filnam[51];
  FILE *fp;
  printf("Input file: "); scanf("%50s", filnam);
  fp = fopen(filnam, "r");
  if (fp == NULL) puts("File not available"), exit(1);
  while (readword(fp)) root = addnode(root);
  fclose (fp);
  return root;
}

main()
{ node *root=NULL, *ptr;
  int i;
  root = buildtree(root);
  puts("\nFrequency distribution:");
  printtree(root);
  for ( ; ; )
  { printf("\nEnter a word, or type @ to stop: ");
    if (scanf("%100s", buffer) != 1 || buffer[0] == '@')
      break;
    for (i=0; buffer[i]; i++) buffer[i] = toupper(buffer[i]);
    ptr = search(root);
    if (ptr == NULL) puts("Does not occur."); else
    printf("Number of occurrences: %d\n", ptr->count);
  }
  return 0;
}
```

Assuming the above text fragment to be available in the file *shakespeare*, we can use program BINTREE.C as follows:

```
Input file: shakespeare
Frequency distribution:
    2 BE
    1 IS
    1 NOT
    1 OR
    1 QUESTION
    1 SHAKESPEARE
    1 THAT
    1 THE
    2 TO
    1 WILLIAM
```

```
Enter a word, or type @ to stop: to
Number of occurrences: 2

Enter a word, or type @ to stop: something
Does not occur.

Enter a word, or type @ to stop: @
```

Program BINTREE.C does not contain a function for node deletion, which is more difficult than most other operations on trees; we will discuss this subject in Section 5.3.

5.2 Perfectly Balanced Binary Trees

It will be clear that we want a binary tree to be reasonably 'balanced'. Even without a definition of this adjective, we feel that the tree shown in Fig. 5.2 is hardly worth calling a binary tree, let alone a balanced binary tree. Of course, searching a degenerated tree of this type is not faster than searching a linked list.

However, this is really a binary tree, and with the numbers (instead of strings, just for a change) shown in the nodes, it is even a binary search tree. A degenerated tree such as this one will be built by program BINTREE.C or any similar program if the objects given in the input file are in ascending order. As we have developed good

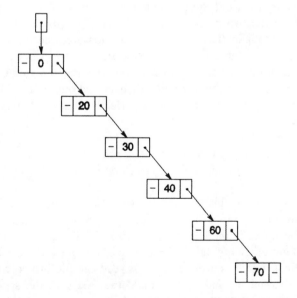

Fig. 5.2. A degenerated binary tree

sorting algorithms in Chapter 2, files with objects in ascending order are not exceptional, so a warning not to use sorted files as input data for this program is in order here. This example makes it clear that we need some definition about how well or how badly a binary tree is balanced. We will distinguish two such definitions.

We call a binary tree *perfectly balanced*, if each node has a left and a right subtree in which the numbers of nodes differ by at most one. The binary tree in Fig. 5.3 is perfectly balanced but the binary tree in Fig. 5.4 is not.

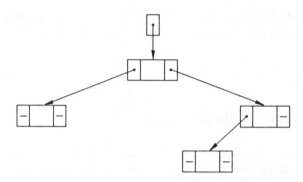

Fig. 5.3. A perfectly balanced binary tree

The tree shown in Fig. 5.4 is an example of a *height-balanced binary tree*, which is a binary tree with the characteristic that for every node the *heights* of its left and right subtrees differ by at most one. A height-balanced binary tree is also called an *AVL tree*, after its inventors Adelson-Velskii and Landis. Every perfectly balanced binary tree is a height-balanced binary tree, but the converse is not true, as Fig. 5.4 shows.

We usually require the two types of balanced trees to be binary search trees. We then have to face the problem that without special measures the trees will lose their balance property if we insert or delete nodes arbitrarily. As we will see in Section 5.4, there is an efficient algorithm for height-balanced binary trees to maintain their balance property. There is no such algorithm for perfectly balanced binary trees. However, with a simple and elegant algorithm, we can build a perfectly balanced binary tree straightaway, provided that:

(1) The objects to be read are given in ascending order (!)
(2) We know in advance how many objects are to be read.

(In Exercise 5.2, at the end of this chapter, we will also use this algorithm to replace a given binary search tree with one that is perfectly balanced.) We assume that all data (including keys) to be stored in the tree are given in a file. To fulfil (1), we can sort this file, which can be done efficiently using, for example, the quicksort method. Requirement (2) is not difficult either, since we can first read the file just to count how may keys there are, then rewind it, and, finally, build the tree with the special algorithm mentioned. A special sorting method such as quicksort is not needed if we use the

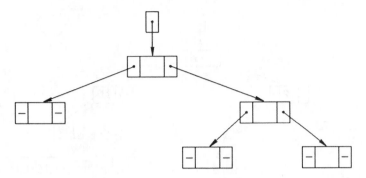

Fig. 5.4. A height-balanced binary tree that is not perfectly balanced

output produced by a function such as **printtree** in Section 5.1, since this output is already sorted. We can in fact regard program BINTREE.C as a sorting program; this way of sorting is called *treesort*.

Program PERFBAL.C is a demonstration program for perfectly balanced binary search trees. First, it asks the user how many integers (in ascending order) will follow. It then reads these integers and stores them in a perfectly balanced binary search tree. Finally, the contents of this tree are printed a way that reflects the tree structure. In the output, the root of the tree is on the left; the usual tree representation is obtained by rotating this tree through 90° clockwise, as the following demonstration shows:

```
How many integers (in ascending order) will follow? 10
11   12   13   14   15   16   17   18   19   20


Here is the resulting perfectly balanced binary
search tree, with its root on the left.
Please turn it 90 degrees clockwise:
```

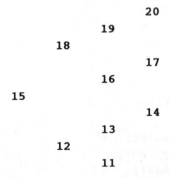

```
                                  20
                             19
                       18
                                  17
                             16
              15
                                  14
                             13
                       12
                             11
```

If we turn this tree as indicated, we obtain the essence of Fig. 5.5.

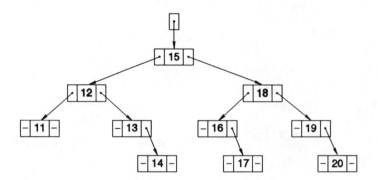

Fig. 5.5. Perfectly balanced binary search tree, built by program PERFBAL.C

Program PERFBAL.C, which does all this, is surprisingly small and simple:

```
/* PERFBAL.C: This program builds a perfectly balanced
             binary search tree.
*/
#include <stdio.h>
#include <stdlib.h>
typedef struct Node {int num; struct Node *left, *right;} node;

node *pbtree(int n)
{   int nleft, nright, nleftplusright=n-1;
    node *p;
    if (n == 0) return NULL;
    nleft = nleftplusright/2;
    nright = nleftplusright - nleft;
    p = (node *)malloc(sizeof(node));
    p->left = pbtree(nleft);
    scanf("%d", & p->num);
    p->right = pbtree(nright);
    return p;
}

void printtree(node *p, int position)
{   if (p != NULL)
    {   printtree(p->right, position+6);
        printf("%*d\n", position, p->num);
        printtree(p->left, position+6);
    }
}
```

```
main()
{   int n;
    node *root;
    printf(
    "How many integers (in ascending order) will follow? ");
    scanf("%d", &n);
    root = pbtree(n);
    puts("\nHere is the resulting perfectly balanced binary");
    puts("search tree, with its root on the left.");
    puts("Please turn it 90 degrees clockwise:\n");
    printtree(root, 6);
    return 0;
}
```

The recursive function **pbtree** builds a perfectly balanced tree containing *n* nodes, where *n* is its argument, and it returns the root of this tree. If, in a recursive call, *n* is zero, the function returns the value **NULL** (or, as we may say, it builds an empty tree). In our example, we call **pbtree** with $n = 10$ in function **main**. We now compute the number of nodes that are to be placed both in the left and in the right subtrees. Since there will be one node (the root node) not belonging to either subtree, there are $10 - 1 = 9$ nodes left for the two subtrees together. We divide this number by 2 and use the truncated quotient in

```
nleft = nleftplusright/2;
```

Thus, we find **nleft** = 4, **nright** = 5. We then create the root node, pointed to by the auxiliary pointer **p**, but we do not yet read the integer to be placed in it. Instead, we first call **pbtree** recursively with **nleft** as an argument, which means that the four numbers 11, 12, 13, 14 are read and placed in the left subtree, which is created at the same time. Only now do we read the integer 15 to be placed in the root node. Finally, we call **pbtree** once more to read the remaining five numbers and to create the right subtree for them. Since **nleft** and **nright** differ by one in this case, the numbers of nodes in the left and the right subtrees will also differ by one, which is required for the tree to be perfectly balanced. In each recursive call, we are again building a tree with two subtrees of about the same size, and so on. In this example, the argument of **pbtree** is 10, which is an even number. If, instead, this number is odd, the two subtrees will have exactly the same number of nodes, which is even better. Thanks to our reading the number for the root node immediately after the construction of the left subtree, the tree will be a binary search tree, provided that the input data is given in ascending order.

Note how the function **printtree** in program PERFBAL.C differs from that with the same name in program BINTREE.C. The call **printtree(root, 6)** in the **main** function says that the integer **root−>num** is to be printed with its least significant digit in the sixth position from the left. The second parameter, **position**, is used as follows in function **printtree**:

```
printf("%*d\n", position, p->num);
```

The asterisk in **%*d** indicates that there is a special argument, **position**, to be used as the field width, so with **position** = 6, this statement works as follows:

```
printf("%6d\n", p->num);
```

In two recursive calls, **position+6** is used as an argument to obtain a proper indentation for the subtrees.

An information system based on a perfectly balanced binary search tree

We will now use a perfectly balanced binary tree in a useful program. The tree will represent a set of items, each consisting of a person's name and a nonnegative number associated with that person, for example, a telephone number or a registration number. We will use type **long int** to admit reasonably long numbers, such as 12345678. The names are used as keys, so they must be unique: we do not admit two persons whose names are spelled exactly the same. Our program will be capable of:

(1) Loading all items from a file and storing them in a perfectly balanced binary search tree.
(2) Reading names from the keyboard to search the tree for the corresponding numbers.
(3) Adding new items.
(4) Deleting items.
(5) Changing the number of an item.
(6) Saving all items by writing them to a file at the end of the session.
(7) Displaying an alphabetically ordered list of all items.

Recall that in Section 4.3 we discussed a similar program based on a linked list. Should that program be too slow for some application, then the program discussed here may be tried instead. However, we will be using a little more memory space, since each node of a binary tree has two pointer members, while each node of a linked list has only one. The names of the files mentioned in points (1) and (6) will be entered by the user. Normally, we will use the same file for both purposes. The items in this file are ordered, that is, the names are in alphabetic order. However, the file may be empty, which will be the case the very first time we use the program. At this initial stage, we add items to an empty set in the same way as we would add items to a nonempty set, using point (3). We then apply point (6) to obtain an ordered file. Thus, instead of first using a conventional text editor to create a file and then sorting this file by another program, we use the very program we are discussing, and begin with an empty tree. Later, we can apply point (1) to build a perfectly balanced binary search tree which will then no longer be empty. To be honest, we must note that the tree may not remain perfectly balanced while we are adding and deleting items. However, as soon as we apply points (6) and (1) again, we start with a fresh, perfectly balanced tree. In practice, the number of updates is usually small compared with the total number of items, so it is most unlikely for the tree to degenerate considerably. The latter may occur only if a great many new items, given in (almost) alphabetic order, are entered during one session. Before we can write a complete program, we have to deal with the *user interface*, that is, we must define how to use it. Since a user may not be familiar with binary trees, we will use the more elementary term *work file* instead. Like a work file used by an editor, our work file is not a permanent file on disk, so its contents are lost at the end of the session, unless they are explicitly saved. We will use the same commands as those discussed in Section 4.3, and only summarize them here. They begin with a period:

.L Load the contents of a permanent file into an empty work file.
.P Print the contents of the work file.
.S Save the work file onto a permanent file.
.Q Quit

The small letters **l**, **p**, **s**, **q** may be used instead of the corresponding capital letters. We can add an item by typing the name, without any internal spaces, then one or more spaces, followed by a number, as, for example,

```
Johnson,P.H.    452319
```

If the name *Johnson,P.H.* already occurs in the work file, the new number overwrites the old one. By typing

```
Johnson,P.H.    /
```

we remove the item with that name. The question mark in

```
Johnson,P.H.    ?
```

means that we want to know Johnson's number.

   This is all the user has to know. As for the implementation of all this, we can borrow useful material both from program INFSYS1.C, listed in Section 4.3, and from our last program, PERFBAL.C. The most difficult new aspect is deletion, mentioned in point (4). If an item is to be deleted, we will not immediately remove the corresponding node in the tree, but instead mark it as unused by setting its number member to −1. The program will behave as if the node really is removed. However, when we save all information onto a disk file, any 'garbage nodes', with a number −1, are ignored, so when we run the program later and load the file, we have a 'clean' perfectly balanced binary search tree again. So the inefficiency of logically deleted nodes that are still occupying memory space is only temporary, in the same way as the tree may temporarily be unbalanced. (We will discuss a more sophisticated way of deleting nodes in Section 5.3.) Recall that in program PERFBAL.C we required the input file to contain the number of input items that are following. Although we could read an input file twice, counting the items in the first scan and using them in the second, there is a more efficient solution. We will count the items as they are entered, and, after the command *.S*, write this item count to the file before the items themselves. As a result of command *.L*, we begin by reading this item count, so that we can use our algorithm for a perfectly balanced tree immediately. During the process of updating the tree, we change the variable **itemcount** accordingly. Since this variable is of type **int**, the size of the tree is limited not only to the available amount of memory, but also to the maximum integer value. Should this be a problem, then using type **long int** for that variable is the obvious solution. It is instructive to compare program INFSYS1.C, of Section 4.3, with our new program, INFSYS2.C. The former uses memory space more efficiently than the latter, but the latter wins on speed.

```
/* INFSYS2.C: An information system based on a
                 perfectly balanced binary search tree.
*/
#include <stdio.h>
#include <stdlib.h>
#include <string.h>
#include <ctype.h>
#define DELETED (-1L)

typedef struct Node
  {char *name; long num; struct Node *left, *right;} node;

long itemcount=0;  /* Number of nodes in tree */

void *getmemory(int n)
{  void *p=malloc(n);
   if (p == NULL) puts("Not enough memory"), exit(1);
   return p;
}

node *getnode(void)
{  return (node *)getmemory(sizeof(node));
}

node *pbtree(FILE *fp, long n)
{  long nleft, nright, nleftplusright=n-1;
   char str[41];
   node *p;
   if (n == 0) return NULL;
   nleft = nleftplusright/2;
   nright = nleftplusright - nleft;
```

```
    p = getnode();
    p->left = pbtree(fp, nleft);
    if (fscanf(fp, "%40s %ld", str, &p->num) != 2)
    {  puts("Error in input file"); return NULL;
    }
    p->name = (char *)getmemory(strlen(str) + 1);
    strcpy(p->name, str);
    p->right = pbtree(fp, nright);
    return p;
}

node *loadtree(void)
{  char filnam[51];
   node *p;
   FILE *fp;
   if (itemcount)
   {  puts("Current set of names and numbers is not empty");
      return NULL;
   }
   printf("File name: "); scanf("%50s", filnam);
   fp = fopen(filnam, "r");
   if (fp == NULL) {puts("Unknown file"); return NULL;}
   if (fscanf(fp, "%ld", &itemcount) == 0)
   {  printf(
      "File %s does not begin with an item count\n", filnam);
      return NULL;
   }
   p = pbtree(fp, itemcount);
   fclose(fp);
   return p;
}

node *add_or_change(char *str, long ii, node *p)
{  int code;
   if (p == NULL) /* Insert */
   {  p = getnode();
      p->name = (char *)getmemory(strlen(str) + 1);
      strcpy(p->name, str);
      p->num = ii;
      p->left = p->right = NULL;
      itemcount++;
   } else
   {  code = strcmp(str, p->name);
      if (code < 0)
```

```
          p->left = add_or_change(str, ii, p->left);
      else
      if (code > 0)
          p->right = add_or_change(str, ii, p->right);
      else
      {  if (p->num == DELETED) itemcount++;
         p->num = ii; /* Insert (if DELETED), or change */
      }
   }
   return p;
}

void printtree(node *p)
{  if (p != NULL)
   {  printtree(p->left);
      if (p->num != DELETED)
         printf("%-40s %8ld\n", p->name, p->num);
      printtree(p->right);
   }
}

node *search(char *str, node *p)
{  int code;
   for ( ; ; )
   { if (p == NULL) return NULL;
     code = strcmp(str, p->name);
     if (code < 0) p = p->left; else
     if (code > 0) p = p->right; else
     return p->num == DELETED ? NULL : p;
   }
}

void writetree(FILE *fp, node *p)
{  if (p != NULL)
   {  writetree(fp, p->left);
      if (p->num != DELETED)
         fprintf(fp, "%s %ld\n", p->name, p->num);
      writetree(fp, p->right);
   }
}

void savetree(node *root)
{  char filnam[51];
   FILE *fp;
```

```
      printf("File name: "); scanf("%50s", filnam);
      fp = fopen(filnam, "w");
      if (fp == NULL) puts("Cannot open output file"); else
      {  fprintf(fp, "%ld\n", itemcount);
         writetree(fp, root);
         fclose(fp);
      }
}

void skiprestline(void)
{ while (getchar() != '\n') ;
}

main()
{  char ch, str[41];
   int busy=1;
   long ii;
   node *root=NULL, *p;
   puts("Enter a name and a (nonnegative) integer, or");
   puts("a name followed either by / or by ?, or");
   puts("one of the commands .Load, .Print, .Save, .Quit");
   puts("There must be blank space after a name, "
        "not within it.");
   while (busy)
   {  printf(">>");
      scanf("%40s", str);
      if (str[0] == '.')
      switch (toupper(str[1]))
      {  case 'L': p = loadtree(); if (p) root = p; break;
         case 'P': puts("Contents:");
                      printtree(root); break;
         case 'Q': busy = 0; break;
         case 'S': savetree(root); break;
         default:  puts("Wrong command. "
         "Use .Load, .Print, .Save, or .Quit");
      } else
      {  if (scanf("%ld", &ii) == 0)
         {  ch = getchar();
            if (ch == '?' || ch == '/')
            {  p = search(str, root);
               if (p == NULL) puts("Unknown name"); else
               if (ch == '?')
                   printf("%-40s %8ld\n", p->name, p->num);
               else                      /* ch == '/' */
```

```
                        {  p->num = DELETED;        /* delete    */
                           itemcount--;
                        }
                  }  else
                  {  puts("A name must be followed by a number, "
                          "a question mark, or a slash.");
                  }
            }  else root = add_or_change(str, ii, root);
      }
      skiprestline();
   }
   return 0;
}
```

5.3 Addresses of Pointers and Node Deletion

We will now see how we can remove nodes from a binary search tree. The way we dealt
with deletion in Section 5.2 may not be satisfactory if a great many deletions and
insertions take place in a single session, during which the data is not saved on disk.
Program INFSYS2.C is already rather complex, so we had better deal with the subject
of node deletion separately in this section. Let us once again develop a complete
program, but this time each node will have only one information member containing an
integer. Throughout this section, we will use a structure type **node** and a pointer type
nodeptr, as defined in:

```
typedef
struct Node {int num; struct Node *left, *right;} node;
typedef node *nodeptr;
nodeptr root, p, *pp;
```

The identifier **nodeptr** denotes type pointer-to-**node**, so **root** and **p** are pointers to
nodes, as they were in previous programs. Then, because of the asterisk in its declaration, **pp** is a pointer to a pointer to a node, however complicated that may sound. The
last of the above four lines is equivalent to

```
node *root, *p, **pp;
```

with two asterisks preceding **pp**. According to this declaration,

pp has type **node,
*pp   has type pointer-to-**node**,
pp   has type pointer-to-pointer-to-**node**.

The double occurrence to 'pointer-to' in type names can easily be avoided by introducing a single identifier, such as **nodeptr**, for a pointer type, as we have done above. Using this new type, we can replace the second and third of the above lines with

    *pp   has type **nodeptr**,
    pp   has type pointer-to-**nodeptr**.

Pointers to pointers, such as **pp**, are not really confusing. After all, pointers (to nodes) are variables, so they have addresses, and if we want to store these addresses in other variables, these variables can only be pointers to pointers.

We will use this new pointer type to solve the problem of removing a node from a tree. We normally want to designate a node by a pointer to that node, and up to now we have been using auxiliary pointer variables to which we copied the pointer values in question. However, a copy of a pointer to some node does not enable us to remove that node from the tree, even if that node is a leaf. For example, if we have a tree of only one node, the root node, and assuming that the statement

    `p = root;`

has been executed, we cannot satisfactorily delete that node using only **p**. The point is that although

    `free(p);`

frees the memory space for the node, this is not sufficient, since we also have to assign the value **NULL** to the variable **root**, and the address of **root** is not given by **p**. In this special case, we could write

    `root = NULL;`

but this would obviously not be correct in more complex situations. Yet we can do the job using only one auxiliary variable. In our example of a tree with only one node, this variable is a pointer to the pointer variable **root**, or, in simpler terms, the value of this variable is the address of the pointer variable **root**. With the above variable declarations, its name is **pp**. After the statement

    `pp = &root;`

variable **pp** contains all information we need. We can now delete the node in question as follows:

    `free(*pp); *pp = NULL;`

The idea of using pointers to pointers is useful not only to delete nodes, but also for other operations on binary search trees. In some programs in the previous section, we used a function search to obtain information stored in the tree, but we did not benefit from this function when we had to insert new nodes, for which, after all, we had to search the tree as well. We will now develop improved functions both for searching and for inserting, based on our new concept of pointers to pointers. (This is not really a digression from our subject, since searching will also be needed in the framework of tree deletion. Besides, searching and inserting are easier subjects than deletion, so we had better deal with them first.) The following function **search** returns a pointer to a pointer member belonging to the tree.

```
nodeptr *search(nodeptr *pp, int x)
{   nodeptr *qq;
    qq = pp;
    while (*qq != NULL  &&  x != (*qq)->num)
        qq = (x < (*qq)->num ? &(*qq)->left : &(*qq)->right);
    return qq;
}
```

If our tree is to be searched for a given integer, say, 123, we can write

```
pp = search(&root, 123);
if (*pp == NULL)
{  ...      /* 123 has not been found */
}  else
{  ...      /*  (*pp)->num == 123, and pp is the address of
                either the variable 'root' or some pointer member
                in a node of the tree.
            */
}
```

It is instructive to verify this for three special cases:

(1) An empty tree. The function **search** returns the address of the variable **root**. We find **NULL** not in the returned value itself, which is an address, but as the contents of the location with that address.
(2) A tree with only one node (the *root node*) containing the given integer 123. The function again returns the address of **root**, but now this address contains a pointer to the root node.
(3) A tree with only one node containing an integer, say, 246, different from the integer 123 searched for. The while-loop in the function **search** is executed once, and since 123 is less than 246, the function returns the value &(*qq) - >**left**, which is the address of the left pointer member of the node. The memory location with this address contains the value **NULL**.

The following function, **insert**, adds a node with a given integer x to the tree in the correct position, that is, if x does not yet occur in the tree. It uses the above function **search** (and the function **getmemory**, which occurs in program INFSYS2.C of the previous section):

```
void insert(nodeptr *pp, int x)
{  nodeptr *qq;
   qq = search(pp, x);
   if (*qq == NULL)
   {  *qq = (node *)getmemory(sizeof(node));
      (*qq)->num = x;
      (*qq)->left = (*qq)->right = NULL;
   }
}
```

We now turn to our main subject, *node deletion*, but before dealing with the deletion of a single node, we will delete entire subtrees, which, surprisingly enough, is simpler! If we are given an integer, say, 123, stored in some node in the tree, we can delete the subtree whose root node is the node just mentioned, by writing, for example,

```
nodeptr *pp;
...
pp = search(&root, 123);
deltree(pp);
```

where the function **deltree** is given below:

```
void deltree(nodeptr *pp)
{  if (*pp != NULL)
   {  deltree(&(*pp)->left); deltree(&(*pp)->right);
      free(*pp);
      *pp = NULL;
   }
}
```

Note that the value returned by **search** is what **deltree** expects as its argument: not a pointer to a node, but the address of such a pointer. It will be clear that the above statements with calls to **search** and **deltree** could have been combined into the single statement

```
deltree(search(&root, 123));
```

After all these preliminaries, we will discuss a function to delete a single node. It is used in the same way as our last function, but instead of deleting an entire subtree, it will delete only the node pointed to by a pointer whose address is given as an argument. So with this new function, **delnode**, we can delete the node containing 123 (if there is such a node) by means of

```
delnode(search(&root, 123));
```

In general, the call

```
delnode(pp);
```

will delete the node pointed to by ***pp**. Using the unary operator ***** once more, we can also say that the latter call deletes the node ****pp**.

Now that we have paid so much attention to matters of notation, we must not forget to find a method of maintaining a binary search tree after we have removed the node in question. Let us first consider the simple case that this node has only one child, as shown in Fig. 5.6, where we want to delete the root node. Both this case and the case with only a left child can be dealt with as follows:

```
p = *pp;
if (p->right == NULL) {*pp = p->left; free(p);} else
if (p->left == NULL) {*pp = p->right; free(p);} else ...
```

(Here ... stands for the more difficult case that the node ***p** has two children). In Fig. 5.6 this program fragment has the effect that pointer **p** will point to the node with the integer 80. There is an even simpler case, namely a node that has neither a left nor a right child, which means that the node is a leaf. The above program fragment works properly in this case as well, as we can easily verify.

If the node in question has two children, we will not really delete the node itself. Instead, we delete one of its descendants, after having copied the data members of the latter node into the former. As we want the tree to remain a binary search tree, we

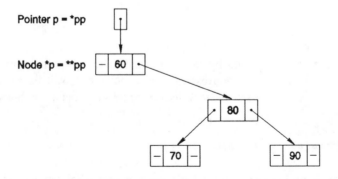

Fig. 5.6. Node to be deleted has only one child

must be very particular about which descendent to choose. We will select the key that would appear as the left neighbor of the key in question, if all keys stored in the tree were written down as an increasing sequence. Starting in the given node (with two children), we first go to its left child and then further downward to the right as far as possible. Thus, of all integers stored in the tree, we find the largest that is less than the one in the given node. This is precisely what we need to maintain a binary search tree. In Fig. 5.7, the tree contains the integers

30   40   50   55   60   <u>90</u>   95

The node containing 90 is to be deleted. Out of all the above integers less than 90, we choose the greatest, 60. By first taking the left child, we restrict ourselves to the subsequence to the left of this selected element, 90. All integers in this subsequence are less than 90. Then, as often as possible, we must go to the right-hand child to find the greatest element of that left subsequence. As a result, we arrive at the desired node with integer 60.

When dealing with node deletion, we must be very careful with the argument of function **delnode**. It is not sufficient for this argument to be (the address of) *any* pointer to the node we want to delete, but it must be the address of the pointer through which we normally gain access to that node. If the node to be deleted is the root node, this pointer is the root of the tree; otherwise it is a pointer stored in the parent of the node in question. Function **delnode** can be found in program PTREE.C, which is intended to be used as a demonstration program.

We borrow the function **printtree** from program PERFBAL.C in Section 5.2. Recall that the tree appears in the output with its root on the left instead of at the top. For each node we print its right subtree before its left one, to obtain the usual tree representations by rotating the printed one clockwise through 90°.

Program PTREE.C shows how pointers to pointer members are used for deleting either an entire subtree or just a node. The program reads a sequence of integers from

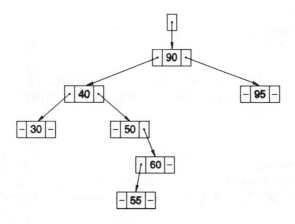

Fig. 5.7. Tree with 60 as the greatest of all keys less than 90

a file to build a binary tree, and then asks the user whether a subtree or a node is to
be deleted and to type in the integer that indicates which subtree or node is meant. It
is also possible to insert new nodes after some nodes or subtrees have been deleted.

```c
/* PTREE.C: Demonstration program for tree deletion,
            using pointers to pointers
*/
#include <stdio.h>
#include <stdlib.h>
#include <ctype.h>

typedef
struct Node {int num; struct Node *left, *right;} node;
typedef node *nodeptr;

void delnode(nodeptr *pp)
{   nodeptr p, q, *qq;
    if (*pp != NULL)
    {   p = *pp;
        if (p->right == NULL) {*pp = p->left; free(p);} else
        if (p->left == NULL) {*pp = p->right; free(p);} else
        {   qq = & p->left;
            while ((*qq)->right != NULL) qq = & (*qq)->right;
            q = *qq;
            *qq = q->left;
            p->num = q->num;
            free(q);
        }
    }
}

nodeptr *search(nodeptr *pp, int x)
{   nodeptr *qq;
    qq = pp;
    while (*qq != NULL  &&  x != (*qq)->num)
        qq = (x < (*qq)->num ? &(*qq)->left : &(*qq)->right);
    return qq;
}

void *getmemory(int n)
{   void *p=malloc(n);
    if (p == NULL) puts("Not enough memory\n"), exit(1);
    return p;
}
```

```
void insert(nodeptr *pp, int x)
{  nodeptr *qq;
   qq = search(pp, x);
   if (*qq == NULL)
   {  *qq = (node *)getmemory(sizeof(node));
      (*qq)->num = x;
      (*qq)->left = (*qq)->right = NULL;
   }
}

void printtree(node *p, int position)
{  if (p != NULL)
   {  printtree(p->right, position+6);
      printf("%*d\n", position, p->num);
      printtree(p->left, position+6);
   }
}

void deltree(nodeptr *pp)
{  if (*pp != NULL)
   {  deltree(&(*pp)->left); deltree(&(*pp)->right);
      free(*pp); *pp = NULL;
   }
}

main()
{  nodeptr root=NULL;
   char ch;
   int x, busy=1;
   puts("Enter a sequence of integers to build a");
   puts("binary search tree, followed by any");
   puts("nonnumeric character:");
   while (scanf("%d", &x) == 1) insert(&root, x);
   getchar();
   puts("Tree with root on the left:\n");
   printtree(root, 6); puts("");
   while (busy)
   {  printf(
      "Enter D (Deletion of node), S (Subtree deletion),\n"
      "I (Insertion), or Q (Quit): ");
      do
      {  ch = getchar(); ch = toupper(ch);
      }  while (ch != 'D' && ch != 'S' &&
                ch != 'I' && ch != 'Q');
```

```
        switch (ch)
        {  case 'D':
               printf("Integer in node to be deleted: ");
               scanf("%d", &x); delnode(search(&root, x));
               break;
           case 'S':
               printf("Integer in root node of subtree: ");
               scanf("%d", &x); deltree(search(&root, x));
               break;
           case 'I':
               printf("Integer for node to be inserted: ");
               scanf("%d", &x); insert(&root, x);
               break;
           case 'Q':
               busy = 0;
        }
        if (busy) {puts(""); printtree(root, 6); puts("");}
     }
     return 0;
}
```

Here is a demonstration of this program. The sets of indented numbers below are
printed by **printtree**. They represent three binary search trees, which should be turned
through 90° clockwise to obtain the usual orientation. The first two of these trees
correspond to our above discussion, illustrated by Fig. 5.7. The third is the result of
deleting a subtree.

```
Enter a sequence of integers to build a
binary search tree, followed by any
nonnumeric character:
90  95  40  30  50  60  55/
Tree with root on the left:

            95
   90
                     60
                        55
                50
           40
              30


Enter D (Deletion of node), S (Subtree deletion),
I (Insertion), or Q (Quit): d
Integer in node to be deleted: 90
```

```
              95
        60
                          55
                  50
              40
                  30
```

```
Enter D (Deletion of node), S (Subtree deletion),
I (Insertion), or Q (Quit): s
Integer in root node of subtree: 40


              95
        60


Enter D (Deletion of node), S (Subtree deletion),
I (Insertion), or Q (Quit): q
```

5.4 AVL Trees

As mentioned in Section 5.2, AVL trees are height-balanced trees. For each node of these trees, the heights of its left and right subtrees differ by at most one. We will now see how we can insert nodes in such a tree while preserving the AVL characteristic. In order to do this efficiently, we will store a *balance factor*, named **bal** and of type **int**, in each node. It will be equal to the height of the right subtree minus that of the left subtree. For the node pointed to by **p**, we can express this as follows:

$$\textbf{p->bal} = height(\textbf{p->right}) - height(\textbf{p->left})$$

Since these two heights differ by at most 1, the value of **p->bal** should be -1, 0, or $+1$. However, during the insertion process, we will temporarily allow the values -2 and $+2$ as well. When this occurs, the tree is no longer balanced, and one or two *rotations* are required to make it balanced again. We distinguish between left and right rotations. Figure 5.8 shows a left rotation, which we will now discuss in detail.

We will write $h(T)$, $h(U)$ and $h(V)$ for the heights of the subtrees T, U and V, respectively (see Fig. 5.8). Also, let us simply write *pbal* and *rbal* instead of **p->bal** and **r->bal**, respectively. The numbers 40 and 50 are examples of keys, and **p** and **r** are auxiliary pointers, which we will also use in our program. Since the given tree is a binary search tree, we have:

- every key in subtree T is less than 40
- every key in subtree U lies between 40 and 50
- every key in subtree V is greater than 50

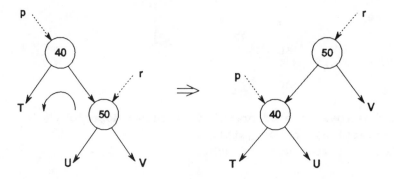

Fig. 5.8. Left rotation

Note that the rotated tree, shown in Fig. 5.8 on the right, is also a binary search tree. Without updating the balance factors, a rotation would be a very simple operation, as the following program fragment shows:

```
typedef
struct Node{int num, bal; struct Node *left, *right;} node;
typedef node *ptr;

void leftrotate(ptr *pp) /* Incomplete version */
{   ptr p=*pp, r;
    *pp = r = p->right;
    p->right = r->left;
    r->left = p;
}
```

For a left rotation of the (sub)tree with a given **root** (of type **ptr**), we write

```
leftrotate(&root);
```

However, we also have to update the balance factors **p->bal** and **r->bal** (which we prefer to write as *pbal* and *rbal*). Both their old and their new values are completely determined by the heights $h(T)$, $h(U)$, and $h(V)$. Unfortunately, these heights are not given. We can only make use of the balance factors, so we have to compute the new balance factors $pbal_{new}$ and $rbal_{new}$ from the old ones $pbal_{old}$ and $rbal_{old}$. Depending on the value of

$$rbal_{old} = h(V) - h(U)$$

(see Fig. 5.8), there are two cases to consider:

If $rbal_{old} \leq 0$, that is, if $h(U) \geq h(V)$ (see Fig. 5.8), we have

$$pbal_{old} = \{h(U) + 1\} - h(T)$$
$$pbal_{new} = h(U) - h(T) = pbal_{old} - 1$$

If $rbal_{old} > 0$, that is, if $h(V) > h(U)$, then

$$pbal_{old} = \{h(V) + 1\} - h(T)$$
$$pbal_{new} = h(U) - h(T) = pbal_{old} - rbal_{old} - 1$$

So much for updating **p–>bal**. We can now immediately use the new value of this balance factor to update **r–>bal**. As illustrated by the new situation (on the right) in Fig. 5.8, the new value of **p–>bal** is computed as follows:

If $pbal_{new} \geq 0$, that is, if $h(U) \geq h(T)$, then

$$rbal_{new} = h(V) - \{h(U) + 1\} = rbal_{old} - 1$$

If $pbal_{new} < 0$, that is, if $h(T) > h(U)$, then

$$rbal_{new} = h(V) - \{h(T) + 1\} = rbal_{old} + pbal_{new} - 1$$

Although these update operations for balance factors may seem rather complicated, their implementation in function **leftrotate** is very simple:

```
void leftrotate(ptr *pp)   /* Final version */
{  ptr p=*pp, r;
   *pp = r = p->right;
   p->right = r->left;
   r->left = p;
   p->bal--;
   if (r->bal > 0) p->bal -= r->bal;
   r->bal--;
   if (p->bal < 0) r->bal += p->bal;
}
```

Figure 5.9 shows a right rotation, with auxiliary pointers **p** and **l**. Writing $lbal$ instead of **l–>bal**, we use

$$lbal_{old} = h(U) - h(T)$$

to find how **p–>bal** is to be updated. This derivation for a right rotation is analogous to the above one for a left rotation:

If $lbal_{old} \geq 0$, we have

$$pbal_{old} = h(V) - \{h(U) + 1\}$$
$$pbal_{new} = h(V) - h(U) = pbal_{old} + 1$$

If $lbal_{old} < 0$, then

$$pbal_{old} = h(V) - \{h(T) + 1\}$$
$$pbal_{new} = h(V) - h(U) = pbal_{old} - lbal_{old} + 1$$

We use this new value of **p->bal** to update **l->bal**:

If $pbal_{new} \leq 0$, then

$$lbal_{new} = \{h(U) + 1\} - h(U) = lbal_{old} + 1$$

If $pbal_{new} > 0$, then

$$lbal_{new} = \{h(V) + 1\} - h(T) = lbal_{old} + pbal_{new} + 1$$

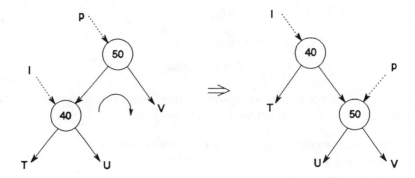

Fig. 5.9. Right rotation

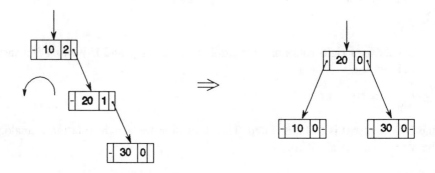

Fig. 5.10. Left rotation required

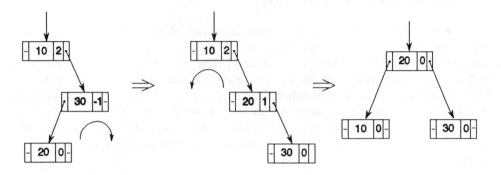

Fig. 5.11. Right rotation followed by left rotation

So much for updating balance factors in rotations. We now have to see in more detail in which situations these rotations are required. If we insert nodes with keys in ascending order, we frequently need a left notation, as Fig. 5.10 shows. Immediately after inserting 30, the tree is out of balance, as the balance factor 2 in the root node shows. A left rotation will then rebalance the tree.

Note that in Fig. 5.10 the balance factor (2) in the root node has the same sign as the balance factor (1) in its right child. If they are -2 and -1 instead of 2 and 1, the situation is analogous but we need a right rotation.

The situation is essentially different in Fig. 5.11. Here the root node has 2 and its right child -1 as balance factors. In this case we need two rotations. We first apply a right rotation to the right subtree (with keys 30 and 20). Then we have the well-known situation with two positive balance factors, so we can subsequently apply a left rotation to the tree itself (with 10 as its root node).

AVL trees and node deletion

So far, we have paid some attention to node insertion. Actually, our demonstration program can also *delete* nodes from an AVL tree in such a way that the tree remains an AVL tree. Node deletion is slightly more complicated than node insertion, so if you want to see how this program works, it is wise to begin with insertion. For deletion we need not only rebalance the tree after each tree update but we may also have to select a leaf and to move its contents, as discussed in Section 5.3 and demonstrated by program PTREE.C. Recall that in that program we followed a certain path in the tree if the node to be deleted had two children. Here we use the same method as in that case, but we now exchange the data stored in two nodes. In a recursive call, we can then delete a node that has no right child.

A demonstration program for AVL trees

Program AVL.C shows how AVL trees grow and shrink. Repeatedly, the user can enter
an integer, either to insert a new node with that integer in it or to delete a node
containing that integer (if there is such a node). The integer is to followed by **I** (or **i**)
in case of insertion and by **D** (or **d**) in case of deletion. Duplicate input values for
insertion are ignored, so the tree actually represents a set. After each of these insertion
or deletion commands, the updated AVL tree is displayed. This is done with the root
on the left: the usual representation is obtained by rotating the displayed tree 90°
clockwise. The letter **Q** (or any other nonnumeric character) can be entered to quit the
program.

```c
/* AVL.C: Demonstration program for AVL trees;
          insertion and deletion of nodes
*/
#include <stdio.h>
#include <stdlib.h>
#include <ctype.h>

typedef
struct Node{int num, bal; struct Node *left, *right;} node;
typedef node *ptr;

void leftrotate(ptr *pp)
{   ptr p=*pp, r;
    *pp = r = p->right;
    p->right = r->left;
    r->left = p;
    p->bal--;
    if (r->bal > 0) p->bal -= r->bal;
    r->bal--;
    if (p->bal < 0) r->bal += p->bal;
}

void rightrotate(ptr *pp)
{   ptr p=*pp, l;
    *pp = l = p->left;
    p->left = l->right;
    l->right = p;
    p->bal++;
    if (l->bal < 0) p->bal -= l->bal;
    l->bal++;
    if (p->bal > 0) l->bal += p->bal;
}
```

```
int insert(ptr *pp, int x)
{  /* Return value: increase in height (0 or 1) after
      inserting x in the (sub)tree with root *pp
   */
   int deltaH=0;
   ptr p=*pp;
   if (p == NULL)
   {  *pp = p = (ptr)malloc(sizeof(node));
      if (p == NULL) puts("Not enough memory"), exit(1);
      p->num = x; p->bal = 0;
      p->left = p->right = NULL;
      deltaH = 1; /* Tree height increased by 1 */
   } else
   if (x > p->num)
   {  if (insert(&p->right, x))
      {  p->bal++; /* Height of right subtree increased */
         if (p->bal == 1) deltaH = 1; else
         if (p->bal == 2)
         {  if (p->right->bal == -1) rightrotate(&p->right);
            leftrotate(pp);
         }
      }
   } else
   if (x < p->num)
   {  if (insert(&p->left, x))
      {  p->bal--; /* Height of left subtree increased */
         if (p->bal == -1) deltaH = 1; else
         if (p->bal == -2)
         {  if (p->left->bal == 1) leftrotate(&p->left);
            rightrotate(pp);
         }
      }
   }
   return deltaH;
}


int delnode(ptr *pp, int x)
/* Return value: decrease in height (0 or -1) of subtree
   with root *pp, after deleting the node with key x.
   (If there is no such node, 0 will be returned.)
*/
{  ptr p=*pp, *qq;
   int deltaH=0;
   if (p == NULL) return 0;
```

```
    if (x < p->num)
    { if (delnode(&p->left, x))
      { p->bal++; /* Height left subtree decreased */
        if (p->bal == 0) deltaH = 1; else
        if (p->bal == 2)
        { if (p->right->bal == -1) rightrotate(&p->right);
          leftrotate(pp);
          if (p->bal == 0) deltaH = 1;
        }
      }
    } else
    if (x > p->num)
    { if (delnode(&p->right, x))
      { p->bal--; /* Height right subtree decreased */
        if (p->bal == 0) deltaH = 1; else
        if (p->bal == -2)
        { if (p->left->bal == 1) leftrotate(&p->left);
          rightrotate(pp);
          if (p->bal == 0) deltaH = 1;
        }
      }
    } else  /* x == p->num */
    { if (p->right == NULL)
      { *pp = p->left; free(p); return 1;
      } else
      if (p->left == NULL)
      { *pp = p->right; free(p); return 1;
      } else
      { qq = & p->left;
        while ((*qq)->right != NULL) qq = & (*qq)->right;
        p->num = (*qq)->num;
        (*qq)->num = x;
        if (delnode(&p->left, x))
        { p->bal++; /* Height left subtree decreased */
          if (p->bal == 0) deltaH = 1; else
          if (p->bal == 2)
          { if (p->right->bal == -1) rightrotate(&p->right);
            leftrotate(pp); deltaH = 1;
          }
        }
      }
    }
    return deltaH;
}
```

```
void printtree(node *p, int position)
{  if (p != NULL)
   {  printtree(p->right, position+6);
      printf("%*d %d\n", position, p->num, p->bal);
      printtree(p->left, position+6);
   }
}

main()
{  int x;
   char ch;
   node *root=NULL;
   puts(
   "\nEach AVL tree displayed by this program has\n"
   "its root on the left. Turn it 90 degrees\n"
   "clockwise to obtain its usual representation.\n");
   for ( ; ; )
   {  printf(
      "Enter an integer, followed by I for insertion\n"
      "or by D for deletion, or enter Q to quit: ");
      if (scanf("%d %c", &x, &ch) != 2) break;
      ch = toupper(ch);
      if (ch == 'I') insert(&root, x); else
      if (ch == 'D') delnode(&root, x);
      printtree(root, 6);
   }
   return 0;
}
```

Here is a demonstration of this program. As you can see, the integers 4, 5, 7, 2, 1, 3, 6, in that order, are inserted, after which the node containing the integer 4 is deleted. Not only these integers but also the balance factors -1, 0, and 1 are printed. Note that in most cases they are zero. Remember, the roots of these trees are on the left, so you must imagine these trees to be turned 90° clockwise to obtain their usual form:

```
Each AVL tree displayed by this program has
its root on the left. Turn it 90 degrees
clockwise to obtain its usual representation.

Enter an integer, followed by I for insertion
or by D for deletion, or enter Q to quit: 4 I
      4 0
```

```
Enter an integer, followed by I for insertion
or by D for deletion, or enter Q to quit: 5 I
            5 0
      4 1

Enter an integer, followed by I for insertion
or by D for deletion, or enter Q to quit: 7 I
            7 0
      5 0
            4 0

Enter an integer, followed by I for insertion
or by D for deletion, or enter Q to quit: 2 I
            7 0
      5 -1
            4 -1
                  2 0

Enter an integer, followed by I for insertion
or by D for deletion, or enter Q to quit: 1 I
            7 0
      5 -1
                  4 0
            2 0
                  1 0

Enter an integer, followed by I for insertion
or by D for deletion, or enter Q to quit: 3 I
                  7 0
            5 1
      4 0
                  3 0
            2 0
                  1 0

Enter an integer, followed by I for insertion
or by D for deletion, or enter Q to quit: 6 I
                  7 0
            6 0
                  5 0
      4 0
                  3 0
            2 0
                  1 0
```

```
Enter an integer, followed by I for insertion
or by D for deletion, or enter Q to quit: 4 D
                    7 0
            6 0
                5 0
       3 0
            2 -1
                1 0
Enter an integer, followed by I for insertion
or by D for deletion, or enter Q to quit: Q
```

Exercises

All functions to be developed in the following exercises are to be complemented by program fragments to demonstrate them. In most cases, program text listed in this chapter can be used for this purpose.

5.1 Write a function which deletes a binary tree and builds a similar one. In the given tree, the information member of each node consists of a pointer to a block of memory, which has been allocated by the standard function **malloc** and contains a (null-terminated) character string. The tree to be built should have the same structure as the original one, but now each node is to contain only an integer as its information member, which denotes the length of the string pointed to in the corresponding node of the original tree. As for the original tree, the memory space used by the tree nodes and that for the character strings should be released by means of the standard function **free**.

In the following exercises, each node in the binary tree in question has an information member which contains only an integer.

5.2 Write a function to transform a given binary search tree into one that is perfectly balanced. The demonstration program should (also) print the heights of the old and the new trees.
    Hint: You can do this in two steps. First, transform the given binary tree into a linked list in which the keys are in ascending order. To do this you can use a recursive function similar to our function **printtree**. Each time, instead of using **free** to delete a node in the tree and **malloc** to create a node in the list, you can change the pointers (using only one of the two pointer members) and leave the data in the node. While building this linked list, you can count how many keys there are. Then, in the second step, you can use a recursive function similar to **pbtree** to build a perfectly balanced binary search tree. Again, you can leave the data in the nodes and change only the pointer members.

5.3 Write a function to determine whether or not a given binary tree is perfectly balanced.

5.4 Write a function to determine the height of a binary tree, see Section 5.1.

5.5 Write a function to determine whether or not a given binary tree is height-balanced.

5.6 Write a function to determine whether or not a given binary tree is a binary search tree.

5.7 Write a function to print all integers stored in a binary tree, along with the levels of all nodes.

5.8 Write a function to print all integers stored in the *leaves* of a given binary tree (ignoring the integers stored in all other nodes).

5.9 Write a function which, for a given binary search tree, swaps the left and right children of every node, and simultaneously replaces each integer i in the tree with $-i$. (The resulting tree is also a binary search tree.)

5.10 Write a function to check whether or not binary trees with balance factors (as discussed in Section 5.4) are AVL trees; in other words, to check the correctness of the balance factors.

6

B-trees

6.1 Building and Searching a B-tree

So far, we have been using only binary trees that existed in main memory. We also want to store trees in *secondary storage*, that is, on disk, and load data from them into main memory only when we need it. There are two reasons for this. First, data in main memory exists only temporarily, whereas on disk it is permanent, and, second, the amount of available main memory will probably be less than the amount of secondary storage. However, disk access is slower than memory access. In order to reduce the number of I/O operations, we will no longer use binary trees, which, as we know, have as many nodes as there are keys. Instead, we want to use larger blocks of data, grouping together several items, each including a key, into one node. We will therefore use multiway trees of a certain type, called *B-trees*. For some fixed number M, each node of a B-tree contains at most $2M$ and at least M items. The latter condition has one exception: the minimum number of items in the root node is 1 instead of M. The constant M is called the *order* of the B-tree.

We will avoid dealing with two new subjects, B-trees and secondary storage, at the same time, so our first B-tree will still be in main memory. Let us, for example, use the following definitions:

```
#define M 2
#define MM 4

typedef
struct Node {int cnt, key[MM]; struct Node *ptr[MM+1];} node;
```

In real applications, we replace M and MM ($= 2M$) with larger values, such as 100 and 200. We always use unique keys, that is, no two items will have the same key. In our example every item will contain no other data than its key, so we will use the terms *item* and *key* interchangeably. In practical applications we usually have more complex items containing other relevant data besides the keys. As with binary search trees, we use the keys to search the tree in an efficient way. In the above declaration of type **node**, each array element **key[i]** can contain a key (or, in the general case, an item that includes a key). The **cnt** member is a counter, which, in contrast to binary trees, is essential in B-trees. For each node, it says how many of the $2M$ data members are actually in use. In our discussion, we will use the simple notations n, k_i and p_i instead of **t->cnt**, **t->key[i]** and **t->ptr[i]**, respectively, where **t** is a pointer to the node under consideration. Thus we have

$$1 \leq n \leq 2M \qquad \text{for the root node}$$
$$M \leq n \leq 2M \qquad \text{for all other nodes}$$

Each node has at most $2M + 1$ children, so there are $2M + 1$ pointer members in each node. However, exactly $n + 1$ of these are actually in use. In other words, a node in which n data items have been stored has precisely $n + 1$ children. Figure 6.1 shows an example of a B-tree. Notice the position of the pointers emanating from each node. For example, the pointer from node [12, 18] to node [14, 15, 16, 17] leaves the former node between 12 and 18, which corresponds to the fact that the numbers 14, 15, 16, 17 in the latter node lie between these two values. Logically, we consider the pointers p_i and the keys k_i in each node to be arranged as follows:

$$p_0, k_0, p_1, k_1, ..., p_{n-1}, k_{n-1}, p_n$$

where

$$k_0 < k_1 < ... < k_{n-1}$$

The values n, though stored in the nodes, are not shown in Fig. 6.1, but for each node, n is equal to the number of integers listed, that is, 1 for the root node and 2, 3, or 4 for the other nodes. The pointer values p_i ($i = 0, 1, ..., n$) stored in a node depend on whether or not that node is a leaf:

-   If the node is a leaf, the value of each pointer p_i in the node is **NULL**.
-   If the node is not a leaf, each pointer p_i points to a child node. For $i = 1, ..., n$, all keys in the child pointed to by p_i are greater than k_{i-1}. Analogously, for $i = 0, ..., n - 1$, all keys in the child pointed to by p_i are less than k_i.

The B-tree of Fig. 6.1 is well-balanced, which is characteristic for B-trees:

All leaves of a B-tree are on the same level.

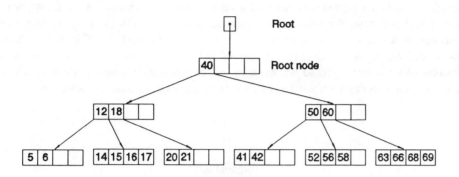

Fig. 6.1. A B-tree of order 2

(As defined in Section 5.1 for binary trees, the level of a node is the length of the path from the root to that node.) Recall that this characteristic did not apply to perfectly balanced binary trees, so B-trees seem to be 'better than perfect'. However, in binary trees we have exactly one data item in each node, which in general makes it impossible to meet a similar requirement about equal path lengths. The nice shape of B-trees is not without its price, since memory space is also allocated for unused data and pointer members. Yet B-trees are elegant and efficient in many applications, especially since there are good algorithms available to manipulate them. Not all of these are particularly simple, however. We will first discuss the insertion of new items.

Let us begin with an empty B-tree, in which we insert four numbers, say, 60, 20, 80, 10. This gives the tree shown in Fig. 6.2(a). There is now only a root node, which contains the following data:

$$n = 4$$
$$p_0 = p_1 = p_2 = p_3 = p_4 = \textbf{NULL}$$
$$k_0 = 10$$
$$k_1 = 20$$
$$k_2 = 60$$
$$k_3 = 80$$

Since n is now equal to MM, there is no room for the next number to be inserted, say 15. Ignoring the limitation to four items for one moment, we write down the augmented sequence

10, 15, 20, 60, 80

(which would appear if there were enough room), to select the item in the middle, 20. We then remove this item, to store it in another node later, and we move the sub-sequence [60, 80] on the right of it to a newly created node. If the node under consideration had a parent which could accommodate the removed item 20, we would store it in that parent. We will consider that situation shortly. In the present case, there is no parent at all, so we have to create another node to store 20. This will be a new root node, which means that the height of the tree increases. This new root node contains one number (20), so we have to use two pointer members. Fortunately, we have two other nodes to point to, namely both the original one, in which we set the

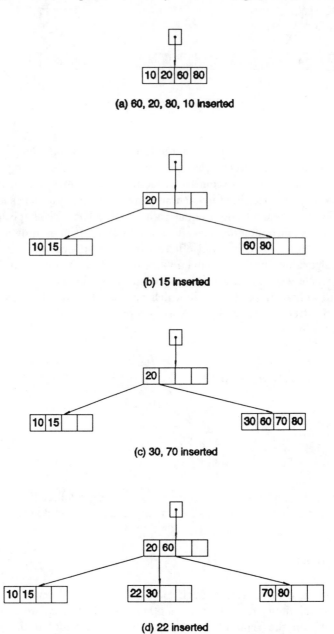

(a) 60, 20, 80, 10 inserted

(b) 15 inserted

(c) 30, 70 inserted

(d) 22 inserted

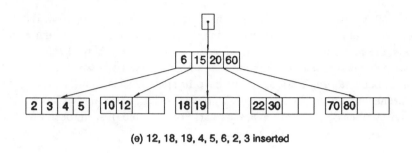

(e) 12, 18, 19, 4, 5, 6, 2, 3 inserted

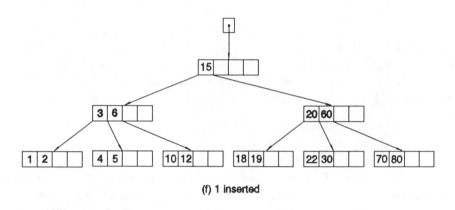

(f) 1 inserted

Fig. 6.2. Growth of a B-tree

count member to 2, and the one created to store 60 and 80. This leads to Fig. 6.2(b). If we now have to insert a new number, say, 30, it might be tempting to store it in the root node, since this node has plenty of room. However, this would not be correct because then the root node would have as many data items as it has children. The general rule is that we always try to insert a new item in a leaf node. So 30 is placed in the right child, which makes it necessary to shift 60 and 80 one position to the right. Let us add another item, say, 70, which will be placed in the same node because it is also greater than 20. This gives the result shown in Fig. 6.2(c). We have now reached the maximum number of data items for that node, so adding another item, say, 22, will cause some item to move upward. To find out which, we again forget about the limitation for one moment, and write down the augmented sequence

22, 30, 60, 70, 80

As we did for the root node, we choose the item (60) in the middle, and split the remaining sequence into

22, 30   and   70, 80

The node 60 is now inserted in the parent node, if possible. In our case, this is indeed possible, so we obtain the tree shown in Fig. 6.2(d). As a result of splitting a leaf node, there is some new room in the leaves for subsequent items. If we keep inserting new items, we will again reach the situation that a leaf is selected in which already $2M$ ($=4$) items have been stored. Then again we have to split that leaf and to move some item to its parent, and so on. In this way, we sooner or later have five leaves, which is the maximum number of children for any parent. For example, if we proceed with the tree of Fig. 6.2(d), and we insert the numbers

   12, 18, 19, 4, 5, 6, 2, 3

in that order, we obtain the tree shown in Fig. 6.2(e). Let us now insert the number 1 in the latter tree. Since 3 is the item in the middle of the sequence 1, 2, 3, 4, 5, obtained by augmenting the bottom-left node, this item 3 is to move upward. We use the remaining items to form the subsequences [1, 2] and [4, 5]. However, the parent node is already full, so this node, too, is to be split. We first write the sequence of five items

   3, 6, 15, 20, 60

and select the element 15, in the middle. Since the parent node in question happens to be the root node, we have to create a new root node to store 15, and at this moment the height of the tree increases again. Figure 6.2(f) shows the resulting tree.

Now that we understand how B-trees grow, we want a program to demonstrate this growth. It will be clear from the above discussion that a function to insert an item in a B-tree will be rather complex. We will actually use two functions. At the higher level, in our **main** function, we write

```
root = insert(x, root);
```

where **x** is the item to be inserted. In this function **insert**, we call the lower-level function **ins** as follows:

```
code = ins(x, t, &xnew, &tnew);
```

To understand how **ins** works, we should remember how we inserted new items ourselves in our above discussion. Recall that we first tried to use a leaf for this purpose. In our program, we arrive at a leaf by means of several recursive calls to **ins**. This explains the second argument, **t**, which is the root of the subtree in which **x** is to be inserted (so **t** is equal to **root** in the above call). We will deal with the third and fourth arguments shortly.

   A recursive call to **ins** may or may not be successful. Function **ins** therefore returns a *status code*, for which we use the following symbolic constants:

SUCCESS:	Insertion successfully completed.
DUPLICATEKEY:	The value **x** has been inserted previously, so the insert request can be ignored.
INSERTNOTCOMPLETE:	See the discussion below.

This last status code occurs when, at the lower level, the insertion has not been a complete success, so that some additional action is required at the current level. The third and fourth arguments then provide us with information about what to do next. There are two possibilities:

(1) The given subtree is empty, that is, **t** = **NULL**. In this case, **x** is assigned to **xnew**, and **NULL** is assigned **tnew**.
(2) The subtree with root **t** could not accomodate **x**. In this case, the node ***t** has been split. A new node has been created and its address has been placed in **tnew**. Recall that if a node was full in our examples, we wrote down an increasing sequence of five integers and selected the one in the middle, which was then placed in the parent node. Here, for the time being, that selected integer is placed in **xnew**.

In both cases (1) and (2), the integer in **xnew** is still to be stored in the tree. If **tnew** is **NULL**, the current node is a leaf, so if there is still room left we are free to place the value of **xnew** in the current node without bothering about pointer members in that node. If a real address of a new node has been placed in **tnew**, the values of both **xnew** and **tnew** are to be stored in the current node, if possible. Note that this is in accordance with the rules for B-trees: in a node that is not a leaf, a new data item can only be inserted if we also insert a new pointer in it. After all, the number of data items must always be exactly one less than the number of pointers to subtrees.

The method we are discussing is similar to an employer who has some work to do and begins by asking his senior employee to do it for him. This employee may have a junior employee working for him. If he has, he in turn delegates the task to this junior employee. In either case, he fulfils his task either completely or incompletely. If necessary, he informs his employer about what still has to be done.

We started the above discussion with the higher-level function **insert**, which is called only in the **main** function, with the root of the entire B-tree as an argument. This means that this function is related to the root node. It is wise to study this function first, because it is simpler than the lower-level function **ins**. Function **insert** calls **ins** as a request to insert the given integer **x** in the root node itself. If this call to **ins** returns **INSERTNOTCOMPLETE**, we create a new root node in **insert**, either because this has not yet been done because we are just starting or because the old root node was full. This means that the height of the B-tree increases by 1.

Let us now turn to the function **ins**, viewed from the inside. Its first line is

```
int ins(int x, node *t, int *y, node **u)
```

As mentioned above, the task of this function is very simple if **t** is equal to **NULL**. Let us now assume that **t** is the address of a node. We then locate the position where the integer x belongs by comparing x with the integers stored in the node. In this way, we find the pointer p_i, indicating the subtree in which we now try to insert x by means of a recursive call to **ins**. If this call is not completely successful, we split the node in the way we did in our examples, using an increasing sequence of $2M + 1$ integers and selecting the one in the middle. We place this selected integer in ***y**. The integers to the right of the selected one are placed in a newly created node, and the address of this new node is placed in ***u**. We now return the value **INSERTNOTCOMPLETE** as a status code.

Program BTREE.C shows further details of B-tree insertion. The program first inserts a given sequence of integers in a B-tree, which initially is empty. In its present form, the program builds a B-tree of order 2, but if a higher order is desired, we have only to alter **M** and **MM** in two **#define**-lines. Once the B-tree has been built, we can enter another integer to search the tree for it. The program prints the complete search path, starting at the root and ending in the node where the integer is stored, or, if we are searching in vain, ending in the leaf where it would have been stored if it had been included in the given input data. This search process is performed in the function **search**. We use binary search, as discussed in Section 2.5, which will increase speed if we choose large values for **M** and **MM**. This program also contains some functions (**delnode** and **del**) for node deletion. This is a new subject, to be discussed in the next section. Facilities for node deletion have already been included in this program to avoid duplication of program text or a too fragmentary presentation.

```
/* BTREE.C: Demonstration program for a B-tree.
            After building the B-tree by entering integers
            on the keyboard, we can update it interactively
            by entering (or deleting) individual integers.
            Instead, we can search the B-tree for a given
            integer. Each time, the tree or a search path is
            displayed.
*/
#include <stdio.h>
#include <stdlib.h>
#include <ctype.h>

#define M 2
#define MM 4

typedef enum {INSERTNOTCOMPLETE, SUCCESS,
    DUPLICATEKEY, UNDERFLOW, NOTFOUND} status;
typedef
struct Node {int cnt, key[MM]; struct Node *ptr[MM+1];} node;

node *root;
```

```
int binsearch(int x, int *a, int n)
/* Search array a[0], a[1], ..., a[n-1] for x.
   Returned value:  0 if x <= a[0],  n if x > a[n-1],
                     or r, where  a[r-1] < x <= a[r]
*/
{  int i, left, right;
   if (x <= a[0]) return 0;
   if (x > a[n-1]) return n;
   left = 0; right = n-1;
   while (right - left > 1)
   {  i = (right + left)/2;
      if (x <= a[i]) right = i; else left = i;
   }
   return right;
}


void found(node *t, int i)
{  printf("Found in position %d of node with contents: ", i);
   for (i=0; i < t->cnt; i++) printf(" %d", t->key[i]);
   puts("");
}


void notfound(int x)
{  printf("Item %d not found\n", x);
}


node *getnode(void)
{  node *p;
   p = (node *)malloc(sizeof(node));
   if (p == NULL) puts("Not enough memory\n"), exit(1);
   return p;
}


status ins(int x, node *t, int *y, node **u)
/*  Insert x in B-tree with root t. If not completely
    successful, the integer *y and the pointer *u
    remain to be inserted.
    Return value:
        SUCCESS, DUPLICATEKEY, or INSERTNOTCOMPLETE
*/
{  node *tnew, *p_final, **p = t->ptr;
   int i, j, xnew, k_final, *n=&(t->cnt), *k = t->key;
   status code;
```

```
/*   Examine whether t is a pointer member in a leaf:
*/
if (t == NULL)
{ *u = NULL; *y = x; return INSERTNOTCOMPLETE;
}


/*   Select pointer p[i] and try to insert x in
     the subtree of which p[i] is the root:
*/
i = binsearch(x, k, *n);
if (i < *n && x == k[i]) return DUPLICATEKEY;
code = ins(x, p[i], &xnew, &tnew);
if (code != INSERTNOTCOMPLETE) return code;

/*   Insertion in subtree did not completely succeed;
     try to insert xnew and tnew in the current node:
*/
if (*n < MM)
{   i = binsearch(xnew, k, *n);
    for (j= *n; j>i; j--)
    {   k[j] = k[j-1]; p[j+1] = p[j];
    }
    k[i] = xnew; p[i+1] = tnew; ++*n; return SUCCESS;
}
/* The current node was already full, so split it. Pass
    item k[M], in the middle of the augmented sequence,
    back through parameter y, so that it can move
    upward in the tree. Also, pass a pointer to the newly
    created node back through u. Return the status code
    INSERTNOTCOMPLETE.
*/
if (i == MM) {k_final = xnew; p_final = tnew;} else
{   k_final = k[MM-1]; p_final = p[MM];
    for (j=MM-1; j>i; j--)
    {   k[j] = k[j-1]; p[j+1] = p[j];
    }
    k[i] = xnew; p[i+1] = tnew;
}
*y = k[M]; *n = M;
*u = getnode(); (*u)->cnt = M;
for (j=0; j < M-1; j++)
{   (*u)->key[j] = k[j+M+1];
    (*u)->ptr[j] = p[j+M+1];
}
```

```
      (*u)->ptr[M-1] = p[MM];
      (*u)->key[M-1] = k_final;
      (*u)->ptr[M] = p_final;
      return INSERTNOTCOMPLETE;
   }

node *insert(int x, node *t)
/*  Driver function for node insertion, called only in the
    main function. Most of the work is delegated to 'ins'.
*/
{  node *tnew, *u;
   int xnew;
   status code;
   code = ins(x, t, &xnew, &tnew);
   if (code == DUPLICATEKEY)
      printf("Duplicate key %d ignored\n", x);
   if (code != INSERTNOTCOMPLETE) return t;
   u = getnode();
   u->cnt = 1; u->key[0] = xnew;
   u->ptr[0] = t; u->ptr[1] = tnew;
   return u;
}

void search(int x, node *t)
{  int i, j, *k, n;
   puts("Search path:");
   while (t != NULL)
   {  k = t->key; n = t->cnt;
      for (j=0; j < n; j++) printf(" %d", k[j]);
      puts("");
      i = binsearch(x, k, n);
      if (i < n && x == k[i]) {found(t, i); return;}
      t = t->ptr[i];
   }
   notfound(x);
}

status del(int x, node *t)
/*  Delete item x in B-tree with root t.
    Return value:
    SUCCESS, NOTFOUND, or UNDERFLOW
*/
{  int i, j, *k, *n, *item,
       *nleft, *nright, *lkey, *rkey, borrowleft, nq, *addr;
```

```
status code;
node **p, *left, *right, **lptr, **rptr, *q, *ql;
if (t == NULL) return NOTFOUND;
n = & t->cnt; k = t->key; p=t->ptr;
i = binsearch(x, k, *n);
if (p[0] == NULL)    /*   *t is a leaf */
{  if (i == *n || x < k[i]) return NOTFOUND;
   /* x is now equal to k[i], located in a leaf: */
   for (j=i+1; j < *n; j++)
   { k[j-1] = k[j]; p[j] = p[j+1];
   }
   --*n;
   return *n >= (t==root ? 1 : M) ? SUCCESS : UNDERFLOW;
}
/*  *t is an interior node (not a leaf):  */
item = k+i; left = p[i]; nleft = & left->cnt;
if (i < *n && x == *item)
{  /*   x found in interior node.  Go to left child     */
   /*   *p[i] and then follow a path all the way to      */
   /*   a leaf, using rightmost branches:               */
   q = p[i]; nq = q->cnt;
   while ((ql = q->ptr[nq]) != NULL)
   { q = ql; nq = q->cnt;
   }
   /* Exchange k[i] with the rightmost item in leaf:    */
   addr = q->key + nq - 1;
   *item = *addr; *addr = x;
}
/* Delete x in subtree with root  p[i]:                 */
code = del(x, left);
if (code != UNDERFLOW) return code;
/* Underflow; borrow, and, if necessary, merge:         */
borrowleft =   i == *n ||
   i > 0 && p[i+1]->cnt == M && p[i-1]->cnt > M;
if (borrowleft)  /* p[i] is rightmost pointer in *p     */
{  item = k+i-1; left = p[i-1]; right = p[i];
   nleft = & left->cnt;
}  else right = p[i+1];
nright = & right->cnt;
lkey = left->key; rkey = right->key;
lptr = left->ptr; rptr = right->ptr;
if (borrowleft)  /* Borrow from left sibling */
{  rptr[*nright + 1] = rptr[*nright];
   for (j = *nright; j>0; j--)
```

```
            {   rkey[j] = rkey[j-1];
                rptr[j] = rptr[j-1];
            }
            ++*nright;
            rkey[0] = *item; rptr[0] = lptr[*nleft];
            *item = lkey[*nleft - 1];
            if (--*nleft >= M) return SUCCESS;
        } else
        if (*nright > M)          /* Borrow from right sibling: */
        {   lkey[M-1] = *item; lptr[M] = rptr[0]; *item = rkey[0];
            ++*nleft; --*nright;
            for (j=0; j < *nright; j++)
            {   rkey[j] = rkey[j+1];
                rptr[j] = rptr[j+1];
            }
            rptr[*nright] = rptr[*nright + 1];
            return SUCCESS;
        }
        /* Merge: */
        lkey[M-1] = *item; lptr[M] = rptr[0];
        for (j=0; j<M; j++)
        {   lkey[M+j] = rkey[j]; lptr[M+j+1] = rptr[j+1];
        }
        *nleft = MM;
        free(right);
        for (j=i+1; j < *n; j++)
        { k[j-1] = k[j]; p[j] = p[j+1];
        }
        return --*n >= (t==root ? 1 : M) ? SUCCESS : UNDERFLOW;
}


node *delnode(int x, node *t)
/* Driver function for node deletion, called only in the
    main function. Most of the work is delegated to 'del'.
*/
{   status code;
    node *newroot;
    code = del(x, t);
    if (code == NOTFOUND) printf("%d not found\n", x);
    if (code != UNDERFLOW) return t;
    /* If underflow, decrease the height of the tree:  */
    newroot = t->ptr[0]; free(t);
    return newroot;
}
```

```
      void printtree(node *p, int position)
      {  int i;
         if (p != NULL)
         {  printf("%*s", position, "");
            for (i=0; i<p->cnt; i++) printf(" %3d", p->key[i]);
            puts("");
            for (i=0; i<=p->cnt; i++)
            printtree(p->ptr[i], position+6);
         }
      }

      main()
      {  int x;
         char ch;
         root = NULL;
         puts(
         "\nB-tree structure will be represented by indentation.");
         puts("Enter some integers, followed by the character /");
         while (scanf("%d", &x) == 1) root = insert(x, root);
         getchar();
         puts(""); printtree(root, 6);
         for ( ; ; )
         {  printf(
            "Enter an integer, followed by I, D, or S (for Insert,\n"
            "Delete and Search), or enter Q to quit: ");
            if (scanf("%d %c", &x, &ch) != 2) break;
            ch = toupper(ch);
            if (ch == 'S') {search(x, root); continue;}
            if (ch == 'I') root = insert(x, root); else
            if (ch == 'D') root = delnode(x, root);
            printtree(root, 6);
         }
         return 0;
      }
```

We can use program BTREE.C to demonstrate how a B-tree is built. The demonstration below first builds the B-tree of Fig. 6.2(e). Then the key 1 is inserted, which results in the B-tree of Fig. 6.2(f). In the output, the structure of these B-trees is reflected by the way indentation is used. All keys stored in one node are printed on the same line. The children of each node follow that line and are shifted six positions to the right. To demonstrate our **search** function, the search path is displayed for each search command. This program can also *delete* items from B-trees, to be discussed in the next section. The following demonstration shows only tree *insertion* and tree *search*:

```
B-tree structure will be represented by indentation.
Enter some integers, followed by the character /
60 20 80 10 15 30 70 22
12 18 19 4 5 6 2 3 /

        6   15   20   60
                2    3    4    5
            10   12
            18   19
            22   30
            70   80
Enter an integer, followed by I, D, or S (for Insert,
Delete and Search), or enter Q to quit: 1 I
        15
                3    6
                        1    2
                        4    5
                    10   12
                20   60
                        18   19
                        22   30
                        70   80
Enter an integer, followed by I, D, or S (for Insert,
Delete and Search), or enter Q to quit: 22 S
Search path:
 15
 20 60
 22 30
Found in position 0 of node with contents:  22 30
Enter an integer, followed by I, D, or S (for Insert,
Delete and Search), or enter Q to quit: Q
```

6.2 Deleting Nodes in a B-tree

Given a key, we now want to search our B-tree, and, if we find an item with this key, we want to remove it from the tree. The basic characteristic concerning the number of items in each node must be maintained during the process of successive deletions. We will use the same type of B-tree as in the previous section, with $M = 2$, so each node will contain at most four data items and five pointers. But, again, our implementation will be more general, so that larger nodes can be obtained by a simple change of the symbolic constant M and MM. In fact, our program BTREE.C already contains functions for deletion, so there is no need for another demonstration program in this

section. Since tree deletion is a rather complex operation, let us not immediately turn
to its implementation, but first consider an example. If we are fortunate enough to find
an item with the given key in a leaf that contains more than M items, we can simply
remove that item, and shift any following items one position to the left. If that leaf
contains precisely the minimum number of items, we still remove the item in question
in the same way, but the function call in which this occurs returns **UNDERFLOW**,
defined as a symbolic constant. In this case, we try to borrow an item from a neigh-
boring sibling (that is, a node with the same parent). Figure 6.3 shows such a situation.
Item 27 has just been deleted, and the node which contained it now contains only one
remaining item, 25, so there is underflow. In the program, we detect this when we are
dealing with the parent node (with items 20, 30, 40), after a recursive call to delete 27
in its child.

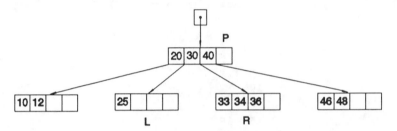

Fig. 6.3. Underflow after deleting item 27 in node L

Although the parent (P) contains three items, we cannot simply use one of these (20
or 30) to fill the gap, since then there would remain two data items and four pointers,
and, as we know, the number of pointers must be only one more than the number of
data items. This is why we need a sibling to borrow an item from. In this example, we
can choose between a left and a right one. Let us, arbitrarily, try the right sibling first,
if there is one (which would not be the case if the removed item had been 46 instead
of 27). If there is no right sibling, we use the left one. We also use the left one if there
are only M items in the right sibling and more than M in the left one. This would be
the case in Fig. 6.3 if there had only been two items, say, 33 and 36, in node R and
three items, say 10, 12, and 15 in the node on the extreme left. Our program will cover
all these cases, but, for the moment, let us restrict our discussion to the case of Fig. 6.3,
where we can borrow an item from the right sibling. We can then focus on the parent
node P, the node L in which underflow has occurred, and the right sibling R.

   We cannot just move 33 from R to L, since that would violate the rule that all keys
in children to the left of 30 must be less than 30, or, more precisely and in the
terminology of the previous section, that all keys in the node pointed to by p_i must be
less than k_i. (Here we have $k_0 = 20$, $k_1 = 30$, $k_2 = 40$, and p_1 pointing to node L.) So
neither item 30 in node P nor item 33 in node R can help us, that is, by themselves. In
combination, however, they can: we move 30 from P to L and then 33 from R to P. The
resulting tree is shown in Fig. 6.4.

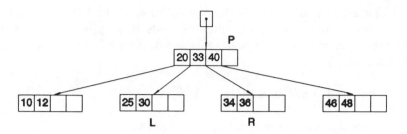

Fig. 6.4. Tree after borrowing an item from node R

Unfortunately, this method does not always work. Here it worked fine because in the original tree (Fig. 6.3) node R contained three items. If R, like the leftmost node, had contained only two items (or, in general, M items) we would not have been able to borrow one of its items without causing underflow in R, which, of course, is just as bad as underflow in L. In that case, we must merge the two nodes L and R into one, as shown in Figs. 6.5 and 6.6.

Since node P has four pointers, it seems that we have a problem, for after merging L and R there will be only three children. To get rid of a pointer in P, we also have to reduce the number of data items in P by one, and, fortunately, we can achieve this by moving the very item 30, used above, to the node resulting from the merge. This is possible because we have exactly M items in R, and, due to underflow, $M - 1$ items in

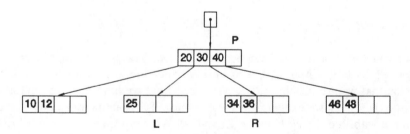

Fig. 6.5. Underflow after deleting item 27 in node L

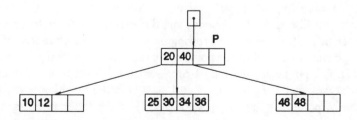

Fig. 6.6. Result after merging L and R

node L. (After all, with more than M items in R, we would have been able to borrow without merging.) Thus, if node L is ***p[i]** and node R is ***p[i+1]**, we let item **k[i]** participate in the merge operation, which means that the total number of items in the resulting node is

$$(M-1) + M + 1 = 2M$$

Figure 6.6 shows the situation after this merge operation.

As we have seen, there are cases in which we solve the underflow problem by borrowing an item from a *left* sibling. One such a case is with underflow occurring in a child on the extreme right, since then there is no right sibling to borrow an item from or to merge with. If the left sibling contains only M items, the result of this borrow operation is that we obtain $M - 1$ items in the left sibling and M items in the node under consideration. If we now call the former L and the latter R, we have a situation similar to the one in Fig. 6.5, and we can apply the same program fragment for merging as before.

In the above discussion we have focused on the data items. Besides these, there are also pointer members in the nodes, and it is time to see what happens with them in the borrow and merge operations. It is true that pointers in leaves are not very interesting because their values are **NULL**, but even with these we must not be inaccurate. More importantly, the above discussion about borrowing and merging applies not only to leaves but also to interior nodes, provided that the pointer members are dealt with properly. To avoid any wordiness and inaccuracy, let us recall that in each node we have data items k_i and pointers p_i in the following logical order:

$$p_0 \ k_0 \ p_1 \ k_1 \ \cdots \ p_{n-1} \ k_{n-1} \ p_n$$

If a node contains its minimum number of items, we have $n = M$, and in the case of underflow we have $n = M - 1$. Let us now consider Fig. 6.3 once again, without the assumption that we are dealing with leaves. In node L, we have $k_0 = 25$, and immediately to the right of k_0 we imagine pointer p_1, which, if L is an interior node, is the root of a subtree with items lying between 25 and 30. We can express this more briefly by saying that p_1 in node L *represents* such items. When borrowing an item from node R to obtain the tree of Fig. 6.4, we assign 30 to k_1 in node L, so p_1 in node L has just the correct pointer value. Returning to Fig. 6.3, we see that pointer p_0 in node R represents items lying between 30 and 33, so this is precisely the pointer we need as p_2 in node L (see Fig. 6.4). Summarizing, when we remedy underflow in node L by borrowing an item from the right sibling R, the pointer on the extreme left in R becomes the rightmost pointer in L. If, instead of borrowing an item, we have to merge two nodes, we can again find out what to do with pointers by thinking of the range of items they represent. In Fig. 6.5, pointer p_0 in node R represents all items between 30 and 34, so this is the pointer we need as p_2 (or, in general, as p_M) in the resulting node, shown in Fig. 6.6. Obviously, pointers p_0 and p_1 ($p_0, ..., p_{M-1}$) in the latter node are the same as those in the original node L. They involve no work at all, since we implement the merge operation by extending the contents of L and disposing of R. It will also be clear that we have to copy the pointers $p_1, ..., p_M$ of node R to use them as $p_{M+1}, ..., p_{2M}$ in the resulting node.

In the above discussion, we suggested that borrowing and merging take place not only for leaves, but also for interior nodes. Consider, for example, Fig. 6.2(f) in the previous section. The node that contains the items 3 and 6 has exactly M items, and so have its three children. If we delete one item in such a child, say, 1 in the leftmost leaf, the two leaves on the left are to be merged into one. The item 3 in the parent node also participates in this merge, so after the merge only 6 remains and we have underflow in this interior node. We now proceed in the same way as we did with underflow in leaves. If the interior node in question has a right sibling with more than M items, we borrow an item from it. If not, as is the case in Fig. 6.2(f), we merge the two nodes, which means that we fetch an item from the parent of the two interior nodes. Again underflow may occur in this parent, in which case we again either borrow or merge, and so on, until we are at the root. Here a special rule applies, namely that a root node is allowed to have less than M items, as long as it has at least one. In Fig. 6.2(f), the root node has only one item, 15, and when this participates in the merge of its two children, the number of items in the root node becomes zero. This is the moment that we say there is underflow in the root node. We then remove the entire node, which decreases the height of the tree. This gives the tree of Fig. 6.2(e). Note that the reduction from Fig. 6.2(f) to Fig. 6.2(e) by deleting item 1 is exactly the reverse action from inserting 1 in the tree, which we did in Section 6.1.

So far, everything started with a deletion in a leaf, and we have seen that this may have far-reaching consequences with regard to the whole tree structure. We still have to consider a deletion which starts in an interior node. For example, let us again use Fig. 6.2(f) and try to delete the item 15 in the root node. We are now faced with a new problem, since a root node must always have at least one item, and we cannot simply borrow an item from its children. Fortunately, this problem can be reduced to deleting an item in a leaf. Recall that in Section 5.3, when dealing with binary search trees, we solved a similar problem by finding a key that was as great as possible but less than the key in the given node. We first went to the left child of that node and then followed the path all the way to a leaf, each time taking the right child. The same method is useful here. If in an interior node item k_i is to be deleted, we find the greatest item that is less than k_i. All items stored in the subtree with root p_i are less than k_i; to find the largest, we follow a path, starting in the node pointed to by p_i, and each time going to the rightmost child, until we arrive at a leaf. The rightmost data item stored in this leaf is the one we are looking for. We can exchange it with the item k_i in the given node, without violating any rule for B-trees. In Fig. 6.2(f) this means that we can exchange the items 15 and 12. Note that it would not have been correct if we had exchanged 15 with item 6 in the left child of the root node, since then in that child the new position of 15 would have been k_1, with p_2 pointing to the smaller items 10 and 12. After the correct exchange of 15 and 12, we can delete item 15 in the usual way because it now resides in a leaf. Further details can be found in the functions **delete** and **del**, which have already been included in program BTREE.C, listed in Section 6.1. The program is useful to demonstrate how a B-tree grows and shrinks by insertions and deletions. After each operation that changes the tree, we can search the tree for some given items. Such a search causes a complete search path to be shown, which enables us to examine the structure of the tree. The best way to learn how B-trees work is to build and modify them on paper or on a blackboard, inserting and deleting items ourselves; program BTREE.C then enables us to check our results step by step.

6.3 B-trees on Disk

In this section we will implement a B-tree as a random-access file (on disk). For most computer systems, this means that the tree can grow much larger than a tree in main memory. At any moment, only a few nodes of the tree will be in memory, but with B-trees this does not imply that only a very limited amount of data should be in memory, since M, the minimum number of items per node, can be as large as we wish. The greater we choose M, the more memory will be used, but the faster the program will run because of less frequent disk access. The program to be developed in this section will enable us to investigate its efficiency experimentally. Though essentially an adaptation of program BTREE.C in Section 6.2, it will deal with one or two files. One file is essential because it accommodates the B-tree itself; the other is an optional input file which contains integers to be stored in the B-tree. In this way, we need no longer supply all input data interactively, but we can also prepare a text file containing integers, as required by the standard function **fscanf**. To create such a file, any text-editor will do, but instead we can use program GENNUM.C, listed below, to generate a random number sequence:

```
/* GENNUM.C  Generation of a text file with integers,
             to be read by DISKTREE.C
*/
#include <stdio.h>
#include <time.h>
#include <stdlib.h>

main()
{  long t;
   int i, n;
   char filnam[51];
   FILE *fp;
   printf("How many integers are to be generated? ");
   scanf("%d", &n);
   printf("Name of output file: "); scanf("%50s", filnam);
   fp = fopen(filnam, "w");
   if (fp == NULL)
   {  puts("Cannot open file");
      exit(1);
   }
```

```
     time(&t);
     srand((int)t);
     /* Generate n integers, in lines of ten: */
     for (i=0; i<n; i++)
     if (fprintf(fp, "%c%d", i%10 ? ' ' : '\n', rand()) == EOF)
     {  puts("Disk writing error");
        exit(1);
     }
     fclose(fp);
     return 0;
}
```

With this program we can easily generate a file of, say, 10000 integers, and our program DISKTREE.C, which we are developing, will be able to read these and insert them in the B-tree, in the same way as it does with integers entered one by one on the keyboard, which, incidentally, will still be possible. Program DISKTREE.C will ask for the names of the two files. The first is the name of the tree file. If it already exists, the B-tree stored in it will be updated, otherwise a new tree file with the given name will be created. The second is the input file discussed above; if it exists, the integers read from it are inserted in the tree, which before this insertion may or may not be empty depending on whether or not a new tree file had to be created. To avoid confusion, it is wise to use different file-name extensions, such as .BIN for the (binary) tree file and .TXT for the optional text file that contains input data. Integers to be inserted can also be entered on the keyboard: at the beginning we can enter a whole sequence of integers, terminated by a nonnumeric character, such as /. Later, we can enter individual integers, followed by one of the characters **I**, **D**, and **S**, for insertion, deletion and search, respectively. Recall that we used similar interactive commands in program BTREE.C in Section 6.2. However, after our entering the quit command, **Q**, the B-tree will not get lost this time, but remain safely in the tree file for subsequent use. Thus the program will be somewhat similar to a text-editor, where we can also either begin with a new file or use an existing file. However, most editors perform a special SAVE operation at the end of a normal edit session, to store the work file onto a permanent file; in contrast to this, program DISKTREE.C will be working with a permanent file all the time.

We now turn to the internal aspects of the program. It will be clear that in a file we cannot use normal pointers, since these have memory addresses as their values, and on disk we use positions, which are (long) integers denoting byte numbers. Recall that in C we can write

```
fseek(fp, pos, SEEK_SET);
fwrite(&buf, size, n, fp);
```

where **pos** is a **long int** value denoting the desired position relative to the beginning of the file. We have

pos = 0   for the first byte
pos = 1   for the second byte

and so on. In the above call to **fwrite**, the first argument **&buf** is the start address in memory from which data is to be written to the file with file pointer **fp**. The number of bytes to be transmitted is the product of **size** and **n**. Thus **pos**, the second argument of **fseek**, can now be used like a pointer; instead of

```
typedef
struct Node {int cnt, key[MM]; struct Node *ptr[MM+1];} node;
node *root, ...
```

we can now use

```
typedef struct {int cnt, key[MM]; long ptr[MM+1];} node;
long root, ...
```

Each element of array **ptr** can contain a file position, and so can the variable **root**. We have now solved the problem of data representation, but there is still a more difficult question to be answered, namely how to find alternatives for the standard functions **malloc** and **free**. If new nodes are to be created, where shall we place them on disk, and if nodes are to be deleted, will there be portions of unused space in the file? To begin with the latter question, we will consider such gaps acceptable, provided that they are reused as soon as any new nodes are to be inserted again. We will therefore insert new nodes in such gaps, if any; otherwise we simply append these nodes to the file. Thus we will not allocate a certain amount of space in advance, and, in principle, there is no limit to the number of nodes in the tree. We want the file to be a complete representation of the tree, which implies that, given only the file, we must be able to find the position of the root node. We will therefore store the root itself, that is, the position of the root node, before all other data in the file. Also, some information about any gaps as a result of deleted nodes must be stored in the file, in order that we can start program execution with an existing file and fill the gaps when nodes are inserted. We will therefore form a *linked list* of these gaps, using pointer member **ptr[0]** to point to a next gap, if any. Note that we are now using the term *pointer* for long integers which denote positions, or, in other words, byte numbers. Let us use −1L, and write this as **NIL**, instead of **NULL** used for real pointers in memory. A linked list of free locations is usually called a *free list*, and we will use the **long int** variable **freelist** as a 'pointer' to the first element of this list. If the list is empty, **freelist** will have the value **NIL**. As long as the program is running, **root** and **freelist** are internal variables, but we reserve room for them at the beginning of the file. At the end of program execution, just before the file is closed, we write their two values in the file. Figure 6.7 shows the file contents for the B-tree of Fig. 6.2(b).

Let us use $M = 2$ again, which means that, except for the root node, there are at least two and at most four items in each node. For a B-tree on disk, such a small value of M will not lead to a very fast program, but, with only integer data items, the program

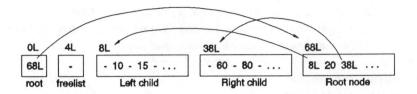

Fig. 6.7. File representation of a B-tree with three nodes

will not be useful for real applications anyway; we will use it only for demonstration purposes, and it is instructive to see how fast or slow it is with $M = 2$. After all, we can then speed it up considerably in a very simple way, namely by choosing larger values for the named constants M and MM, such as $M = 1000$ and $MM = 2000$. As Fig. 6.7 shows, the root node may not be the first node in the file. In fact the situation shown here with the root node at the end of the file will occur more frequently, which follows from the way B-trees grow. As this root node will be needed quite often, it will be worthwhile to have a copy of it available in main memory, although it must be said that this requirement complicates the program considerably. We will use the function **readnode**, which normally reads a node from the file, but uses instead the internal variable **rootnode** if the given pointer to the desired node happens to be equal to the variable **root**. Function **readnode** should not be confused with **getnode**; the latter is to return the position of a newly created node, so it plays the role of **malloc** in program BTREE.C. It first tries to obtain an element of the free list of gaps, mentioned above. If this free list is empty, there are no such gaps, so we go to the end of the file and write a node there with no well-defined contents; this may seem odd, but we need it to reserve room, so that any subsequent call of **getnode** should not return the same location. Further details can be found in the program text itself; complex as it is, the program is easy to use, and it may be instructive to run it on various machines to see how it behaves. As mentioned above, we can speed it up considerably by increasing the values of M and MM (where MM stands for $2M$).

```
/*  DISKTREE.C:
    Demonstration program for a B-tree on disk. After
    building the B-tree by entering integers on the
    keyboard or by supplying these as a text file, we can
    update it interactively by entering (or deleting)
    individual integers. Instead, we can search the
    B-tree for a given integer. Each time, the tree or a
    search path is displayed. In contrast to BTREE.C,
    program DISKTREE.C writes, reads, and updates nodes on
    disk, using a binary file. The name of this file is to
    be entered on the keyboard. If a B-tree file with that
    name exists, that B-tree is used; otherwise such a
    file is created.
```

```
        Caution:
            Do not confuse the (binary) file for the B-tree with
            the optional text file for input data. Use different
            file-name extensions, such as .BIN and .TXT.
*/
#include <stdio.h>
#include <stdlib.h>
#include <ctype.h>

#define M 2
#define MM 4
#define NIL (-1L)

typedef enum
{   INSERTNOTCOMPLETE,
    SUCCESS,
    DUPLICATEKEY,
    UNDERFLOW,
    NOTFOUND
}   status;

typedef struct {int cnt, key[MM]; long ptr[MM+1];} node;
node rootnode;
long start[2], root=NIL, freelist=NIL;
FILE *fptree;

void error(char *str)
{   printf("\nError: %s\n", str);
    exit(1);
}

void readnode(long t, node *pnode)
{   if (t == root) { *pnode = rootnode; return; }
    if (fseek(fptree, t, SEEK_SET)) error("fseek in readnode");
    if (fread(pnode, sizeof(node), 1, fptree) == 0)
        error("fread in readnode");
}

void writenode(long t, node *pnode)
{   if (t == root) rootnode = *pnode;
    if (fseek(fptree, t, SEEK_SET)) error("fseek in writenode");
    if (fwrite(pnode, sizeof(node), 1, fptree) == 0)
                        error("fwrite in writenode");
}
```

```
long getnode(void)
{  long t;
   node nod;
   if (freelist == NIL)
   {  if (fseek(fptree, 0L, SEEK_END))
         error("fseek in getnode");
      t = ftell(fptree);
      writenode(t, &nod);        /* Allocate space on disk */
   }  else
   {  t = freelist;
      readnode(t, &nod);         /* To update freelist:    */
      freelist = nod.ptr[0];
   }
   return t;
}


void found(long t, int i)
{  node nod;
   printf("Found in position %d of node with contents: ", i);
   readnode(t, &nod);
   for (i=0; i < nod.cnt; i++) printf(" %d", nod.key[i]);
   puts("");
}


void notfound(int x)
{  printf("Item %d not found\n", x);
}


int binsearch(int x, int *a, int n)
/*  Search array a[0], a[1], ..., a[n-1] for x.
    Return value:
        0 if x <= a[0],  n if x > a[n-1],
        or r, where  a[r-1] < x <= a[r]
*/
{  int i, left, right;
   if (x <= a[0]) return 0;
   if (x > a[n-1]) return n;
   left = 0; right = n-1;
   while (right - left > 1)
   {  i = (right + left)/2;
      if (x <= a[i]) right = i; else left = i;
   }
   return right;
}
```

```
status search(int x)
{  int i, j, *k, n;
   node nod;
   long t = root;
   puts("Search path:");
   while (t != NIL)
   {  readnode(t, &nod);
      k = nod.key; n = nod.cnt;
      for (j=0; j < n; j++) printf(" %d", k[j]);
      puts("");
      i = binsearch(x, k, n);
      if (i < n && x == k[i]) {found(t, i); return SUCCESS;}
      t = nod.ptr[i];
   }
   return NOTFOUND;
}


status ins(int x, long t, int *y, long *u)
/* Insert x in B-tree with root t. If not completely
   successful, the integer *y and the pointer *u
   remain to be inserted.
*/
{  long tnew, p_final, *p;
   int i, j, xnew, k_final, *n, *k;
   status code;
   node nod, newnod;
   /* Examine whether t is a pointer member in a leaf:
   */
   if (t == NIL) {*u = NIL; *y = x; return INSERTNOTCOMPLETE;}
   readnode(t, &nod);
   n = & nod.cnt; k = nod.key; p = nod.ptr;
   /*  Select pointer p[i] and try to insert x in
       the subtree of which p[i] is the root:
   */
   i = binsearch(x, k, *n);
   if (i < *n && x == k[i]) return DUPLICATEKEY;
   code = ins(x, p[i], &xnew, &tnew);
   if (code != INSERTNOTCOMPLETE) return code;

   /* Insertion in subtree did not completely succeed;
      try to insert xnew and tnew in the current node:
   */
   if (*n < MM)
   {  i = binsearch(xnew, k, *n);
```

```
          for (j= *n; j>i; j--)
          { k[j] = k[j-1]; p[j+1] = p[j];
          }
          k[i] = xnew; p[i+1] = tnew; ++*n;
          writenode(t, &nod); return SUCCESS;
      }

      /* The current node was already full, so split it. Pass
         item k[M] in the middle of the augmented sequence
         back through parameter y, so that it can move
         upward in the tree. Also, pass a pointer to the newly
         created node back through u. Return INSERTNOTCOMPLETE,
         to report that insertion was not completed:
      */
      if (i == MM) { k_final = xnew; p_final = tnew; } else
      {  k_final = k[MM-1]; p_final = p[MM];
         for (j=MM-1; j>i; j--)
         {  k[j] = k[j-1]; p[j+1] = p[j];
         }
         k[i] = xnew; p[i+1] = tnew;
      }
      *y = k[M]; *n = M;
      *u = getnode(); newnod.cnt = M;
      for (j=0; j < M-1; j++)
      {  newnod.key[j] = k[j+M+1];   newnod.ptr[j] = p[j+M+1];
      }
      newnod.ptr[M-1] = p[MM];   newnod.key[M-1] = k_final;
      newnod.ptr[M] = p_final;
      writenode(t, &nod); writenode(*u, &newnod);
      return INSERTNOTCOMPLETE;
   }

status insert(int x)
/* Driver function for node insertion, called only in the
   main function. Most of the work is delegated to 'ins'.
*/
{  long tnew, u;
   int xnew;
   status code = ins(x, root, &xnew, &tnew);
   if (code == DUPLICATEKEY)
      printf("Duplicate key %d ignored\n", x); else
   if (code == INSERTNOTCOMPLETE)
   {  u = getnode();
      rootnode.cnt = 1; rootnode.key[0] = xnew;
```

```
            rootnode.ptr[0] = root; rootnode.ptr[1] = tnew;
            root = u;
            writenode(u, &rootnode);
            code = SUCCESS;
      }
      return code; /* Return value: SUCCESS or DUPLICATEKEY */
}


void freenode(long t)
{  node nod;
   readnode(t, &nod);
   nod.ptr[0] = freelist;
   freelist = t;
   writenode(t, &nod);
}


void rdstart(void)
{  if (fseek(fptree, 0L, SEEK_SET)) error("fseek in rdstart");
   if (fread(start, sizeof(long), 2, fptree) == 0)
      error("fread in rdstart");
   readnode(start[0], &rootnode);
   root = start[0]; freelist = start[1];
}


void wrstart(void)
{  start[0] = root; start[1] = freelist;
   if (fseek(fptree, 0L, SEEK_SET)) error("fseek in wrstart");
   if (fwrite(start, sizeof(long), 2, fptree) == 0)
      error("fwrite in wrstart");
   if (root != NIL) writenode(root, &rootnode);
}


status del(int x, long t)
/* Delete item x in B-tree with root t.
   Return value:
      SUCCESS, NOTFOUND, or UNDERFLOW
*/
{  int i, j, *k, *n, *item, *nleft, *nright,
   *lkey, *rkey, borrowleft=0, nq, *addr;
   status code;
   long *p, left, right, *lptr, *rptr, q, ql;
   node nod, nod1, nod2, nodL, nodR;
   if (t == NIL) return NOTFOUND;
   readnode(t, &nod);
```

```
n = & nod.cnt; k = nod.key; p=nod.ptr;
i = binsearch(x, k, *n);
if (p[0] == NIL)     /*   *t is a leaf */
{ if (i == *n || x < k[i]) return NOTFOUND;
   /* x is now equal to k[i], located in a leaf: */
   for (j=i+1; j < *n; j++)
   { k[j-1] = k[j]; p[j] = p[j+1];
   }
   --*n;
   writenode(t, &nod);
   return *n >= (t==root ? 1 : M) ? SUCCESS : UNDERFLOW;
}
/*   *t is an interior node (not a leaf):   */
item = k+i; left = p[i]; readnode(left, &nod1);
nleft = & nod1.cnt;
if (i < *n && x == *item)
{ /* x found in interior node.                           */
   /* Go to left child *p[i] and then follow a path      */
   /* all the way to a leaf, using rightmost branches: */
   q = p[i]; readnode(q, &nod1); nq = nod1.cnt;
   while (q1 = nod1.ptr[nq], q1 != NIL)
   { q = q1; readnode(q, &nod1); nq = nod1.cnt;
   }
   /* Exchange k[i] with the rightmost item in
      that leaf:
   */
   addr = nod1.key + nq - 1;
   *item = *addr; *addr = x;
   writenode(t, &nod); writenode(q, &nod1);
}
/* Delete x in subtree with root  p[i]:                  */
code = del(x, left);
if (code != UNDERFLOW) return code;
/* Underflow; borrow, and, if necessary, merge:        */
if (i < *n) readnode(p[i+1], &nodR);
if (i == *n || nodR.cnt == M)
{ if (i > 0)
   { readnode(p[i-1], &nodL);
      if (i == *n || nodL.cnt > M) borrowleft = 1;
   }
}
if (borrowleft)       /* Borrow from left sibling */
{ item = k+i-1; left = p[i-1]; right = p[i];
   nod1 = nodL;
```

```
      readnode(right, &nod2);
      nleft = & nod1.cnt;
} else
{ right = p[i+1];    /* Borrow from right sibling */
      readnode(left, &nod1);
      nod2 = nodR;
}
nright = & nod2.cnt;
lkey = nod1.key; rkey = nod2.key;
lptr = nod1.ptr; rptr = nod2.ptr;
if (borrowleft)
{ rptr[*nright + 1] = rptr[*nright];
      for (j = *nright; j>0; j--)
      { rkey[j] = rkey[j-1]; rptr[j] = rptr[j-1];
      }
      ++*nright;
      rkey[0] = *item; rptr[0] = lptr[*nleft];
      *item = lkey[*nleft - 1];
      if (--*nleft >= M)
      { writenode(t, &nod); writenode(left, &nod1);
         writenode(right, &nod2);
         return SUCCESS;
      }
} else
if (*nright > M)          /* Borrow from right sibling: */
{ lkey[M-1] = *item; lptr[M] = rptr[0]; *item = rkey[0];
      ++*nleft; --*nright;
      for (j=0; j < *nright; j++)
      { rptr[j] = rptr[j+1]; rkey[j] = rkey[j+1];
      }
      rptr[*nright] = rptr[*nright + 1];
      writenode(t, &nod); writenode(left, &nod1);
      writenode(right, &nod2);
      return SUCCESS;
}
/* Merge: */
lkey[M-1] = *item; lptr[M] = rptr[0];
for (j=0; j<M; j++)
{ lkey[M+j] = rkey[j]; lptr[M+j+1] = rptr[j+1];
}
*nleft = MM;
freenode(right);
for (j=i+1; j < *n; j++) {k[j-1] = k[j]; p[j] = p[j+1];}
--*n;
```

```
      writenode(t, &nod); writenode(left, &nod1);
      return *n >= (t==root ? 1 : M) ? SUCCESS : UNDERFLOW;
}

status delnode(int x)
/* Driver function for node deletion, called only in the
     main function. Most of the work is delegated to 'del'.
*/
{  long newroot;
   status code = del(x, root);
   if (code == UNDERFLOW)
   {  newroot = rootnode.ptr[0]; freenode(root);
      if (newroot != NIL) readnode(newroot, &rootnode);
      root = newroot; code = SUCCESS;
   }
   return code; /* Return value: SUCCESS or NOTFOUND */
}

void printtree(long t)
{  static int position=0;
   int i, *k, n;
   node nod;
   if (t != NIL)
   {  position += 6;
      readnode(t, &nod);
      k = nod.key; n = nod.cnt;
      printf("%*s", position, "");
      for (i=0; i<n; i++) printf(" %3d", k[i]);
      puts("");
      for (i=0; i<=n; i++) printtree(nod.ptr[i]);
      position -= 6;
   }
}

main()
{  int x, code=0;
   char ch, treefilnam[51], inpfilnam[51];
   FILE *fpinp;
   puts("\nB-tree structure will be represented by "
        "indentation.");
   printf("Enter name of (old or new) binary file for "
          "the B-tree: ");
   scanf("%50s", treefilnam);
   fptree = fopen(treefilnam, "r+b");
```

```
          if (fptree == NULL)
          { fptree = fopen(treefilnam, "w+b"); wrstart();
          } else
          { rdstart(); printtree(root);
          }
          puts("Enter a (possibly empty) sequence of integers, "
               "followed by /:");
          while (scanf("%d", &x) == 1) {insert(x); code = 1;}
          getchar(); puts("");
          if (code) printtree(root);
          printf("Are integers to be read from a text file? (Y/N): ");
          scanf(" %c", &ch);
          while (getchar() != '\n') ; /* Rest of line skipped */
          if (toupper(ch) == 'Y')
          { printf("Name of this text file: ");
            scanf("%50s", inpfilnam);
            fpinp = fopen(inpfilnam, "r");
            if (fpinp == NULL) error("File not available");
            while (fscanf(fpinp, "%d", &x) == 1) insert(x);
            fclose(fpinp);
            printtree(root);
          }
          for ( ; ; )
          {  printf(
             "Enter an integer, followed by I, D, or S (for Insert,\n"
             "Delete and Search), or enter Q to quit: ");
             code = scanf("%d", &x);
             scanf(" %c", &ch); ch = toupper(ch);
             if (code)
             switch (ch)
             {  case 'I': if (insert(x) == SUCCESS) printtree(root);
                          break;
                 case 'D': if (delnode(x) == SUCCESS) printtree(root);
                          else puts("Not found");
                          break;
                 case 'S': if (search(x) == NOTFOUND)
                               puts("Not found");
                          break;
             }  else
             if (ch == 'Q') break;
          }
          wrstart();
          return 0;
      }
```

To see how this program can be used, let us use a very simple example. Suppose that we have a text file with input data, possibly produced by program GENNUM.C. When this program was executed with the (very small) number 3 as input, it generated the sequence

```
15532 5495 7095
```

in a file named *gennum.txt*. This file is used in the following demonstration of program DISKTREE.C:

```
B-tree structure will be represented by indentation.
Enter name of (old or new) binary file for the B-tree: test.bin
Enter a (possibly empty) sequence of integers, followed by /:
1 2 3 4 5 6/


            3
                1    2
                4    5    6
Are integers to be read from a text file? (Y/N): Y
Name of this text file: gennum.txt
            3    6
                1    2
                4    5
            5495 7095 15532
Enter an integer, followed by I, D, or S (for Insert,
Delete and Search), or enter Q to quit: 20 I
            3    6
                1    2
                4    5
            20 5495 7095 15532
Enter an integer, followed by I, D, or S (for Insert,
Delete and Search), or enter Q to quit: 2 D
            6
                1    3    4    5
            20 5495 7095 15532
Enter an integer, followed by I, D, or S (for Insert,
Delete and Search), or enter Q to quit: Q
```

At the very beginning of this session, there was no file *test.bin*, so this file was created. After this demonstration, this file contains the last B-tree (with 6 in its root node). If we run the program again, with *test.bin* as the name of the binary file, we begin with this B-tree instead of an empty one as we did above.

Exercises

In the following exercises, the same node type as in Section 6.1 is to be used. Write a main program to show that each function works properly.

6.1   Write a function to count how many data items have been stored in a given B-tree.

6.2   Write a function to determine the height of a B-tree.

6.3   Write a function to delete an entire B-tree.

6.4   Write a function which takes a B-tree and builds a new one containing the same integers as the given B-tree, except for those which are a multiple of 3. For example, if the given B-tree contains the integers 1, 4, 6, 7, 12, 20, 23, 24, then the new one will contain only the integers 1, 4, 7, 20, 23.

7

Tries

7.1 Introduction

In the trees of Chapters 5 and 6, each node contained one or more key values, and we have seen that this principle may require special measures to prevent those trees from becoming unbalanced or even degenerated. Obviously, if a tree is to be searched efficiently, the nodes must contain certain values that enable us to decide which branch to take, and, up to now, we have taken it for granted that those values must be existing key values. However, this is not absolutely necessary. Instead of using a complete key in each comparison, we can compare only a certain portion of it. This idea is the basis of a special type of tree, called a *trie*. This peculiar word is derived from the two words *tree* and *retrieval*, and, in spite of this derivation, *trie* is often pronounced as *try*, to distinguish it from *tree* in spoken language. To understand what a trie is about, let us consider a not unrealistic example. Our keys will be character strings, consisting of capital letters only, for example:

```
A
ALE
ALLOW
AN
ANY
ANYTHING
```

We will use the individual characters of the string to determine how to branch. All interior nodes, called *branch nodes*, will have 27 pointer members and an integer member to be discussed later. The leaves, also called *data nodes*, will consist of the

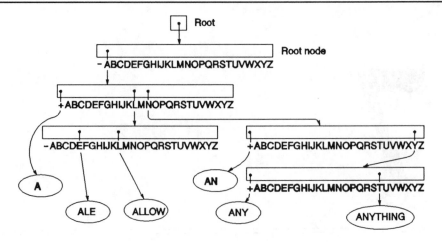

Fig. 7.1. A trie

complete information records; each of them contains a key and, possibly, some other information associated with the key. In the branch nodes, there is a pointer member for each of the letters A, ..., Z. The main rule is that branching on the ith level in the trie is determined by the ith character of the key. Figure 7.1 shows the trie for the above six words.

If, for example, we search the trie for the word *ALE*, we take the branch that corresponds to the letter A in the root node, then the branch corresponding to L, and, finally, the one corresponding to E. We find the key *ALLOW* similarly, but here we need only the first three letters, since there is no other key beginning with those letters. We say that *ALL* is a *prefix* of the key *ALLOW*, which, in contrast to the prefix *AL*, determines this key uniquely. Similarly, *ANYT* is a prefix that uniquely determines the key *ANYTHING*. At first sight, the complete key *ANY* seems to be a prefix of longer keys that begin with these three letters, such as *ANYTHING*. However this is not the case, because we consider terminating null characters (on which C string handling is based) to belong to the key. The key *ANY* will therefore consist of four characters. The fourth, '\0', differs from the fourth character 'T' in the key *ANYTHING*. Thus, our keys should be read as

```
A\0
ALE\0
ALLOW\0
AN\0
ANY\0
ANYTHING\0
```

In every branch node, there is also a pointer member that corresponds to this null character; in Fig. 7.1 these pointer members are denoted by + if they contain a real pointer. This explains the pointers to the data nodes for the keys A, AN, ANY. If these pointer members contain **NULL**, this is denoted in Fig. 7.1 by −. In this example, there is a minus sign in the branch node at the bottom left, which indicates that there is no key *AL*. (There is always a minus sign in the root node, because a plus sign here would correspond to an empty key, which does not make sense.)

Of course, we must be able to tell branch nodes from data nodes. We will therefore include an integer member in each branch node; this member will be located at the very beginning of each branch node, and it will always have the value 0. As for the data nodes, they represent variable-length strings, for which we will allocate memory elsewhere in the usual way. Besides a pointer to such a character string, we include a nonzero integer to distinguish data nodes from branch nodes, and this integer will be the first member of each data node. Thus, we will be able to tell branch nodes from data nodes: the former begin with integer 0 and the latter with a nonzero integer. It may seem to be a waste of memory space to use an entire integer instead of only one bit for this; however, reserving only a single bit would result in allocating at least an entire byte on most machines. Furthermore, we will use this integer for another purpose, namely as a count member, indicating how many occurrences of the word have been read.

There is a little problem associated with using two distinct node types. Each pointer in a branch node can point either to another branch node or to a data node. Fortunately, one pointer type can be converted to another by means of a cast. In particular, ANSI C offers the possibility of using **void**-pointers, intended to be used as *generic pointers*. Generic pointers can point to objects of different types, or, in other words, they enable us to use *polymorphic* data structures. Note how the following **typedef** declarations declare the two structure types **branchnode** and **datanode** as well as the two pointer types **brptr** and **dataptr**:

```
#define NBRANCHES ('Z'-'A'+2) /* = 27 with ASCII */
typedef struct {int num; void *ptr[NBRANCHES];} branchnode;
typedef struct {int num; char *key;} datanode;
typedef branchnode *brptr;
typedef datanode *dataptr;
```

With ASCII values for characters, the members of a branch node have the following meaning:

num: 0 (to indicate that the node is a branch node)
p[0]:   a pointer corresponding to **'\0'**,
p[1]:   a pointer corresponding to **'A'**,

    . . .

p[26]:   a pointer corresponding to **'Z'**.

(With character values other than ASCII, the characters **'A'** to **'Z'** may not be consecutive, so that array **ptr** will have more than 27 elements. Although our discussion is based on ASCII values, our program will also be correct if these do not apply.)

7.2 A Demonstration Program

We will now discuss program TRIE.C, which builds, prints, and searches a trie of the type we are discussing. The program will read words from a file and store them in a trie. Each data node will contain a word and a count member, the latter indicating how many occurrences of the word have been read. Thus the value of each count member is at least 1, which makes it a suitable means to distinguish data nodes from branch nodes. Internally, all names will consist of capital letters only: we will convert any small letters to the corresponding capital letters. The words are separated by sequences of any characters other than letters. After the trie has been built, we will print all words, just to show that we can easily traverse our trie and list the keys in alphabetic order. Finally, we will demonstrate searching the trie for keys entered on the keyboard; the special word *STOPSEARCH* will be interpreted as an end signal, not as a key to search for. Since function **insert** in program TRIE.C is rather intricate, it is strongly recommended to study the functions **main**, **printtrie**, and **found** first. A discussion of function **insert** follows this program.

```
/*   TRIE.C: A demonstration program for tries
*/
#include <stdio.h>
#include <stdlib.h>
#include <string.h>
#include <ctype.h>

#define MAXWORDLENGTH 80
#define NBRANCHES ('Z'-'A'+2) /* = 27 with ASCII */

typedef struct {int num; void *ptr[NBRANCHES];} branchnode;
typedef struct {int num; char *key;} datanode;
typedef branchnode *brptr;
typedef datanode *dataptr;

void error(char *str)
{  printf("\nError: %s\n", str); exit(1);
}

void printtrie(void *p)
{  dataptr dp=(dataptr)p;
                         /* Suppose p points to a data node */
   void *q;
   int k;
   if (dp->num)          /* num > 0: p points to a data node  */
       printf("%5d %s\n", dp->num, dp->key);
```

```
      else      /* num = 0: p points to a branch node */
          for (k=0; k<NBRANCHES; k++)
             if ((q = ((brptr)p)->ptr[k]) != NULL) printtrie(q);
}

dataptr found(void *p, char *word)
{  int i=0, k;
   char ch;
   dataptr dp=(dataptr)p;      /* In case of a data node    */
   brptr bp=(brptr)p;          /* In case of a branch node  */
   while (p != NULL && bp->num == 0)
   {  ch = word[i++]; k = (ch ? ch-'A'+1 : 0);
      if (k < 0 || k >= NBRANCHES) return NULL;
      p = bp->ptr[k]; bp = (brptr)p;
   }
   dp = (dataptr)p;
   return (p == NULL ? NULL :
           strcmp(word, dp->key) == 0 ? dp : NULL);
}


brptr newbrnode(void)
{  brptr bp;
   int k;
   bp = (brptr)malloc(sizeof(branchnode));
   if (bp == NULL) error("Not enough memory");
   bp->num = 0;
   for (k=0; k<NBRANCHES; k++)
      bp->ptr[k] = NULL;
   return bp;
}


dataptr newdatanode(char *word)
{  char *pch;
   dataptr dp;
   dp = (dataptr)malloc(sizeof(datanode));
   pch = (char *)malloc(strlen(word)+1);
   if (dp == NULL || pch == NULL)
      error("Not enough memory");
   strcpy(pch, word);
   dp->num = 1;
   dp->key = pch;
   return dp;
}
```

```
void insert(void **pp, char *word, int i)
/*  Insert 'word' in a trie. Parameter pp contains the
    address of the root of this trie. If *pp points to
    a branch node, use word[i] for branch selection.
*/
{ char ch, ch1;
  brptr bp, bp1;
  dataptr dp;
  int k, k1;
  for ( ; ; )
  { if (*pp == NULL)
    { *pp = (void *)newdatanode(word); break;
    }
    bp = *(brptr *)pp;     /* In case of a branch node */
    dp = *(dataptr *)pp;   /* In case of a data node   */
    ch = word[i];
    k = (ch ? ch-'A'+1 : 0);
    if (bp->num == 0) pp = & bp->ptr[k];  /* Branch node */
    else /* Data node */
    { if (strcmp(word, dp->key) == 0)
      { dp->num ++; break;
      }
      bp1 = newbrnode(); *pp = (void *) bp1;
      ch1 = dp->key[i];  /* Char. in existing data node */
      k1 = (ch1 ? ch1-'A'+1 : 0);
      bp1->ptr[k1] = (void *)bp;
      pp = & bp1->ptr[k];
    }
    i++;
  }
}


int getword(FILE *fp, char *str)
{ int ch, i=0;
  /* Skip non-alphabetic characters: */
  while (ch = getc(fp), ch != EOF && !isalpha(ch)) ;
  /* Read letters into str, if any: */
  while (isalpha(ch))
  { str[i++] = toupper(ch); ch = getc(fp);
    if (i > MAXWORDLENGTH) error("Word too long");
  }
  str[i] = '\0';
  return i;
}
```

```
main()
{   FILE *fp;
    char filnam[51], word[MAXWORDLENGTH+1];
    void *root;
    dataptr q;
    puts("This program can read any text file. Then for any");
    puts("word (consisting of at most 80 letters) you can");
    puts("ask how often that word occurs in this file.");
    printf("Input file: "); scanf("%50s", filnam);
    fp = fopen(filnam, "r");
    if (fp == NULL) error("File not available");
    root = NULL;
    while (getword(fp, word) > 0)
        insert(&root, word, 0);
    fclose(fp);
    printf("\nContents of trie:\n");
    if (root != NULL) printtrie(root);
    while
    (printf("\nEnter a word, or type STOPSEARCH to stop: "),
     getword(stdin, word), strcmp(word, "STOPSEARCH"))
    {   q = found(root, word);
        if (q == NULL) printf("Key not found\n"); else
            printf("Key found; count member = %d\n", q->num);
    }
    return 0;
}
```

There are many occurrences of the two pointer types **brptr** and **dataptr** in this program. With

```
brptr bp;
dataptr dp;
```

the variables **bp** and **dp** can be used as pointers to branch nodes and data nodes, respectively. Thus, we can use

bp->num, bp->ptr, dp->num, dp->key

but not **bp->key** or **dp->ptr**.

The functions **printtrie** and **found** should now be studied carefully, not only because they are interesting themselves, but also as a preparation for the more difficult function **insert**. As the call

```
insert(&root, word, 0);
```

in the main program shows, the first argument of **insert** is the address of a pointer variable. This enables this function to assign an address to that variable. Within the function, we use the notation **pp** for the address of the pointer, so if **pp** is not **NULL**, then ***pp** is that pointer itself. After assigning ***pp** to the local variables **bp** and **dp**, we use **bp** if ***pp** points to a branch node and **dp** if it points to a data node. The second argument of **insert** is the word to be inserted, and the third denotes the next character position of this word, to be used in a comparison. There are several cases to consider, which is why this function is more complex than the rest of the program. If ***pp** is equal to **NULL**, we create a new data node for the word to be inserted and assign the address of this node to ***pp**. Otherwise, we compute the index **k** corresponding to **word[i]** as follows:

```
ch = word[i];
k = (ch ? ch-'A'+1 : 0);
```

Then if the node under consideration is a branch node (pointed to by **bp**), we assign the address of **bp->ptr[k]** to **pp** and increase **i** by 1. This means that we take one step on the search path of the trie. We then repeat the whole process.

If, on the other hand, the node under consideration is a data node, we test to see if the given word is identical with the word in that data node. If so, we simply increase the count member **num** by one, after which our task is completed. If these two words are different, we insert a new branch node:

```
bp1 = newbrnode(); *pp = (void *) bp1;
```

For example, suppose that we find *ALLOW* in an existing data node. In accordance with Fig. 7.1, suppose that we have reached this node by using the second *L*. This implies that **i** = 3; we now compute **ch1 = dp->key[3]** = **'O'**. Then in the new branch node the address of the data node, available in **dp**, is placed in the pointer element corresponding to **'O'**. This is shown in Figs. 7.2 and 7.3.

Recall that we have reached the data node *ALLOW* because the contents of **word** also begin with *ALL*. Suppose this is the word *ALLIGATOR*. Then it will be clear that after one more step in the updated trie this word will be in a new data node, pointed to by the new branch node that also points to *ALLOW*, as shown in Fig. 7.3.

If **word** contains *ALLOY* instead of *ALLIGATOR*, with **ch** = **'O'** instead of **'I'**, the situation is different because the pointer for *O* is already in use for *ALLOW*. In this case yet another branch node will be necessary. In general, inserting a new branch node may be required several times. Fortunately, this is no problem, because all program statements of function **insert** are inside a loop. This loop can terminate in two ways, either by finding a pointer member **NULL** or by finding the word to be inserted already present in the trie.

Function **getword** in program TRIE.C skips all non-alphabetic characters and converts lower case letters to capital. Thanks to this function, we can use any text file as input for this program. To illustrate this, here is a demonstration in which the

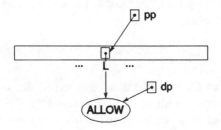

Fig. 7.2. Situation before inserting ALLIGATOR

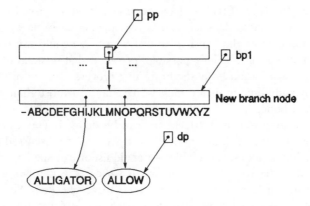

Fig. 7.3. Situation after inserting ALLIGATOR

program is supplied with its own source code (that is, file TRIE.C) as input data. Since there are a great many distinct words in this file, the middle part of the alphabetic list of words is replaced here with three dots:

```
This program can read any text file. Then for any
word (consisting of at most 80 letters) you can
ask how often that word occurs in this file.
Input file: TRIE.C
Contents of trie:
   13 A
    1 ADDRESS
    1 ALPHABETIC
    3 ANY
      ...
    1 YOU
    1 Z
```

```
Enter a word, or type STOPSEARCH to stop: ANY
Key found; count member = 3

Enter a word, or type STOPSEARCH to stop: STOPSEARCH
```

Not only words in the input file but also those entered on the keyboard are converted to capital letters, so, for example, we could have entered the word *any* instead of *ANY*.

It should be noted that tries are not particularly economical with memory space. Besides data nodes, there are branch nodes, which use much space, especially in our type of trie with 27 pointer members in each of them. Instead of using arrays with 27 elements, we could use linked lists, but then much space would be required for pointers. Besides, searching such linked lists would take more time than selecting elements in our arrays. However, the type of trie we have been discussing is very efficient with respect to time. Tries are suitable data structures for spelling-checking programs. The data nodes would then contain the words of a dictionary. We could use only branch nodes (and no data nodes at all). This is possible, provided that, instead of a unique prefix, all letters of each word are used in the branching process. But, unfortunately, we would then need many additional branch nodes, which may cost more than we would gain by omitting the data nodes.

We have not discussed how trie nodes can be deleted. This can be done, and is considerably simpler than deleting nodes in a B-tree, as we discussed in Section 6.2. If the option of deleting nodes is available, we could use it in a spelling checker. We have just suggested that the trie should contain all words of a dictionary, so that we can search the trie for each word in the text that is to be checked. Alternatively, we can proceed the other way round: we can store each word of the text in question (only once) in a trie and then search the trie for each word in the dictionary. Each time a word is found, we delete it from the trie, so that the trie gradually shrinks. When all words of the dictionary have been searched for, any remaining words in the trie are just those which do not occur in the dictionary. Obviously, this method is feasible only if the dictionary is very limited in size. A curious point is that in this way we do not benefit from the alphabetic order of the dictionary. This observation suggests yet another method, namely, *traversing* the trie (rather than searching it), so that we encounter all words of our text in alphabetic order, and, at the same time scanning the dictionary sequentially, each time comparing a word in the trie with a word in the dictionary.

There is another aspect of tries that deserves our attention, namely that a trie is a very suitable means to search for all words with a given prefix. For example, we may want to enter *COM* to obtain a list of words beginning with this prefix, such as

COMMAND, COMPILER, COMPUTE, COMPUTER, COMPUTING

As a final remark, it should be mentioned that we can implement a trie on disk rather than in memory, as we did for B-trees in Section 6.3. This will slow down the search process considerably, but, provided that it is still fast enough for our application, we may benefit from this method because of the large capacity of disks. Another favorable point is the permanent nature of disk files, compared with data in main memory.

Exercises

7.1 In the tries in this chapter, we used arrays of 27 pointer members because we distinguished only the 26 capital letters. If, instead, we have to distinguish all printable ASCII characters, we had better use linked lists instead of those arrays. Write a demonstration program for such a trie.

7.2 Write a demonstration program which manipulates a trie on disk.

7.3 Write an extension to program TRIE.C in Section 7.2, to delete words of a trie.

7.4 Write a program to traverse a trie, printing all words stored in it in alphabetic order.

7.5 Investigate the various ways of constructing a spelling checker by means of a trie, as suggested near the end of this chapter. Examine analytically how running time will depend on:

(a) the size of the text to be checked,
(b) the number of distinct words in this text,
(c) the size of the dictionary.

Choose the method that seems best for your purposes and write a program for it.

7.6 Write a program to find all words in a trie which have a given prefix.

8

Graphs

8.1 Directed and Undirected Graphs

The term *graph* is used for a set of *vertices* (or *nodes*), along with a set of *edges*, each of which connects a pair of vertices. We may consider each edge between two vertices i and j to be the ordered pair i, j, and we then say that we have a *directed* graph. Alternatively, we can use only unordered pairs (i, j), in which case we are dealing with an *undirected* graph. We have in fact been dealing with directed graphs for a long time, since linked lists and trees are special cases of them. In a directed graph, we usually represent each edge $<i, j>$ by an arrow, pointing from i to j. Obviously, for two distinct vertices i and j, the pairs $<i, j>$ and $<j, i>$ represent two distinct edges. In an undirected graph, the pairs (i, j) and (j, i) are two different notations for the same edge. Incidentally, we can regard an undirected graph as a directed graph in which each

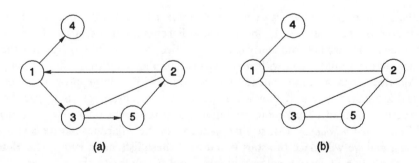

Fig. 8.1. (a) Directed graph; (b) undirected graph

edge $<i, j>$ is accompanied by an edge $<j, i>$; the notation (i, j) then represents this pair of edges. In Fig. 8.1(a) we have a directed graph, with vertices labelled 1, 2, 3, 4, 5 and edges $<1, 3>$, $<1, 4>$, $<3, 5>$, $<5, 2>$, $<2, 3>$, $<2, 1>$. Figure 8.1(b) shows an undirected graph. A network of pipes through which water can flow in one direction is an example of a directed graph; the pipes are then drawn as arrows and the points of connection as vertices. If in each pipe the water can flow in both directions, we have an undirected graph.

Graph theory is an extensive branch of mathematics with many interesting theorems and useful applications. Also, there are good books on data structures, including those by Horowitz & Sahni (1977) and Aho, Hopcroft & Ullman (1983), which discuss internal representations of graphs and associated algorithms. Since in the present book we focus on programming in the C language, we will select one application of graphs, and work this out in a complete, efficient and possibly useful program. It is about *project planning* by means of a directed graph, also called an *activity network*. But let us first see how we can represent directed graphs internally. From now on, we will use the term *graph* for what actually is a directed graph.

8.2 Graph Representations

An elegant but rather expensive means of representing a graph is a so-called *adjacency matrix*. For a graph with n vertices, numbered 1, 2, ..., n, the corresponding adjacency matrix has n rows and n columns. If $<i, j>$ is an edge in the graph, the matrix element on the ith row and the jth column is 1, otherwise it is 0. For example, the adjacency matrix for the graph of Fig. 8.1(a) is

$$\begin{pmatrix} 0 & 0 & 1 & 1 & 0 \\ 1 & 0 & 1 & 0 & 0 \\ 0 & 0 & 0 & 0 & 1 \\ 0 & 0 & 0 & 0 & 0 \\ 0 & 1 & 0 & 0 & 0 \end{pmatrix}$$

Since the given graph contains an edge from vertex 1 to vertex 3, the third element in the first row of the matrix is 1, and so on. Adjacency matrices in the form of two-dimensional arrays are not frequently used in practice, because for large graphs they use too much memory space, and with many algorithms they lead to quadratic computing time. Matrices such as those under consideration, with a large proportion of zero elements, are called *sparse*. If they are large, it may be advantageous to use dynamic data structures instead of two-dimensional arrays to represent them. Here we will use linked lists, called *adjacency lists*, so that each row of the adjacency matrix corresponds to one list, and we will place the start pointers of these lists in an array. The elements of the lists contain at least a column number and a pointer to the next list element. Figure 8.2 shows such adjacency lists for the graph of Fig. 8.1(a).

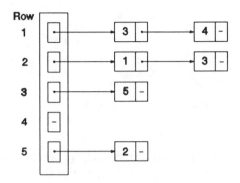

Fig. 8.2. Adjacency lists for the graph of Fig. 8.1(a)

Each element in an adjacency list represents in fact an edge. Adjacency lists such as those shown in Fig. 8.2 are an excellent means to find all immediate *successors* of a given vertex. For example, we find the edges <1, 3> and <1, 4> by traversing the first linked list. However, these lists do not provide an efficient way of finding all immediate *predecessors* of a given vertex. If, for example, we want to find all immediate predecessors of vertex 2, we would have to scan all linked lists, to find the number 2 in the final one, as the only immediate successor of vertex 5. To find predecessors, we had better use *inverted* adjacency lists. These contain the vertex numbers of immediate predecessors instead of immediate successors; all immediate predecessors of vertex 1 are in the first list, and so on. We will use inverted adjacency lists in Section 8.4.

8.3 Topological Sorting; Detecting Cycles

In Fig. 8.1(a), the edges <2, 3>, <3, 5>, <5, 2> form a *cycle*: if we start at vertex 2 and we follow these three edges, we arrive at vertex 2 again. In many applications we have to deal only with so-called *acyclic graphs*, which have no cycles. With an acyclic graph, we can write all its vertex numbers in a sequence, in such a way that for any edge <*i, j*> vertex number *i* precedes vertex number *j* in this sequence. Such a sequence is called a *topological order*. Note that there may be several topological orders for the same graph. For example, each of the sequences

    1, 2, 3, 4

and

    1, 3, 2, 4

is a topological order for the graph shown in Fig. 8.3 (and there are no others for this graph).

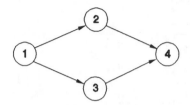

Fig. 8.3. An acyclic graph that has two topological orders

Although a graph may have many topological orders, we normally want only one. As a preparation for the next sections, we will now develop a program which may be applied to any (directed) graph; it will detect the occurrence of cycles, if any, and it will produce a topological order of the vertex numbers if the graph is acyclic. We will use adjacency lists similar to Fig. 8.2, with one extension. We will use an array **a**, whose elements are structures, each containing both a pointer **a[i].link**, pointing to an adjacency list, and an integer member **a[i].count**. The latter is intended primarily to indicate how many immediate predecessors the vertex corresponding to that array element has. That integer is called the *in-degree* of the vertex in question. Figure 8.4 shows array **a** and the adjacency lists for the graph of Fig. 8.3. The integers that denote in-degrees are surrounded by parentheses, to distinguish them from vertex numbers.

So far, we have hardly paid any attention to the way our vertices are numbered. If, for each edge $<i, j>$, we required number i to be less than number j, our task would be very simple. First, this condition would exclude the possibility of cycles, and second, we would obtain a topological order simply by sorting all vertex numbers. However, we will not impose that requirement on our vertex numbering, because in practical applications alterations may be necessary, and the requirement $i < j$ might force us to renumber a great many vertices if we had to insert one somewhere in the middle of the graph. Our vertex numbering will be almost completely free, the only restriction being that the range of numbers used should not be too large for the amount of memory that is available. After all, the range of these numbers will be the range of our subscripts and, depending on our computer system, we have to reckon with certain limitations with respect to the maximum array size. Instead of a normal array, we will use a pointer,

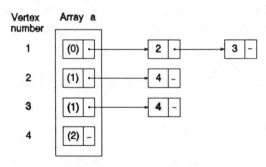

Fig. 8.4. Adjacency lists for the graph of Fig. 8.3.

pointing to some allocated area of memory which is just as large as we need. Thus, we again benefit from the well-known equivalence of arrays and pointers in the C language. Although we think in terms of array **a**, the variable **a** is actually a pointer, declared in:

```
typedef struct Edge {int num; struct Edge *next;} edge;
typedef struct {int count; edge *link;} vertex;
...
vertex *a;
```

Let us denote the user's vertex numbers by capital letters I and J. We will read them from a file, which enables us to scan them more than once. We first determine the smallest and the greatest values (*minimum* and *maximum*) of all given vertex numbers. After this first scan, we compute

$$n = maximum - minimum + 1$$

which is the number of array elements that we will allocate. Internally, we then use vertex numbers i, j, related to I, J as follows:

$$i = I - minimum$$
$$j = J - minimum$$

The smallest and the greatest internal vertex numbers are now 0 and $n - 1$, respectively. (Of course, in the output we reconstruct the user's vertex numbers I and J again by adding *minimum* to i and j.) For example, for the graph of Fig. 8.5 we have:

$$minimum = 100$$
$$maximum = 130$$
$$n = 31$$

so the internal vertex numbers are 0, 10, 20, 30, and we allocate memory for **a[0]**, **a[1]**, ..., **a[30]**. Since a subset of the reserved array elements **a[0]**, ..., **a[n−1]** may not be used, we will mark those elements by a code. Now we realize that each count member

a[i].count

is primarily intended for the in-degree of vertex i, as mentioned above, and, as such, can have only a nonnegative value. This opens the possibility to store a negative value in these members as a code indicating the absence of vertex i in the graph. Let us use the symbolic constant **ABSENT** = −2 for this code (−1 having a different meaning, as we will see shortly). Thus, in the above example, all count members except those of **a[0]**, **a[10]**, **a[20]**, and **a[30]**, are equal to **ABSENT**.

As for the topological order we want, we begin with all vertices with zero count members. This means that these vertices have zero in-degree, that is, they have no predecessors, so they are to come first in a topological order. Our algorithm works as

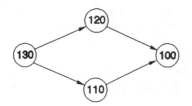

Fig. 8.5. Graph with large vertex numbers

follows. We begin by replacing these zero count members with subscript values, in such a way that the array elements for all vertices without predecessors form a linked list (to be distinguished from the adjacency lists). This linked list does not require any additional memory space allocated by **malloc**, but, instead, we use elements of array **a** as nodes. The subscript values stored in their count members act as 'pointers'. An integer variable **start** is the start pointer of the list. At the end of the list we use the value **NIL** = −1 instead of **NULL**. For example, if we have

```
start = 34
a[34].count = 87
a[87].count = 22
a[22].count = NIL
```

then the vertices 34, 87, 22 have no predecessors. Note that our algorithm is destructive, since we actually alter the count members. We even go a step further and gradually reduce the graph, each time deleting vertices that have no predecessors, until, in an acyclic graph, there are no vertices left. If, in this way, we do not get rid of all vertices, that is, if at some moment there are still vertices in the graph but each of them has at least one predecessor, then the graph has a cycle. The list of vertices with no predecessors will be used as a linked stack: insertions and deletions occur only at the head of the list. This stack will grow and shrink all the time; when we are deleting a vertex, we place all its immediate successors on the stack, since these successors will be vertices without a predecessor after that deletion. Our program, TOPOL.C, reads a file containing number pairs $<I, J>$ for each edge of the graph. Its output consists of either all vertex numbers in a topological order or a message saying that there is a cycle.

```
/* TOPOL.C: Topological sorting; the presence of any
            cycles will be detected.
*/
#include <stdio.h>
#include <stdlib.h>

typedef struct Edge {int num; struct Edge *next;} edge;
typedef struct {int count; edge *link;} vertex;
#define STRUCTSIZE sizeof(vertex) /* = sizeof(edge) */
```

```
#define NIL (-1)
#define ABSENT (-2)

void error(char *str)
{ printf("Error: %s\n", str); exit(1);
}

main()
{  FILE *fp;
   char filnam[51];
   int n, i, j, k, I, J, start, first=1, minim, maxim,
      min1, max1;
    vertex *a;
    edge *p;
   printf("Input file: "); scanf("%50s", filnam);
   fp = fopen(filnam, "r");
   if (fp == NULL) error("File not available");

   /* Determine minimum and maximum vertex numbers: */
   while (fscanf(fp, "%d %d", &I, &J) == 2)
   {  if (I < J) {min1 = I; max1 = J;}
            else {min1 = J; max1 = I;}
      if (first)
      {  minim = min1; maxim = max1; first = 0;
      }  else
      {  if (min1 < minim) minim = min1;
         if (max1 > maxim) maxim = max1;
      }
   }
   fclose(fp);

   /* Build adjacency lists: */
   n = maxim - minim + 1;
   a = (vertex *)malloc(n * STRUCTSIZE);
   if (a == NULL) error("Vertex-number range too large");
   for (i=0; i<n; i++)
   {  a[i].count = ABSENT; a[i].link = NULL;
   }
   fp = fopen(filnam, "r");
   while (fscanf(fp, "%d %d", &I, &J) == 2)
   {  i = I - minim; j = J - minim;
      if (a[i].count == ABSENT) a[i].count = 0;
      if (a[j].count == ABSENT) a[j].count = 0;
      p = (edge *)malloc(STRUCTSIZE);
```

```
      if (p == NULL) error("Not enough memory");
      p->num = j; p->next = a[i].link;
      a[i].link = p;
      a[j].count++;
   }
   fclose(fp);

   /* Form a linked stack of nodes that have no
      predecessor:
   */
   start = NIL;
   for (i=0; i<n; i++)
   if (a[i].count==0) {a[i].count = start; start = i;}

   /* Print vertex numbers in topological order: */
   for (i=0; i<n; i++)
   {  while (a[i].count == ABSENT) i++;
      if (start == NIL) error("There is a cycle");
      /* Take a vertex from the stack, print it,
         and decrease the in-degree of all its
         immediate successors by 1; as soon as the
         updated in-degree of a successor is zero,
         place it on the stack: and dispose of
         the (edge) node in the adjacency list.
      */
      j = start; start = a[j].count;
      J = minim + j;
      printf("%d ", J);
      while ((p = a[j].link) != NULL)
      {  k = p->num;
         a[k].count--;
         if (a[k].count == 0)
         {  a[k].count = start; start = k;
         }
         a[j].link = p->next;
         free(p);
         /* In the adjacency list we have disposed of a node
            that we don't need any longer.
         */
      }
   }
   puts("");
   return 0;
}
```

Note the loop starting with

```
/* Print vertex numbers in topological order: */
for (i=0; i<n; i++)
{  while (a[i].count == ABSENT) i++;
```

As a result of the inner (while) loop, the variable i will have only real vertex numbers as values in the program fragment that follows. However, the vertices are not dealt with in the order of these *i*-values. Instead, we always use the top of the linked stack containing all vertices that have no predecessor. Each time, we unstack the vertex that is to be deleted, but, at the same time, we stack its immediate successors if these, as a consequence of this deletion, no longer have any predecessors. If the linked stack is empty before we have done this *n* times, we have a situation where there are still vertices left each of which has a predecessor, which means that there is a cycle. If our input file contains the four lines

```
120      100
130      110
110      100
130      110
```

which correspond to the graph of Fig. 8.5, we obtain the following topological order as output:

```
130 110 120 110
```

Instead of this extremely simple example, we could have used a very large graph without any problems as to computing time, because the algorithm that we have been using is very efficient. If the graph contains *n* vertices and *e* edges, running time is $O(n + e)$, in other words, it is *linear* in the size of the problem. This is worth mentioning, since there are many graph problems where we can do no better than 'try all possibilities', which normally leads to exponential growth rate.

8.4 Activity Networks; Critical Path Method

An important application of graphs is in project planning and scheduling. Some well-known techniques in this area are *CPM* (Critical Path Method) and *PERT* (Performance Evaluation and Review Technique). A project consists of a number of activities, some of which are related to one another. For example, when we are building a house, it is obvious that the construction of its roof cannot take place until its walls are ready. There are two possibilities to place activities in a graph: we can use either the vertices or the edges for them. Let us choose the edges for this purpose. Besides the vertex pair $<i, j>$ each activity also has a given *duration*, which is an estimate of the time that activity will take, and a *description*, which, technically speaking, is a string of, say, at most 80 characters. In the framework of project planning, we use the terms *activities* and *events* instead of *edges* and *vertices*, respectively. Figure 8.6 shows an *activity network*, for a simple project. Two components A and B are involved in manufacturing a certain product; we have only to place an order to obtain component A, but it is estimated that the article will be delivered as many as 50 days after the order has gone out. Things are more complex for component B. We have to build it ourselves, which takes 20 days. Then we have to test it (25 days) and to correct the errors (15 days). Also, we have to write a user's guide (60 days), but for some reason the person who is to do this can start writing only after B has been built.

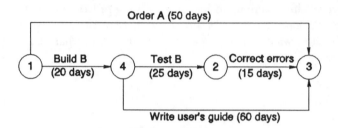

Fig. 8.6. An activity network

Events 1 and 3 denote the start and the completion of the entire project, respectively. Note that this network includes two activities $<i, j>$ for which i is greater than j. Some time ago, there were real CPM programs that admitted only activities $<i, j>$ for which i is less than j. This restriction would exclude any cycles; it would make the task of obtaining a topological order extremely easy and would therefore simplify our program considerably. Instead, we will allow vertices to be numbered freely, but it is nevertheless a good idea from the planner's point of view to begin with a network with $i < j$ for all activities $<i, j>$, so the network shown in Fig. 8.6 is not a good example for project managers. However, when activities are to be inserted in a complex network, the user of a more tolerant program like ours will appreciate that he need not worry about vertex numbers. Incidentally, the danger of introducing cycles should not be exaggerated: they can also be avoided simply by drawing all activities as arrows pointing more or less from left to right, as is usual in practice. If, in spite of this good advice, cycles should occur, then our program will detect them. (It would not be fair if we, as programmers, imposed the restriction $i < j$ on all activities $<i, j>$, using the argument about cycles as a pretext for our inability to solve an interesting programming problem!)

If all activities start as soon as possible, each event i occurs at its *earliest event* time, $ee(i)$. In our example, we have:

$ee(1) = 0$
$ee(2) = 45$
$ee(3) = 80$
$ee(4) = 20$

Note that even for this very simple project we have to be careful. We cannot take just any path from event 1 to event 3, but we have to find the longest path, or, as we say, the *critical path*, which consists of the activities <1, 4> and <4, 3>.

In general, we have $ee(j) = 0$ for all events j that have no predecessors. If event j has one or more predecessors, its earliest event time $ee(j)$ is the maximum value of

$$ee(i) + \text{duration of } <i, j>$$

where all immediate predecessors i of event j are to be considered. To compute these values efficiently, we traverse all events in a topological order (1, 4, 2, 3 in the example), using an algorithm similar to the one on which program TOPOL.C in Section 8.3 was based. We therefore also use similar data structures, that is, array **a** for the events and adjacency lists with a node for each activity, see Fig. 8.7.

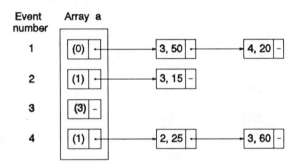

Fig. 8.7. Adjacency lists for the network of Fig. 8.6

For each activity, its duration is stored in its node. (Remember that each activity, that is, each edge in the activity network, uniquely corresponds to a node of an adjacency list.) Again, the parenthesized integers in the array elements **a[i]** denote the in-degree of vertex i, and are called **a[i].count** in the program. Though not included in Fig. 8.7, each element **a[i]** also contains two integer members **a[i].ee** (earliest event) and **a[i].le** (latest event, to be discussed shortly). Initially, all members **ee** are set to zero. We now traverse the events in a topological order, using a linked stack and each time deleting events that have no predecessors. However, we do not destroy the members **ee** and **le** as we are deleting events. When dealing with event i, we update the earliest event times of all its successors j. Using the notation $ee(i)$ as an abbreviation for **a[i].ee**, we test, for each of these successors, to see if the sum

$$ee(i) + \text{duration of } <i, j>$$

is greater than the current value of $ee(j)$, and, if so, we assign that greater value to $ee(j)$. The greatest value of all earliest event times thus computed is the time needed for the entire project.

In the example of Fig. 8.6, we see that the activities $<1, 3>$, $<4, 2>$, $<2, 3>$ do not lie on the critical path $(1, 4, 3)$. It is not absolutely necessary for them to begin as early as possible. For example, the activity $<2, 3>$ may begin as late as 15 days before the completion time (80) of the entire project, so instead of at time $ee(2) = 45$, we may start at time 65, without any danger of delaying the project (provided that all duration times are exact values instead of estimates). Again focusing on the events, rather than on the activities, we can compute their latest event times $le(i)$. The value of $le(i)$ is the minimum value of

$$le(j) - \text{duration of } <i, j>$$

where all immediate successors j of event i are to be considered. We compute the latest event times in a backward scan, which is analogous to the forward scan in which we computed the earliest event times. We therefore need *inverted adjacency lists*, as shown in Fig. 8.8.

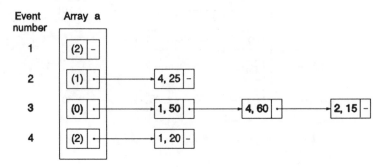

Fig. 8.8. Inverted adjacency lists for the network of Fig. 8.6

We will use the same array **a** as before. The nodes of the old adjacency lists were deleted when we were computing the earliest event times. (Recall that the earliest event times themselves are stored in array **a**, so we did not destroy them when we were deleting the adjacency lists.) We now build the inverted adjacency lists. In the new situation, each array element **a[j]** contains the start pointer of a linked list in which the numbers of all predecessors i of event j are stored. Each node of the list starting at **a[j].link** corresponds to an activity $<i, j>$. A parenthesized integer **a[j].count** denotes the *out-degree* of vertex j, that is, the number of immediate successors of vertex j. Initially, we set all members **le** to the time needed for the entire project, and we form a linked stack of all events that have no successor. Working with this stack in the same way as in the forward scan, we deal with all events in a reverse topological order, and, when dealing with event j, we update the latest event time of all its predecessors i as follows. If the difference

$$le(j) - \text{duration of } <i, j>$$

is less than the current value of $le(i)$ we assign that difference to $le(i)$. After this backward scan, we have computed both the earliest event times and the latest event times of all events, and we can find them in array **a**. However, in the program output there is a line for each activity, not for each event. For every activity $<i, j>$, with duration d, we therefore define its *earliest start time* $EST(i, j)$, its *earliest completion time* $ECT(i, j)$, its *latest start time* $LST(i, j)$, and its *latest completion time* $LCT(i, j)$ as follows:

$$EST(i, j) = ee(i)$$
$$ECT(i, j) = ee(i) + d$$
$$LST(i, j) = le(j) - d$$
$$LCT(i, j) = le(j)$$

The meanings of these quantities are as their names indicate. For example, *LST* denotes the latest time the activity may start without delaying the completion time of the entire project. If, for some activity, the earliest start time is equal to the latest start time, then that activity is said to lie on a *critical path*. We also define the *(free) slack* as

$$SLACK(i, j) = LST(i, j) - EST(i, j)$$

Thus, any activity on a critical path has zero slack. Note that we may instead define

$$SLACK(i, j) = LCT(i, j) - ECT(i, j),$$

since we have

$$LST(i, j) - EST(i, j) = \{le(j) - d\} - ee(i)$$
$$LCT(i, j) - ECT(i, j) = le(j) - \{ee(i) + d)\}$$

so both expressions for $SLACK(i, j)$ are equivalent.

We now want to write a program to compute all these quantities for a given project. For each activity of a project, we will read the two relevant event numbers, the duration and a description, from a file. For example, this file may have the following contents for the network shown in Fig. 8.6:

```
1   3     50 Place order A
1   4     20 Build B
4   2     25 Test B
2   3     15 Correct
4   3     60 User's guide
```

With this data in some file, we want the program to inquire the name of this file and then to produce the following output:

I	J	DUR	EST	LST	ECT	LCT	SLACK		DESCRIPTION
1	3	50	0	30	50	80	30		Place order A
1	4	20	0	0	20	20	0	<--	Build B
4	2	25	20	40	45	65	20		Test B
2	3	15	45	65	60	80	20		Correct
4	3	60	20	20	80	80	0	<--	User's guide

Lines with an arrow pointing to a slack value 0 denote activities lying on a critical path. The order in which the activities are listed is based on the input file. We read this file in a third scan (after the two scans for the computation of *ee* and *le*), and we copy each line, together with the computed items found in array **a**. In this way, we need not store all descriptions in main memory: in the first and the second scans we simply skip them, and in the third scan we print each description immediately after reading it, which in the case of a large project saves a good deal of memory space. In real critical path programs we can usually specify the order in which the output lines are to be printed. For example, we may want them to appear with the slack in ascending order. After our discussion of some sorting methods in Chapter 2, this should not be a difficult problem. The above output has actually been produced by program CPM.C, listed below.

```
/* CPM.C: Critical Path Method.
           The program asks for an input file, containing
           a line for each activity with two (integer)
           event numbers, a duration (integer), and an
           optional description. The range of the event
           numbers influences the amount of memory needed.
           Apart from this, there are no limitations
           imposed on the number of events or on the way
           they are numbered, nor are there any
           restrictions on the number of activities or on
           their order in the input file, except for memory
           limitations of the machine on which the program
           runs. If the available amount of memory should
           be exceeded, or if the network should contain a
           cycle, the program gives an error message and
           stops.
*/
#include <stdio.h>
#include <stdlib.h>
typedef
struct Activity
    {int num, dur; struct Activity *next;} activity;
typedef struct {int count, ee, le; activity *link;} event;
#define NIL (-1)
```

```
#define ABSENT (-2)

void error(char *str)
{  printf("Error: %s\n", str); exit(1);
}

main()
{  FILE *fp;
   char filnam[51], descript[80];
   int n, i, j, k, I, J, t1, d, start, first=1, minim,
       maxim, min1, max1, tmax=0, est, lst, ect, lct,
       slack;
   event *a;
   activity *p;
   printf("Input file: "); scanf("%50s", filnam);
   fp = fopen(filnam, "r");
   if (fp == NULL) error("File not available");

   /* Determine minimum and maximum event numbers: */
   while (fscanf(fp, "%d %d %d", &I, &J, &d) == 3)
   {  fgets(descript, 80, fp); /* Skip text, if any */
      if (I < J) {min1 = I; max1 = J;}
           else {min1 = J; max1 = I;}
      if (first)
      {  minim = min1; maxim = max1; first = 0;
      } else
      {  if (min1 < minim) minim = min1;
         if (max1 > maxim) maxim = max1;
      }
   }
   fclose(fp);
   n = maxim - minim + 1;
   a = (event *)malloc(n * sizeof(event));
   if (a == NULL) error("Event number range too large");
   for (i=0; i<n; i++)
   {  a[i].count = ABSENT; a[i].ee = 0;
      a[i].link = NULL;
   }

   /* Build adjacency lists: */
   fp = fopen(filnam, "r");
   while (fscanf(fp, "%d %d %d", &I, &J, &d) == 3)
   {  fgets(descript, 80, fp); /* Skip text, if any */
      i = I - minim; j = J - minim;
```

```
        if (a[i].count == ABSENT) a[i].count = 0;
        if (a[j].count == ABSENT) a[j].count = 0;
        p =
        (activity *)malloc(sizeof(activity));
        if (p == NULL) error("Not enough memory");
        p->num = j; p->dur = d; p->next = a[i].link;
        a[i].link = p;
        a[j].count++;
    }
    fclose(fp);

/*  Form a linked stack of events that have no
    predecessors:
*/
    start = NIL;
    for (i=0; i<n; i++)
        if (a[i].count==0)
        { a[i].count = start; start = i;
        }

/* Compute earliest event time (ee) for each node: */
    for (i=0; i<n; i++)
    {  while (a[i].count == ABSENT) i++;
        if (start == NIL) error("There is a cycle");
        j = start; start = a[j].count;
        while ((p = a[j].link) != NULL)
        {  k = p->num;
            a[k].count--;
            t1 = a[j].ee + p->dur;
            if (t1 > a[k].ee) a[k].ee = t1;
            if (t1 > tmax) tmax = t1;
            if (a[k].count == 0)
            {  a[k].count = start; start = k;
            }
            a[j].link = p->next;
            free(p);
        }
    }

/* Build inverted adjacency lists: */
    for (j=0; j<n; j++)
        if (a[j].count != ABSENT)
        { a[j].le = tmax; a[j].count = 0; a[j].link = NULL;
        }
```

```
fp = fopen(filnam, "r");
while (fscanf(fp, "%d %d %d", &I, &J, &d) == 3)
{  fgets(descript, 80, fp); /* Skip text, if any */
   i = I - minim; j = J - minim;
   p = (activity *)malloc(sizeof(activity));
   if (p == NULL) error("Not enough memory");
   p->num = i; p->dur = d; p->next = a[j].link;
   a[j].link = p;
   a[i].count++;
}
fclose(fp);

/*  Form a linked stack of nodes that have no
    successors:
*/
start = NIL;
for (j=0; j<n; j++)
   if (a[j].count == 0)
   {  a[j].count = start; start = j;
   }
/* Compute latest event time (le) for each node: */
for (j=0; j<n; j++)
{  while (a[j].count == ABSENT) i++;
   i = start; start = a[i].count;
   while ((p = a[i].link) != NULL)
   {  k = p->num; a[k].count--;
      t1 = a[i].le - p->dur;
      if (t1 < a[k].le) a[k].le = t1;
      if (a[k].count == 0)
      {  a[k].count = start; start = k;
      }
      a[i].link = p->next;
      free(p);
   }
}

puts("Output:\n\n\n");
printf("%3s %3s %4s %5s %4s %5s %4s  %s\n\n",
 "I", "J", "DUR", "EST", "LST", "ECT", "LCT",
 "SLACK     DESCRIPTION");
fp = fopen(filnam, "r");
while (fscanf(fp, "%d %d %d", &I, &J, &d) == 3)
{  fgets(descript, 80, fp); /* Read text, if any */
   i = I - minim; j = J - minim;
```

```
        est = a[i].ee; lct = a[j].le;
        ect = est + d; lst = lct - d; slack = lst - est;
        printf("%3d %3d %4d %5d %4d %5d %4d %5d %3s %s",
               I, J, d, est, lst, ect, lct, slack,
               slack ? "    " :  "<--", descript);
    }
    return 0;
}
```

Exercises

8.1 If we require i to be less than j for all edges $<i, j>$ in a directed graph, then the graph will have no cycles and we can easily find a topological order of all vertices. Write a program to demonstrate this. Do not use adjacency lists or an adjacency matrix.

8.2 Write a simple CPM program in the spirit of Exercise 1, allowing only activities $<i, j>$ with $i < j$.

8.3 Replace the tabular output of program CPM.C with graphical output in the form of line segments for the activities, each having a length proportional to its duration, and placed in its proper position based on a horizontal time axis.

8.4 Extend program CPM.C, so that, in case of a cycle, the vertex numbers of the cycle are printed.

8.5 Write a program which, for any directed graph, lists all vertices that are (not necessarily immediate) successors of a given vertex. The input data for this program consists of a file with a pair $<i, j>$ for each edge, as shown at the end of Section 8.3, along with a number entered on the keyboard, denoting the vertex whose successors are desired.

9

Fundamentals of Interpreters and Compilers

This chapter deals with a well-defined infinite set of character strings that represent arithmetic expressions. In formal language theory such a set of strings (not necessarily consisting of arithmetic expressions) is called a *language*, so this word has a special technical meaning, to be distinguished from what we call a 'language' in everyday life. Whether or not a given string belongs to the language in question is determined by certain formation rules, also called *grammar* or *syntax rules*. For example, the C language can be defined as the set of all possible C programs. In this case, and for programming languages in general, there are also *semantic rules*, which define the actions to be performed when the programs are executed. We will define the Very Simple Language VSL. This is not just a language in the sense of formal language theory, but each element of the language is a simple arithmetic expression with a very clear meaning, namely a computation in accordance with elementary arithmetic and resulting in an integer. Although it may be a bit pretentious, we will talk about VSL *programs*. Our goal will be to *implement* this new language, or, as we may say, we are interested in VSL *implementations*. As may be expected in this book, we will present such implementations in the form of C programs. Depending on how they work, we call these C programs either *interpreters* or *compilers*.

The present chapter is included in this book for two reasons. First, as we use real interpreters and compilers quite often, it is good to have some idea about how they work, and basic principles are always best explained by simple examples, hence our Very Simple Language. Second, there are computer applications where the user can enter some arithmetic expression, so that the program can read this character by character and subsequently either interpret it or convert it to some internal format. This chapter will be helpful in developing programs for such applications.

9.1 Syntax Diagrams for a Very Simple Language

The language that we will be dealing with consists of VSL programs. Here are three examples:

```
{3 - 5}
{1 - 2 * ((9 - 5 + 1 - 2 * 3) - 2)}
{8}
```

A VSL program is written as an *expression*, as defined below, surrounded by a pair of braces { }. An expression consists of one or more *terms* separated by addition and subtraction operators (+ and −). Similarly, each term consists of one or more *factors*, separated by multiplication operators (*). Finally, each factor consists of either a one-digit integer or an expression surrounded by parentheses. A verbal description like this would do for VSL, but not for a real programming language. We therefore normally use a more formal means for syntactic definitions, such as a set of *syntax diagrams*. Fig. 9.1 shows syntax diagrams for VSL. (It will be clear that in the last diagram the three dots denote the remaining seven digits 2, 3, 4, 5, 6, 7, 8.) The first diagram says that a program consists of three components, namely an open brace ({), an expression, and a close brace (}), in that order. In these syntax diagrams, symbols in circles, such as { in

are *primitive* or *terminal symbols*: they may occur literally in a program, whereas names such as *expression* in

Expression

denote *syntactic categories*, also known as *nonterminal symbols*. In a complete set of syntax diagrams (such as Fig. 9.1), there is a syntax diagram for every nonterminal symbol that is used.

A VSL program can be quite complex, as shown by the following example, consisting of two lines:

```
{((1 + 8 * (9 - 1) * 5 - (2 + (3 * 4))) *
(7 - (3 - 1)) + 1) * 2}
```

In spite of this, the syntactic description of VSL is very simple. This is because our syntax diagrams are *recursive*; indirectly, we define an expression in terms of itself, since an expression contains a term, a term contains a factor, and a factor may again contain an expression. It is therefore quite natural to use recursive functions when we are writing a program to process expressions, as the next section will show.

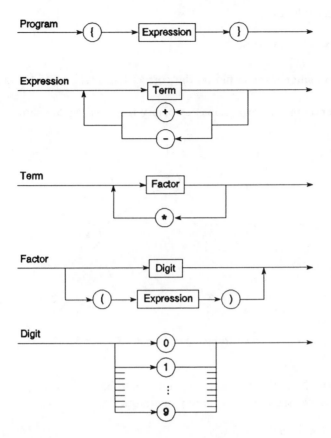

Fig. 9.1. Syntax diagrams for VSL

We have not explicitly discussed any precedence rules for the three operators +, −, *, but the above syntactic descriptions, both in words and in syntax diagrams, clearly suggest that * has higher precedence than + and −. After all, a term is composed of factors, not the other way round. For example, since each of two lines

    2 * 4 * 1
    7 * 5

denote a term and because terms are separated by + and −, the line

    2 * 4 * 1 + 7 * 5

represents an expression consisting of two terms separated by +. This makes it clear that this expression is to be read as

    (2 * 4 * 1) + (7 * 5)

and not, for example, as

    (2 * 4 * 1 + 7) * 5

Incidentally, the latter form would be the correct interpretation if * and + had equal precedence.

We can represent our expressions as binary trees, as Fig. 9.2 shows.

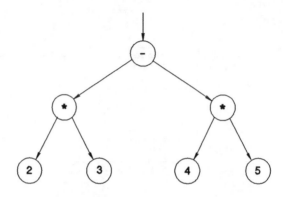

*Fig. 9.2. Binary tree for 2 * 3 – 4 * 5*

This tree clearly shows that the minus operator is to be applied to the terms 2 * 3 and 4 * 5. Note that we are using only *binary* operators, so

    {2 * 3 – 4 * 5}

must not be written

    {–4 * 5 + 2 * 3}

because we do not implement the *unary* operator –, used in the last line. Another point worth observing is that our operators are *left-associative*. This is relevant for operators with the same precedence, as + and – in our language VSL. For example, the expression

    9 – 3 + 1

means

    (9 – 3) + 1

and not

    9 – (3 + 1)

We can see the difference between the second and the third of these three expressions very clearly by examining their binary trees. Since **9 − 3 + 1** and **(9 − 3) + 1** have exactly the same meaning, they correspond to the same binary tree, shown in Fig. 9.3(a). The tree for the expression **9 − (3 + 1)** is different, as Fig. 9.3(b) shows.

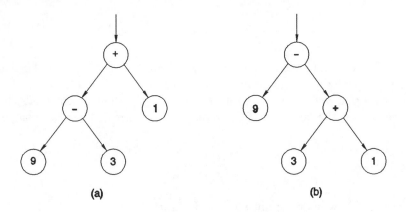

(a)   (b)

Fig. 9.3. Binary trees for: (a) 9 − 3 + 1; (b) 9 − (3 + 1)

9.2 A Source-text Interpreter

When designing a programming language, we have to define it not only *syntactically*, but also *semantically*, that is, each valid language construct must be given a *meaning* in terms of the operations to be performed. In our case, the language is so simple that the meaning of VSL programs can be expressed in few words. We want the given expression to be evaluated according to the usual arithmetic rules and the resulting integer to be printed. For example, the program

```
{9 − 2 * 4}
```

means that the product of 2 and 4 is to be subtracted from 9 and that the resulting value, 1, is to be printed.

In this section, we will write a C program which accepts any VSL program and performs the actions prescribed by it, so with the VSL program **{9 − 2 * 4}** as input, the output of our C program will be **1**. We will call this C program an *interpreter*, and, more specifically, a *source-text* interpreter. The term *source text* is used here for VSL programs to distinguish them from any code derived from them, as we will discuss after this section.

Our method of analyzing source text is known as *recursive descent*, because it is based on a hierarchy of recursive functions. In principle, there is a function for each syntactic category, such as *factor*. Each of these functions has a well-defined task, which can be expressed in terms of its input data and its return value. For example, each time the function **factor** is called, it reads one factor, which may be a simple or a more complex one, such as these two examples:

```
5
(3 - 4 * 5 - (3 + 6 * 2))
```

(Note that, according to Section 9.1, there would not be a factor on the last line if the outer pair of parentheses were omitted.) Not only does function **factor** *read* a factor; it also *evaluates* it and returns its (integer) value. For example, if it reads the factor consisting of only the character **'5'**, it returns the integer 5, which we compute in C as

```
'5' - '0'
```

In case of the above more complex factor, it returns

$$3 - 20 - 15 = -32$$

Although each integer in VSL consists of only one character, the output can be any integer, such as -32 in the last example. If the input is incorrect, we will print an error message and stop program execution. Blanks and newline characters will be allowed in the input, which enables us to write VSL programs on more than one line. When reading characters, it is sometimes convenient to look one character ahead, or, equivalently, to push one character back into the input stream. In C we normally do this by using **ungetc**. Our approach will be slightly different because each time we read a character (using **getc**) we will also display it (using **putc**), and we must prevent the same character from being displayed twice. Instead of **ungetc**, we will therefore use a global variable **buf** as a character buffer of our own. The advantage of this is that we can initially set it to zero, and use its contents only if it is nonzero. In this way, **getc** reads each character only once, so that it will not be duplicated in the output.

Logically, function **next** reads the next character; physically, it reads that character from the input file (using **getc**) only if the variable **buf** is zero. If this variable is nonzero, its value is taken instead, and it is set to zero. There is also function **nextis**, which we use to examine whether a given character can be read from the input stream. If this is the case, **nextis** reads this character and returns 1; if not, it returns 0. This is implemented by reading a character and placing it back into **buf** if it is not identical with the given character. This way of reading characters conditionally is very convenient in programs that analyze their input character by character. For example, a VSL term consists of one or more factors separated by *, so to read a term we begin by reading a factor; if this is followed by *, another factor must follow, and so on. Our function **term** can therefore be extremely simple:

```
int term(void)
{  int x = factor();
   while (nextis('*')) x *= factor();
   return x;
}
```

Program INTERPR.C shows further details; it should be studied in connection with the
syntax diagrams in Section 9.1.

```
/* INTERPR.C: A source-text interpreter for VSL
*/
#include <stdio.h>
#include <stdlib.h>
#include <ctype.h>

FILE *fp;
int buf=0;

void error(char *str)
{  printf("\nError: %s\n", str); exit(1);
}

int next(void)
{  int ch;
   do
   {  if (buf) {ch = buf; buf = 0;} else
      {  ch = getc(fp);
         if (ch == EOF) error("End of file reached");
         putchar(ch);
      }
   }  while (isspace(ch));
   return ch;
}

int nextis(char chgiven)
{  char ch=next();
   if (ch != chgiven) buf = ch;
   return ch == chgiven;
}

int factor(void)
{  int x, expression(void);
   char ch=next();
   if (isdigit(ch)) x = ch - '0'; else
```

```
      if (ch == '(')
      {  x = expression();
         if (!nextis(')')) error("')' expected");
      } else error("Digit or '(' expected");
      return x;
  }


  int term(void)
  {  int x;
     x = factor();
     while (nextis('*')) x *= factor();
     return x;
  }


  int expression(void)
  {  int x = term();
     for ( ; ; )
     {  if (nextis('+')) x += term(); else
        if (nextis('-')) x -= term(); else break;
     }
     return x;
  }


  main()
  {  char filnam[51];
     int x;
     puts("This program reads an input file, containing");
     puts("a VSL program, such as, for example, {3-2*5}\n");
     printf("Name of input file: ");
     scanf("%50s", filnam);
     fp = fopen(filnam, "r");
     if (fp == NULL) error("File not available");
     puts("\nVSL program read from file:\n");
     if (!nextis('{')) error("Open brace ({) expected");
     x = expression();
     printf("\n\nComputed value: %d\n", x);
     if (!nextis('}')) error("Close brace (}) expected");
     return 0;
  }
```

Program INTERPR.C reads a VSL program from a file prepared by the user, and it also prints each character read from this file, so in the following demonstration we need not list the contents of file *test* separately:

```
This program reads an input file, containing
a VSL program, such as, for example, {3-2*5}

Name of input file: test
VSL program read from file:

{ 2
  + 3 * 4 * (7 - 2 - 1)
  - (1 + 2)
}

Computed value: 47
```

9.3 Conversion from Infix to Postfix

We usually place a binary operator *between* its two operands, as in 8 − 3, for example, and we call this *infix* notation. Instead, we may place the same operator either before or after its operands, and we use the terms *prefix* and *postfix* for these notations. Thus we have:

```
−  8  3    prefix
8  −  3    infix
8  3  −    postfix
```

The usual notation of functions with arguments is essentially prefix notation; for example, if we define the function **subtract** and write

```
subtract(8, 3)
```

to represent the difference 8 − 3 = 5, we can regard the function name **subtract** as an operator, written before its operands 8 and 3. However, in the framework of compiler construction, we are more interested in postfix notation, which, incidentally, is also known as *reverse Polish*. Postfix expressions can be evaluated very straightforwardly, as Section 9.4 will show. For the time being, let us assume that they are useful, so that it makes sense to perform automatic conversion from infix to postfix. If an infix expression is represented by a binary tree, as shown in Figs. 9.2 and 9.3, we can find the corresponding postfix expression by traversing this tree (and its subtrees) as follows:

1. Traverse the left subtree.
2. Traverse the right subtree.
3. Use the root node of the (sub-)tree.

Applying this to the left and the right subtrees in Fig. 9.2, we obtain 2 3 * and 4 5 *, respectively. For the entire tree, we find the postfix expression

    2   3   *   4   5   *   −

Note that we do not need any parentheses in postfix notation. For example, Figs. 9.3(a) and 9.3(b) lead to:

Infix	*Postfix*
9 − 3 − 1	9 3 − 1 −
9 − (3 − 1)	9 3 1 − −

Fortunately, it will not be necessary to build a real binary tree because we do not need all information in the tree at the same time. However, we will use recursion, which is closely related to trees, as we have seen in Section 1.5. The basic idea of our method is quite simple. Let us focus on a term, which has infix form

$$f_1 * f_2 * f_3 * \ldots * f_n$$

where $f_1, \ldots, f_n$ are factors. To transform this into postfix, all we need is a function (to be called **term**) which reads this from an input file and writes the desired form

$$f_1 \, f_2 * f_3 * \ldots f_n *$$

to an output file. So first we have to copy factor f_1, which is always present. If an asterisk follows, we read it, but we postpone writing it until we have copied f_2; in other words, we read * f_2 and write f_2 *. Similarly, if an asterisk follows, both * and f_3 are read in that order and written in the reverse order, and so on. Using function **nextis** in the same way as in program INTERPR.C (see Section 9.2) and file pointer **fpout** for the output file, we can write this function **term** as follows:

```
void term(void)
{   factor();
    while (nextis('*'))
    {   factor(); putc('*', fpout);
    }
}
```

This function really does what we have said above, provided that function **factor**, used here, performs its copying task properly. If the factor to be copied is a only a digit, it is to be copied literally. For example, if the input is

    3 * 8

then the digit 3 is copied by the first call of **factor**, before the while-loop is entered. In the inner part of the loop, there is another call of **factor**, which copies 8. The important point to be noticed is that the asterisk is read before copying 8, but is written after it, so that the output is

    3 8 *

In case of more complex factors, they must not be copied literally, but, instead, they must in turn be converted from infix to postfix. For example, if one of these factors is read as

    (9 – 5)

it is to be written as

    9 5 –

So we do not write the parentheses in the output, and we deal with the remaining infix expression 9 – 5 in a way that is similar to the way we would deal with 9 * 5. Program POSTFIX.C shows further details.

```
/* POSTFIX.C:
        Conversion from infix to postfix; the program
        reads a VSL program, which has the form

           { expression }

        The given expression is converted to postfix, and
        written to another file. The names of both files
        are to be supplied by the user.
*/
#include <stdio.h>
#include <stdlib.h>
#include <ctype.h>

FILE *fpin, *fpout;
char buf;

void error(char *str)
{  printf("\nError: %s\n", str);
   exit(1);
}
```

```
int next(void)
{   int ch;
    do
    {   if (buf) {ch = buf; buf = 0;} else
        {   ch = getc(fpin);
            if (ch == EOF) error("End of file reached");
            putchar(ch);
        }
    }  while (isspace(ch));
    return ch;
}


int nextis(char chgiven)
{   char ch=next();
    if (ch != chgiven) buf = ch;
    return ch == chgiven;
}


void factor(void)
{   void expression(void);
    char ch=next();
    if (isdigit(ch)) putc(ch, fpout); else
    if (ch == '(')
    {   expression();
        if (!nextis(')')) error("')' expected");
    }  else error("Digit or '(' expected");
}


void term(void)
{   factor();
    while (nextis('*'))
    {   factor(); putc('*', fpout);
    }
}


void expression(void)
{   term();
    for ( ; ; )
    {   if (nextis('+')) {term(); putc('+', fpout);} else
        if (nextis('-')) {term(); putc('-', fpout);} else
            break;
    }
}
```

```
main()
{   char filnam[51];
    int ch;
    puts("This program reads an input file, containing");
    puts("a VSL program, such as, for example, {3-2*5}\n");
    printf("Name of input file:  ");
    scanf("%50s", filnam);
    fpin = fopen(filnam, "r");
    if (fpin == NULL) error("File not available");
    printf("Name of output file: ");
    scanf("%50s", filnam);
    fpout = fopen(filnam, "w");
    if (fpout == NULL) error("Cannot open output file");
    puts("\nVSL program read from file:\n");
    if (!nextis('{')) error("Open brace ({) expected");
    expression();   /* This call does most of the work! */
    if (!nextis('}')) error("Close brace (}) expected");
    fclose(fpin);
    fclose(fpout);
    puts("\n\nContents of output file (postfix):");
    fpout = fopen(filnam, "r");
    while (ch = getc(fpout), ch > 0) putchar(ch);
    return 0;
}
```

The results are first placed in an output file, which we will use in Section 9.4. Then they are copied to the screen, so that we can immediately see what the result is. There are only digits and operators in the output file, no white-space characters. This causes no ambiguity at all because all integers in VSL consist of only one digit. Thus, in the following demonstration, 34 stands for the two integers 3 and 4:

```
This program reads an input file, containing
a VSL program, such as, for example, {3-2*5}

Name of input file:  infix.txt
Name of output file: postfix.txt
VSL program read from file:

{ 3 * 4 - 5 * 6
  - 7 * (4 + 2 + 2)
}

Contents of output file (postfix):
34*56*-742+2+*-
```

9.4 A Postfix Interpreter

It is now time to see why postfix expressions are useful. In Section 9.3, we did not compute the integer values associated with the given infix expressions. Instead, we produced postfix expressions, and these might seem to be of little use if we want the integer values, as computed in Section 9.2. We will now discuss how to evaluate postfix expressions, and we will see that this can be done extremely simply. The main tool to be used is a *stack*. Scanning a given postfix expression from left to right, we place each operand on this stack, so that each time the stack height increases by 1. Whenever, during this scan, we encounter an operator, we apply the corresponding operation to the two most recent operands on the stack, and the result of that operation will replace these two operands, so that the stack height decreases by 1. For example, with the VSL program

```
{5 – 3 – 4 – 7 * 3}
```

as input, program POSTFIX.C gives the postfix expression

```
53–4–73*–
```

as output, and this gives rise to the successive stack contents shown in Fig. 9.4.

							3		
	3		4			7	7	21	
5	5	2	2	–2	–2	–2	–2	–2	–23

*Fig. 9.4 Successive stack contents, when evaluating 53 – 4 – 73 * –*

In each column, we find the stack elements $s[0]$, $s[1]$, ..., from bottom to top. We begin with $s[0] = 5$, as shown in the first column. Then 3, the second character of the postfix expression, is placed in $s[1]$, as the second column shows. We now encounter the minus operator (–) in the postfix expression, so we compute

5 – 3 = 2

and place the result in $s[0]$ (see the third column) so that it replaces the values 5 and 3. The important thing is that if we proceed in this way, we end with $s[0] = -23$, which is just the value we want as the result of the given VSL program. Thus, if $s[t]$ is the next free stack location, each integer i in the postfix expression will be pushed on the stack as follows:

```
s[t++] = i;
```

Also, each operator +, -, or * performs an operation symbolically denoted by

```
t--;  s[t-1] •= s[t];
```

where the dot (·) denotes one of the above three operators. In every (infix or postfix) expression with only binary operators, the number of operators is one less than the number of operands. For example, in the above expression we have five operands and four operators. Each operand causes the stack pointer **t** to be increased by one and each operator causes it to be decreased by one. Altogether, this means that the final value of **t** is one higher than its initial value. So if initially we have **t** = 0, then we end with **t** = 1. The latter implies that **s[1]** is the next free location, so the result is **s[0]**. We will assume that there is a file with a correct postfix expression, produced by program POSTFIX.C. Then program POSTINT.C is a postfix interpreter, which reads the given file and computes the desired integer result.

```
/* POSTINT.C:
     A postfix interpreter, which interprets the
     postfix expression produced by POSTFIX.C.
*/
#include <stdio.h>
#include <stdlib.h>
#define STACKSIZE 20
int t, s[STACKSIZE]; /*  Initially, t = 0  */

void error(char *str)
{  printf("\n\nError: %s\n", str);
   exit(1);
}

void push(int i)
{  if (t == STACKSIZE)
      error(
      "STACKSIZE too small for this postfix expression");
      s[t++] = i;
}

void add(void)
{  t--; s[t-1] += s[t];
}

void subtract(void)
{  t--; s[t-1] -= s[t];
}
```

```
void multiply(void)
{  t--; s[t-1] *= s[t];
}

main()
{  FILE *fp;
   int ch;
   char filnam[51];
   printf("Name of input file (postfix): ");
   scanf("%50s", filnam);
   fp = fopen(filnam, "r");
   if (fp == NULL) error("File not available");
   puts("The given postfix expression is");
   while (ch = getc(fp), ch > 0)
   {  putchar(ch);
      if (ch >= '0' && ch <= '9') push(ch-'0'); else
      if (ch == '+') add(); else
      if (ch == '-') subtract(); else
      if (ch == '*') multiply(); else break;
   }
   if (t != 1) error("Incorrect postfix expression");
   printf("\nComputed result: %d\n", s[0]);
   return 0;
}
```

Let us use the last example of Section 9.3 to demonstrate this program. Recall that our VSL program was

```
{3 * 4 - 5 * 6 - 7 * (4 + 2 + 2)}
```

so we eventually have to compute:

$$12 - 30 - 7 * 8 = -74$$

Executing program POSTINT.C, and supplying the file *postfix.txt*, produced by program POSTFIX.C on the basis of this example, we obtain this desired result:

```
Name of input file (postfix): postfix.txt
The given postfix expression is
34*56*-742+2+*-
Computed result: -74
```

It will be clear that we can combine the programs POSTFIX.C and POSTINT.C, and it is then not difficult to develop a program that we can use in the same way as

INTERPR.C in Section 9.2. Program INTERPR.C interprets the source code immediately, whereas the combined new program uses a postfix expression as intermediate code. For a real programming language, the latter method is more efficient. Real interpreters usually first produce some intermediate code, which is subsequently interpreted. This has the advantage that in loops, where the same type of computation is done repeatedly, the relatively time-consuming task of processing the original source text, and performing all kinds of syntactic checks, is done only once; after this stage, we have intermediate code available, which can be interpreted more rapidly than the source text. However, if we are not dealing with a complete programming language, but have instead only to interpret arithmetic expressions, even though these may be more realistic than those in VSL, it is not particularly advantageous to use postfix expressions as intermediate code, so direct interpretation of the source text, in the spirit of Section 9.2, should be seriously considered.

9.5 Object Program and Run-time System

In the previous section we saw that there may be good reasons to separate the actual computation from the syntactic analysis, and to interpret intermediate code rather than the given source code. We can go a significant step further in this direction. Instead of generating intermediate code that has to be interpreted, we can generate executable code, consisting of real program text. Traditionally, a real compiler translates a program from source text into machine code. This can be done by first producing assembly language, and subsequently transforming this to machine code. Automatically generated assembly-language code is not the same as machine code, but its purpose is similar, and it is fundamentally different from intermediate code as used in Section 9.4. Although the task of producing machine code is delegated to an assembler (which relieves the task of the compiler), the final result will be an autonomous program, which has full control over the machine. Note that this is not the case when we are using an interpreter; the intermediate code then acts merely as input data; we do not transfer control to it. Thus, the distinction between an interpreter and a (code-generating) compiler can be summarized as follows. An interpreter keeps control over the machine, and performs actions prescribed by its input data, which is either source text or intermediate code. A compiler, on the other hand, produces code that will eventually result in an independent program. Let us use the term *object program* for such code, even though it does not yet have the form of machine code. Before writing a compiler to produce object programs, we have to think about the structure of these object programs themselves. To keep our discussion machine-independent, we will not use real assembly language (let alone machine code). Instead, our object programs will consist of C text. This might seem odd, since C is a high-level language, and, indeed, it would be no use to transform a VSL program into an almost identical C program. However, the object programs that we generate will have the structure of assembly-language programs. For example, consider the following VSL program:

```
{9 - 2 * 4 + 5}
```

Rewriting this in postfix would give

```
9 2 4 * - 5 +
```

Instead, the given VSL program will be translated into the object program that starts after the following comment:

```
/* OBJECT.C: Sample object program
*/


main()
{ void push(int i), add(void),
        subtract(void), multiply(void),
        printresult(void);
   push(9);
   push(2);
   push(4);
   multiply();
   subtract();
   push(5);
   add();
   printresult();
   return 0;
}
```

Note the resemblance between this and the above postfix expression. This object program is in fact a syntactically correct C module, which can be compiled by any (ANSI) C compiler. Instead of producing assembly language, to be processed by a standard assembler, our VSL compiler will produce C code, to be processed by a standard C compiler. An object module such as OBJECT.C has the same structure as an assembly-language module that consists only of subroutine calls. With some imagination we may therefore consider our object programs to be expressed in a machine-independent assembly language, which in turn is only a means to present machine code in a reasonably readable form. Consequently, our object modules, though expressed in C for reasons of readability, are essentially no different from object modules in machine code.

To form a ready-to-run program, we have to supply an additional program module, which we call a *run-time system*. We will express this also in C, but again we will be using only very simple and low-level C-language concepts, so that run-time system RTS.C may be regarded as being expressed in a very readable machine code:

```
/* RTS.C: A run-time system for VSL
*/
#include <stdio.h>
#include <stdlib.h>

#define STACKSIZE 20
int t, s[STACKSIZE]; /*  Initially, t = 0  */

void error(char *str)
{  printf("\n\nError: %s\n", str); exit(1);
}

void push(int i)
{  if (t == STACKSIZE)
   error(
   "STACKSIZE too small for this postfix expression");
   s[t++] = i;
}

void add(void)
{   t--; s[t-1] += s[t];
}

void subtract(void)
{   t--; s[t-1] -= s[t];
}

void multiply(void)
{   t--; s[t-1] *= s[t];
}

void printresult(void)
{  if (t != 1) error("Incorrect object program");
   printf("Result: %d\n", s[0]);
}
```

If we compile object program OBJECT.C and we link it together with the compiled version of RTS.C, we obtain an executable program, which, when executed, gives the output

```
Result: 6
```

Recall that we used

```
{9 - 2 * 4 + 5}
```

as input for our compiler, so the above result is what we expect.

It should be noted that our run-time system does not depend on the particular VSL program that we are dealing with. It need therefore be compiled only once, so its compiled version, say, RTS.OBJ, is a constant component, whereas, for each VSL program that we want to deal with, we have to generate a program OBJECT.C, the variable component. The name we chose for the latter reflects that it is an object program generated by our VSL compiler, to be discussed in Section 9.6. Curiously enough, the 'object program' OBJECT.C is a source program for the standard C compiler. This might seem confusing, but we should not forget that we are expressing our 'object programs' in C merely for reasons of readability. If, instead, we had expressed them immediately in machine language then we would have avoided any confusion of this kind.

9.6 A VSL compiler

There is only one thing that remains to be done, namely translating a given VSL program, such as

```
{9 - 2 * 4 + 5}
```

into the corresponding object program, such as OBJECT.C in Section 9.5. Since this object program is essentially a postfix expression, such as

```
9 2 4 * - 5 +
```

in a different notation, and since in Section 9.3 we have already written program POSTFIX.C to produce postfix, our remaining task is extremely simple. All we have to do is to alter the code-generating parts of POSTFIX.C. In this way, we obtain:

```
/* COMPILER.C:
        This program reads a VSL program, and translates it into
        the VSL object program OBJECT.C. The latter is a C
        program with the structure of an assembly-language
        program. After compiling OBJECT.C by a standard C
        compiler, it is to be linked together with the compiled
        version of RTS.C, see Section 9.5. Program COMPILER.C has
        been derived from POSTFIX.C, discussed in Section 9.3.
*/
#include <stdio.h>
#include <stdlib.h>
#include <ctype.h>
```

```
FILE *fpin, *fpout;
int buf=0;

void error(char *str)
{  printf("\nError: %s\n", str); exit(1);
}

int next(void)
{  int ch;
   do
   {  if (buf) {ch = buf; buf = 0;} else
      {  ch = getc(fpin);
         if (ch == EOF) error("End of file reached");
         putchar(ch);
      }
   }  while (isspace(ch));
   return ch;
}


int nextis(char chgiven)
{  char ch=next();
   if (ch != chgiven) buf = ch;
   return ch == chgiven;
}

void factor(void)
{  void expression(void);
   char ch=next();
   if (isdigit(ch))
      fprintf(fpout, "   push(%c);\n", ch); else
   if (ch == '(')
   {  expression();
      if (!nextis(')')) error("')' expected");
   }  else error("Digit or '(' expected");
}

void term(void)
{  factor();
   while (nextis('*'))
   {  factor();
      fprintf(fpout, "   multiply();\n");
   }
}
```

```
void expression(void)
{  term();
   for ( ; ; )
   {  if (nextis('+'))
      {  term();
         fprintf(fpout, "    add();\n");
      }  else
      if (nextis('-'))
      {  term();
         fprintf(fpout, "    subtract();\n");
      }  else break;
   }
}

void write_beginning(void)
{  fprintf(fpout, "main()\n"
        "{  void push(int i), add(void),\n"
        "          subtract(void), multiply(void),\n"
        "          printresult(void);\n");
}

void write_end(void)
{  fprintf(fpout, "    printresult();\n"
        "    return 0;\n}\n");
}

main()
{  char filnam[51];
   int ch;
   puts("This program reads an input file, containing");
   puts("a VSL program, such as, for example, {3-2*5}\n");
   printf("Name of input file:  ");
   scanf("%50s", filnam);
   fpin = fopen(filnam, "r");
   if (fpin == NULL) error("File not available");
   fpout = fopen("OBJECT.C", "w");
   puts("\nVSL program read from file:\n");
   if (!nextis('{')) error("Open brace ({) expected");
   write_beginning();
   expression();
   write_end();
   if (!nextis('}')) error("Close brace (}) expected");
   fclose(fpin);
   fclose(fpout);
```

```
        puts("\n\nContents of output file OBJECT.C:\n");
        fpout = fopen("OBJECT.C", "r");
        while ((ch = getc(fpout)) != EOF) putchar(ch);
        return 0;
    }
```

For a demonstration, let us use the same file INFIX.TXT as in Sections 9.3 and 9.4, where we used the programs POSTFIX.C and POSTINT.C to compute the value −74. Here, too, we need two steps. We first run the above compiler, to obtain:

```
This program reads an input file, containing
a VSL program, such as, for example, {3-2*5}

Name of input file:  infix.txt
VSL program read from file:

{ 3 * 4 - 5 * 6
  - 7 * (4 + 2 + 2)
}

Contents of output file OBJECT.C:

main()
{   void push(int i), add(void),
         subtract(void), multiply(void),
         printresult(void);
    push(3);
    push(4);
    multiply();
    push(5);
    push(6);
    multiply();
    subtract();
    push(7);
    push(4);
    push(2);
    add();
    push(2);
    add();
    multiply();
    subtract();
    printresult();
    return 0;
}
```

After compiling this and linking the result together with (the compiled version RTS.OBJ of) RTS.C, see Section 9.5, we obtain an executable program which when executed gives the expected output:

```
Result: -74
```

Exercises

In each of the following exercises, a new set of syntax diagrams is to be drawn. Then the language in question may be implemented in three ways:

(1) By a source-text interpreter, see Section 9.2.
(2) By both a conversion from infix to postfix and a postfix interpreter, see Sections 9.3 and 9.4.
(3) By both a compiler producing an object program and a run-time system, see Sections 9.5 and 9.6.

Since the methods (1)–(3) are applicable to each of the following four exercises, there are in fact twelve distinct exercises.

9.1 Extend the language VSL to admit also integers of more than one decimal digit, and implement the extended language.

9.2 Extend VSL to admit the binary operators / and %, which, respectively, yield the quotient and the remainder of an integer division. Implement the extended language.

9.3 Extend VSL to admit the unary minus operator. Since we have

```
    (-a) * b  =  -(a * b)
```

you may regard the expression

```
    - a * b
```

either as the product of $-a$ and b or as the negated product of a and b (where a and b stand for decimal digits). This means that you must make a choice: you can apply the new minus operator either to a factor or to a term, whichever you prefer. If you apply it to a factor (and define the result to be a factor as well), you will admit constructions such as

```
    3 * - - -(4 * 5)
```

Such constructions are not valid if the unary minus operator is applied to a term, since then − cannot immediately follow *****. It is instructive to notice the difference between C and Pascal in this regard. In any postfix output a unary minus operator must be represented by a different character, say **$**, to distinguish it from a binary minus operator; it is placed after its operand. For example, depending on the choice mentioned above, the postfix equivalent of − **a * b** is either

a $ b *

or

a b * $

Implement the extended language.

9.4   Define and implement the 'Very Logical Language' VLL. Every expression in VLL may contain:

- the characters **0** and **1** (to be regarded as *false* and *true*, respectively),
- the operators **!**, **&**, **|**, with the same meaning and precedence as in the C language,
- parentheses, with their usual meaning.

About C and C++

A.1 Function Declarations

All programs in this book are in ANSI C and at the same time in C++. This is possible because these two languages have much in common, as Fig. A.1 illustrates. Although not recommended, the old way of declaring and defining functions is still supported by ANSI C. For example, we could write

```
int f();          /* Old-style declaration of f */

int f(i) int i;  /* Old-style definition of f  */
{ ...
}
```

The new way of writing this is

```
int f(int i);    /* New-style declaration of f */

int f(int i)     /* New-style definition of f  */
{ ...
}
```

This new style is *recommended* in ANSI C and even *mandatory* in C++. The same applies to the convention of declaring every function before it is used. New-style function declarations, such as the one shown above, are also called *function prototypes*. Unlike C, the C++ language does not allow us to use functions that are not declared,

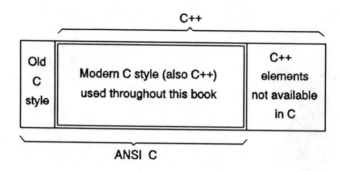

Fig. A.1. ANSI C and C++

so as far as function declarations are concerned, good style is obligatory in this language. A function definition also counts as a declaration, so if we define a function before we use it there is no need for a separate declaration. This principle has been used in most programs in this book. However, there are three exceptions. We really need separate function declarations in these cases:

(1) For standard library functions. These are declared in standard header files. For example, for any program that uses **strcmp** (to compare strings) there is a line

```
#include <string.h>
```

The header file *string.h* contains a prototype for function **strcmp**.

(2) For functions that are used in modules other than those in which they are defined. For example, in Section 1.4, there is a module ACCESS_TWO.C, in which the declaration

```
void accessfunction(void);
```

occurs. This function, **accessfunction**, must be declared here because it is used in this module but defined in module ACCESS_ONE.C. In practice we often prefer to declare our functions in header files of our own, as is done in Section 1.9 for our functions **readint** and **writeint**. The header file *intio.h* can be regarded as the *interface* between *applications*, such as INTCOPY.C and the *implementation*, INTIO.C (see Section 1.9). Such header files are also very suitable for declaring new types and defining symbolic constants. This way of dividing programs into the three components mentioned is particularly attractive in C++. More information about this can be found in *C++ for Programmers* (Chapter 7: Object-oriented Programming) listed in the Bibliography.

(3) For functions that use indirect recursion. This applies, for example, to the functions **expression**, **term** and **factor**, which occur in program INTERPR.C, discussed in Section 9.2. In this program, **expression** calls **term**, which calls **factor**, which may call **expression**. Here we really need a separate function declaration, for which we can use

```
int expression(void);
```

in **factor**. Then no other function prototypes are required if we define these three functions in the order **factor**, **term**, **expression**.

Note that we insist on writing **void** between parentheses in the definitions and the declarations of functions that have no parameters. If, instead of the above function declaration, we wrote

```
int expression();
```

then in C++ the meaning of this declaration would be the same as that with **void** between parentheses, while in C this would be an old-style declaration, which gives no information about any parameters. A serious drawback of the old style is that no checks on the types and the number of parameters are performed, nor is there any automatic type conversion, for example, from **int** to **float**. Lack of type checking and conversion for function arguments has given old C a bad reputation as a programming language for beginners. All this is much better with the new style, which is therefore strongly recommended in ANSI C and even mandatory in C++.

In every C (or C++) program there is a function **main**. Unless there are program arguments, it is very usual for **main** functions to be written as

```
main()
{  ...
}
```

This notation is not in accordance with what we have just been discussing, since there is no keyword **void** between the parentheses. No return type is specified either. In such cases, type **int** is assumed, hence the statement **return 0;** which is normally written at the end of our **main** functions. There are some C and C++ compilers that give a warning or even a fatal error if this return statement is omitted. If you do not like using the old style for the **main** function, you may write

```
int main(void)
{  ...
}
```

This is perhaps a more logical form than the usual one, but it has no real advantages. Since **main** is a very special function, we may as well use a special notation for it.

A.2 Remaining Pitfalls in ANSI C and C++

If we declare (or define) functions as discussed above, there are relatively few pitfalls that remain. Let us discuss some of them.

The equal sign

A single equal sign (=) denotes assignment, while a double equal sign is used for comparisons. Unlike most other languages, C and C++ allow us to write assignments as expressions, so if, instead of

```
if (x == a) ...
```

we wrote

```
if (x = a) ...
```

there would be no syntactical error. During execution, the value of **a** would be assigned **x**, and the statement represented here by three dots would be executed if **a** was nonzero.

The operator & in calls to scanf

There would be a serious error in the following program if the ampersand (&) in the call to **scanf** were omitted:

```
#include <stdio.h>

main()
{   int i=0;
    scanf("%d", &i);
    return 0;
}
```

The integer that is read is placed in the memory location with the address given here as second argument of **scanf**. If we wrote

```
scanf("%d", i);
```

in this program, that integer would be placed in the memory location with address 0, because of the initialized declaration **int i=0;**. This can a have disastrous effect. It goes without saying that omitting **=0** in the declaration of **i** would not improve this program. Although type checking normally takes place, as discussed in Section A.1, function **scanf** is an exception because its number of arguments is variable. Incidentally, that is one of the reasons why C++ offers a new set of I/O facilities, with the header file *iostream.h* instead of *stdio.h*.

Memory access violation

There is no array-bound checking in C or C++. After declaring

```
int a[100], i, *p;
```

we can expect all sorts of trouble if we assign a value to **a[i]** for **i** < 0 or **i** > 99. The same applies to assigning a value to ***p** without first assigning an appropriate value to pointer **p**.

B

Program Index by Chapter

For quick reference, here is a summary of some programs and functions that you may find useful or interesting. Page numbers are given in parentheses. Most modules mentioned below are complete, ready-to-run programs. If not, the description will indicate this.

Chapter 1: Programming Style, Iteration and Recursion

Chapter 2: Array and File Manipulation

Chapter 3: Some Combinatorial Algorithms

Chapter 4: Linked Lists

Chapter 5: Binary Trees

Bibliography

Aho, A.V., J.E. Hopcroft, and J.D. Ullman (1983) *Data Structures and Algorithms*, Reading, MA: Addison-Wesley.

Ammeraal, L. (1991) *C for Programmers, Second Edition*, Chichester: John Wiley.

Ammeraal, L. (1991) *C++ for Programmers*, Chichester: John Wiley.

Atkinson, L.V. (1980) *Pascal Programming*, Chichester: John Wiley.

Bellman, R.E. (1957) *Dynamic Programming*, Princeton, NJ: Princeton University Press.

Berge, C. (1958) *The Theory of Graphs and its Applications*, New York, NY: John Wiley.

Esakov, J., and T. Weiss (1989) *Data Structures - An Advanced Approach Using C*, Englewood Cliffs, NJ: Prentice-Hall.

Gonnet, G.H. (1984) *Handbook of Algorithms and Data Structures*, London: Addison-Wesley.

Horowitz, E., and S. Sahni (1977) *Fundamentals of Data Structures*, Bath: Pitman.

Kernighan, B.W., and D.M. Ritchie (1988) *The C Programming Language, Second Edition*, Englewood Cliffs, NJ: Prentice-Hall.

Knuth, D.E. (1968) *The Art of Computer Programming, Vol. I: Fundamental Algorithms*, Reading, MA: Addison-Wesley.

Knuth, D.E. (1969) *The Art of Computer Programming, Vol. II: Seminumerical Algorithms*, Reading, MA: Addison-Wesley.

Knuth, D.E. (1973) *The Art of Computer Programming, Vol. III: Sorting and Searching*, Reading, MA: Addison-Wesley.

Kruse, R. L., (1987) *Data Structures and Program Design*, Englewood Cliffs, NJ: Prentice-Hall.

Stroustrup, B. (1986) *The C++ Programming Language*, Reading, MA: Addison-Wesley.

Wirth, N. (1976) *Algorithms + Data Structures = Programs*, Englewood Cliffs, NJ: Prentice-Hall.

Index